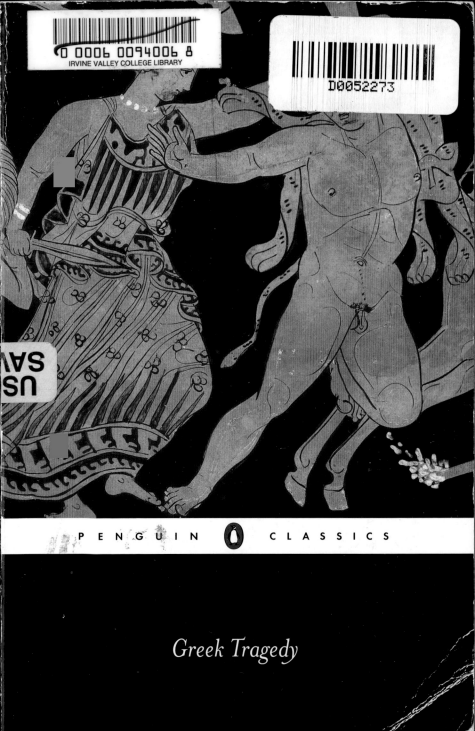

PENGUIN (CLASSICS

Greek Tragedy

PENGUIN CLASSICS

GREEK TRAGEDY

AESCHYLUS was born of a noble family at Eleusis near Athens in 525 BC. He took part in the Persian Wars, and his epitaph, said to have been written by himself, represents him as fighting at Marathon. At some time in his life he appears to have been prosecuted for divulging the Eleusinian mysteries, but he apparently proved himself innocent. Aeschylus wrote more than seventy plays, of which seven have survived: *The Suppliants*, *The Persians*, *Seven Against Thebes*, *Prometheus Bound*, *Agamemnon*, *The Choephori* and *The Eumenides*. He visited Syracuse more than once at the invitation of Hieron I and he died at Gela in Sicily in 456 BC. Aeschylus was recognized as a classic writer soon after his death, and special privileges were decreed for his plays.

ARISTOPHANES, an Athenian citizen, was born in c. 448–445 BC and died between 387 and 380 BC. Little is known about his life, but there is a portrait of him in Plato's *Symposium*. He is presented as a well-liked and convivial person, who 'divides his time between Aphrodite and Dionysus'. His eleven surviving comedies are *Archarnians* (425), *Knights* (424), *Clouds* (423), *Wasps* (422), *Peace* (421), *Birds* (414), *Lysistrata* (411), *The Thesmophoriazusae* (411), *Frogs* (405), *The Ecclesiazusae* (c. 392) and *Plautus* (388).

ARISTOTLE was born at Stagira, in the dominion of the kings of Macedonia, in 384 BC. For twenty years he studied at Athens in the Academy of Plato, on whose death in 347 he left, and, some time later, became tutor of the young Alexander the Great. When Alexander succeeded to the throne of Macedonia in 335, Aristotle returned to Athens and established his school and research institute, the Lyceum, to which his great erudition attracted a large number of scholars. After Alexander's death in 323, anti-Macedonian feeling drove Aristotle out of Athens, and he fled to Chalcis in Euboea, where he died in 322. His writings, which were of extraordinary range, profoundly affected the whole course of ancient and medieval philosophy, and they are still eagerly studied and debated by philosophers today. Very many of them have survived and among the most famous are the *Ethics* and the

Politics, both of which are published in Penguin Classics, together with *The Athenian Constitution*, *De Anima*, *The Art of Rhetoric* and *Poetics*.

EURIPIDES was an Athenian born in 484 BC. A member of a family of considerable rank, he avoided public duties as far as possible, and devoted his life to the work of a dramatist. His popularity is attested by the survival of seventeen of his plays and by abundant other evidence; though it was partly due to his audience's inability to penetrate the irony of his character-drawing. His unpopularity is equally clear from the constant attacks made upon him in the comedies of Aristophanes, and by the fact that in fifty years he was awarded first prize only four or five times. At the age of seventy-three he found it necessary to leave Athens; he went into voluntary exile at the court of Archelaus, king of Macedon. It was during these last months that he wrote what many consider his greatest work, *The Bacchae*. When the news of his death reached Athens in 406 Sophocles appeared publicly in mourning for him.

SOPHOCLES was born at Colonus, just outside Athens, in 496 BC, and lived ninety years. His long life spanned the rise and decline of the Athenian Empire; he was a friend of Pericles, and though not an active politician he held several public offices, both military and civil. The leader of a literary circle and friend of Herodotus, he was interested in poetic theory as well as practice, and he wrote a prose treatise *On the Chorus*.

Sophocles first won a prize for tragic drama in 468, defeating the veteran Aeschylus. He wrote over a hundred plays for the Athenian theatre, and is said to have come first in twenty-four contests. Only seven of his tragedies are now extant, these being *Ajax*, *Antigone*, *Oedipus Rex*, *Women of Trachis*, *Electra*, *Philoctetes*, and the posthumous *Oedipus at Colonus*. Fragments of other plays remain, showing that he drew on a wide range of themes; he also introduced the innovation of a third actor in his tragedies. He died in 406 BC.

SHOMIT DUTTA was educated at the Royal Grammar School, High Wycombe, University College Oxford, and King's College London. He has taught classics at Radley College and Harrow School, and is currently completing a D Phil on Aristophanes and Greek tragedy. He has taught at Oxford and various schools, worked as a freelance arts reviewer, and published a translation of Sophocles' *Ajax*.

MALCOLM HEATH was born in London in 1957 and was educated in Harrow and at Oxford University. He was a lecturer in Greek for a year at the University of St Andrews and has been Reader in Greek Language and Literature at Leeds University since 1991. Apart from numerous articles, he has also published *The Poetics of Greek Tragedy* (1987), *Political Comedy in Aristophanes* (1987), *Unity in Greek Poetics* (1989) and *Hermogenes on Issues: Strategies of Argument in Later Greek Rhetoric* (1995).

PHILIP VELLACOTT translated the following volumes for the Penguin Classics: the complete plays of Aeschylus, the complete plays of Euripides, and a volume of Menander and Theophrastus. He was educated at St Paul's School and Magdalene College, Cambridge, and for twenty-four years taught classics (and drama for twelve years) at Dulwich College. He lectured on Greek drama on ten tours in the USA, and spent four terms as Visiting Lecturer in the University of California at Santa Cruz. He wrote a number of books including *Sophocles and Oedipus* (1971), *Ironic Drama: A Study of Euripides' Method and Meaning* (1975) and *The Logic of Tragedy: Morals and Integrity in Aeschylus' Oresteia* (1984). Philip Vellacott died in 1997.

E. F. WATLING was educated at Christ's Hospital and University College, Oxford. His translations of Greek and Roman plays for the Penguin Classics include the seven plays of Sophocles, nine plays of Plautus, and a selection of the tragedies of Seneca. He died in 1990.

SIMON GOLDHILL is Professor of Greek at Cambridge University and a Fellow of King's College where he is Director of Studies in Classics. He has published widely on many aspects of Greek literature, especially tragedy. He is in great demand as a lecturer all over the world, and is a frequent broadcaster on radio and television on classical matters.

Greek Tragedy

Edited and with Notes by SHOMIT DUTTA
With an Introduction by SIMON GOLDHILL

PENGUIN BOOKS

PENGUIN BOOKS

Published by the Penguin Group
Penguin Books Ltd, 80 Strand, London WC2R ORL, England
Penguin Group (USA) Inc., 375 Hudson Street, New York, New York 10014, USA
Penguin Books Australia Ltd, 250 Camberwell Road, Camberwell, Victoria 3124, Australia
Penguin Books Canada Ltd, 10 Alcorn Avenue, Toronto, Ontario, Canada M4V 3B2
Penguin Books India (P) Ltd, 11, Community Centre, Panchsheel Park, New Delhi – 110 017, India
Penguin Group (NZ), Cnr Airborne and Rosedale Roads, Albany, Auckland 1310, New Zealand
Penguin Books (South Africa) (Pty) Ltd, 24 Sturdee Avenue, Rosebank 2196, South Africa

Penguin Books Ltd, Registered Offices: 80 Strand, London WC2R ORL, England

www.penguin.com

Agamemnon first published in this translation 1956
Reprinted with revisions 1959
Oedipus Rex first published in this translation 1947
Medea first published in this translation 1963
Extracts from *Frogs* first published in this translation 2004
Poetics first published 1996

This compilation first published 2004

6

Agamemnon copyright © Philip Vellacott, 1956, 1959
Oedipus Rex copyright 1947 by E. F. Watling; renewal copyright © E. F. Watling 1974
Medea copyright © Philip Vellacott, 1963
Frogs copyright © Shomit Dutta, 2004
Poetics copyright © Malcolm Heath, 1996
Compilation, Chronological Table, A Note on the Texts, Prefaces, Genealogical Tables and
Notes copyright © Shomit Dutta, 2004
Introduction and Further Reading copyright © Simon Goldhill, 2004
All rights reserved

The moral right of the editors and translators has been asserted

Set in 10.25/12.25 pt PostScript Adobe Sabon
Typeset by Rowland Phototypesetting Ltd, Bury St Edmunds, Suffolk
Printed in England by Clays Ltd, St Ives plc

www.greenpenguin.co.uk

Penguin Books is committed to a sustainable future
for our business, our readers and our planet.
The book in your hands is made from paper
certified by the Forest Stewardship Council.

Contents

Chronological Table

Only some of the plays of Aeschylus and Euripides (and only a few of Sophocles') can be firmly dated. In some cases definite dates can be given on the basis of external evidence or references within the plays. Otherwise, the primary method of dating extant tragedies is the analysis of metrical tendencies (these give a reliable indication of the approximate date of a particular play to within a few years). In the case of Aristophanes' comedies the situation is much clearer; we know dates for all of his surviving plays (and some lost or fragmentary ones). The table below gives dates, with varying degrees of certainty, for selected plays by Aeschylus, Sophocles, Euripides and Aristophanes. Certain key historical dates are also included.

Year (BC)

c. 536–532 Founding of the tragic competition	
525 Birth of Aeschylus	
	510 Democracy established in Athens (by Cleisthenes)
496 Birth of Sophocles	
	490 Persian invasion under Darius; Greek victory at Marathon
c. 480 Birth of Euripides	480 Persian invasion under Xerxes; Greek naval victory off Salamis
	479 Greek victory at Plataea ends Persian invasion

472 Aeschylus' *Persians*
468 Sophocles' first competition
  (first prize)
467 Aeschylus' *Laius,**
  Oedipus, *Seven Against*
  Thebes, Sphinx†

462 Athenian democracy
  radically reformed (by
  Ephialtes)

458 Aeschylus' *Agamemnon,*
  Libation Bearers, Eumenides,
  Proteus†
456 Death of Aeschylus
455 Euripides' first competition
  (third prize)
c. 445 Birth of Aristophanes
438 Euripides' *Alcestis* and
  *Telephus**
431 Euripides' *Medea*

431 Start of Peloponnesian War
  between Athens and Sparta
430 Great plague in Athens
429 Death of Pericles

428 Euripides' *Hippolytus*
428–425? Sophocles' *Oedipus*
  Rex
427 Aristophanes' first play
  Babylonians‡
425? Euripides' *Andromache*
425 Aristophanes' *Acharnians*
424 Aristophanes' *Knights*
423 Aristophanes' *Clouds*
  (original version)
422 Aristophanes' *Wasps*
422–417 Euripides' *Electra* §

*These plays are either lost or fragmentary
†These are lost or fragmentary satyr-plays
‡Only a few fragments of this play survive.
§The dates of both Euripides' and Sophocles' *Electra* are very much a matter
of conjecture; there is even disagreement over which play is the earlier of the
two.

421 Aristophanes' *Peace*

421 Death of Cleon (demagogue attacked in Aristophanes' early plays); Peace of Nicias (short-lived)

420–10 Sophocles' *Electra*
415 Euripides' Trojan trilogy (incl. *Trojan Women*)
414 Aristophanes' *Birds*

413 Athenian naval expedition to Sicily ends in disastrous defeat.

412 Euripides' *Helen*; *Iphigenia at Tauris* (approximate date)
411 Aristophanes' *Lysistrata* and *Thesmophoriazusae*
409 Sophocles' *Philoctetes*
408 Euripides' *Orestes*
406/5 Aristophanes' *Frogs*; deaths of Euripides and Sophocles
c. 405 Euripides' *Bacchae* and *Iphigenia at Aulis* (performed posthumously)
401? Sophocles' *Oedipus at Colonus* (performed posthumously)

404 Defeat of Athens by Sparta; start of Spartan hegemony
399 Execution of Socrates

c. 392 Aristophanes' *Assembly Women*
388 Aristophanes' *Wealth*
c. 387–80 Death of Aristophanes

384 Birth of Aristotle
336 Accession of Alexander the Great
323 Death of Alexander the Great
322 Death of Aristotle

Introduction*

by Simon Goldhill

The Festival of Dionysus

What we call 'Greek Tragedy' is really Athenian tragedy. All the plays which survive today and which are included in this Penguin volume were written in one city, Athens, in one short, remarkable period – the last seventy years of the fifth century BC. This context is crucial for understanding tragedy as a dramatic event, and for appreciating how these plays have had such a lasting effect on the Western imagination.

The fifth century was one of the most extraordinary eras of social, political and cultural change the West has known. It saw the invention of democracy, as well as the first writing of history, philosophy, medical science and rhetoric. We are all its heirs. It also witnessed the first performances of tragedy. It is fundamental that Athenian tragedy takes place in a city that is a democracy – the first democracy – and in a society that knew it was undergoing rapid and often painful cultural change. Tragedy is fully a part both of this new political system and of this extraordinary explosion of cultural innovation.

Let us look first at how the Athenians watched tragedy. It is a long way from any modern Western experience of theatre although many artists, like Richard Wagner with the Bayreuth Festival, have tried to recapture its spirit. Each of the tragedies in this volume was produced for a single performance in a competition held at the festival of the Great Dionysia, a religious celebration in honour of the god Dionysus held annually in

---

*Readers are warned that the plots of the plays in this volume are disclosed in this Introduction.

Athens over four consecutive days at the end of February and the beginning of March.[1] Eventually these plays became so famous that they were re-performed in Athens and in other cities by repertory companies; they became part of the school curriculum, and were read and studied by critics and philosophers like Aristotle, whose *Poetics* became one of the most influential texts for the understanding of tragedy for later European thinking. From their first performances, the tragic plays entered the public imagination, as is vividly demonstrated by Aristophanes' *Frogs*, a popular comedy which mocks the tragic language of Aeschylus and Euripides in particular. (Both Aristotle's *Poetics* and Aristophanes' *Frogs* are included in this volume, as important ancient commentaries on the tragedies.) But in the fifth century, tragedians wrote with the expectation of a single significant performance in a competition before the citizens of Athens. There were no 'long runs', no theatres to attend except at festival time, and no range of plays from which to pick and choose.

Each year, a leading state bureaucrat, the archon, chose three playwrights to enter the tragedy competition and five playwrights to enter the comedy competition. We don't know what criteria he used for his choice, but the fact that Aeschylus, Sophocles and Euripides each were selected so often indicates that reputation may have played a considerable role. Each tragic playwright had to write three tragedies and a satyr-play. The satyr-play ended the sequence and was a farcical play that had a chorus of satyrs – drunken, lascivious figures, half-goat half-man, who were worshippers of Dionysus, the god whose realm encompassed wine and release as well as theatre. The trilogy of tragedies always ended with this release of Dionysiac wildness.

Each playwright had the same chorus members for each of his plays, and the same three actors. The chorus was made up of citizens – fifteen of them by the time of Sophocles and Euripides[2] – and the actors too were full citizens (rather than a disreputable *demi-monde* as has so often been the case in the Western tradition). These citizens needed funding for rehearsal time, and the plays with their lavish costumes and effects were expensive to produce. When the playwrights were chosen, the State also appointed a wealthy individual to fund each playwright's offering. This sort of taxation was known as a 'liturgy', and the sponsor was called a *chorêgos*, literally, 'the chorus director'. Victory in the competition was as much the triumph of the *chorêgos* as it was that of the playwright. When a playwright was chosen it was called 'being granted a chorus'. In this way, plays were chosen and funded by the State for the State festival.

The festival began with the sort of processions and sacrifices that any Greek would recognize as a usual part of religious celebration. A large crowd gathered to watch a procession of chosen representatives from different areas of city life, dressed in their finery, carrying sacred objects and leading sacrificial animals towards the theatre. This was called a *pompê* (from which comes the English word 'pomp'). It marked out the day as special and the rituals as a collective activity. A smaller group of citizens also gathered on another day in the Odeion, a large building built by the great statesman Pericles for artistic performances. Here the playwrights presented their choruses in costume and announced the plays to be performed. When Euripides died in 406, Sophocles, his old rival, presented his chorus in mourning, rather than in their usual splendour, to mourn his fellow artist.

These events, along with choral competitions, meetings and other processions, all took place on days before or after the plays were performed. What made the Great Dionysia and its tragedies so extraordinary was the day when the plays themselves started. The festival began at dawn, in the open-air theatre at the foot of the Acropolis. The audience was huge – estimates vary between 14,000 and 16,000. The vast majority of this audience was citizens: adult males with the right to vote, heads of households. This was the biggest collection of citizens in the calendar. The Assembly, the most important political body of democracy, regularly had around 6,000 attending; courts fewer still. The only occasion to match the size of such a gathering as the Great Dionysia might be the Olympic Games, or a major battle. The Great Dionysia was truly an occasion for the whole State.

A citizen was issued with a ticket by the authorities of the local State organization, the *deme*. Some of these little lead tokens are still to be seen in the Athens museum. The ticket cost two obols, about a day's wages for a manual labourer, but there was a fund, called the Theoric Fund, which paid the two obols to any citizen who wished. We are not sure exactly when the fund was first established, but it stemmed from the same ideological commitment that paid citizens to attend jury service and to row in the navy. Going to the theatre was seen as part of a citizen's duties and privileges, like jury or military service, and no citizen should be prevented by poverty from attending. Indeed, so important was the Theoric Fund that it was against the law even to propose to change the law which established it. Even in the wars against Philip of Macedon in the mid-fourth century, when finances were desperate, it was not possible to touch State funding for the theatre. For the Athenians, going to the theatre was a civic duty.

Where did the citizen sit in the theatre? The lead tickets are each stamped with the name of one of the ten tribes of Athens. (Each *deme* was part of a tribe, and each citizen thus belonged to a tribe.) This has led many scholars to believe that the citizens sat in tribal divisions: that is, that ten of the wedges of seats in the theatre were reserved each for one of the tribes, the socio-political divisions of the State. This would match other seating arrangements. A central block of 500 seats was reserved for the Council, the executive body of government. The first row was reserved for visiting ambassadors, priests and other dignitaries. One further section was reserved for *ephebes* – young men on the point of joining the armed forces. (We will see the role of these *ephebes* and the ambassadors shortly.) Another wedge was reserved for *metics* who were the resident aliens, foreigners without full citizenship rights. Seating marked out the audience according to socio-political position, age and status – when a citizen walked into the theatre, he walked into a map of the city. He took his place in a picture of the political organization of the city: the theatre represented the city to itself.

The question of whether there were any women present is an extraordinarily vexed issue. There is no single clear statement from the ancient world that says conclusively either that women definitely did attend or definitely did not attend theatre. All the scraps of indirect evidence are particularly difficult to interpret. It is clear that if any women attended, they were very few in number and not the 'intended audience' of the plays. But since women were wholly excluded from the Assembly, the Law Court and the Gymnasium in Athens, and since the Great Dionysia was a major political occasion of the city, it is perhaps more likely that women were not present at all. But it is annoyingly impossible to be certain on this issue.

Before the plays were performed for this great gathering of citizens, four rituals took place, which show in a vivid way how the Great Dionysia became a political showpiece of the Athenian calendar. The first was most simple. As with most Greek festivals, there was a sacrifice – piglets were slaughtered and their blood sprinkled around the playing area – and libations of wine were poured to the gods. What is surprising, however, is who poured the libations: for brought on stage to perform this ritual were the ten generals, that is, the ten most important military and political leaders of the State. The ten generals came together for such rituals very rarely, and usually for something evidently related to their role (a sacrifice for 'peace', say), but every year they opened the drama festival. The festival opened under the authority of the State, embodied in its leaders.

The second ritual was the announcement of the names of civic benefactors who had been awarded a crown during the year for services to the State. Athens was always a fiercely competitive society, where men struggled for honour in the public gaze. So this ceremony was clearly a moment of great personal glory for the citizen named before the citizen body. But it is interesting that the Greek writers who discuss this occasion talk about it in different terms. They see it as an occasion at which the city gave thanks, and encouraged all citizens to do their duty. This view depends on a standard democratic tenet: that a citizen's actions are evaluated according to how they contribute to the city. This ceremony is thus seen as a way of projecting and promoting the values of the city.

The third ritual was stranger still. Slaves carried in a large amount of silver and paraded it around the theatre. This was the 'parade of tribute'. All our existing tragedies come from the period of the Athenian Empire. Athens had become the dominant imperialist power of the Mediterranean by virtue of its naval power. It could compel cities to join its League – to become allies, as it was known – and the cost of being an ally was the payment of tribute. This money, ostensibly to protect against attack by Persia, was used to build an even bigger fleet (and for building the Parthenon and other symbols of imperialist power). The allies were forced to send their tribute to Athens in February, and their ambassadors were invited to the theatre to watch their silver paraded around the theatre.

This spectacle was designed to parade the power and might of Athens, to declare its position as the dominant military and political force in the Mediterranean. It was a state occasion to glorify the State.

The fourth ceremonial was the 'parade of war orphans'. In Athens, if a boy's father died fighting for the State, he was brought up at State expense. When the end of maintained childhood was reached, and the boy was ready, as a man, to join the armed forces, he was presented with armour by the State, and together these *ephebes* ('young men') were paraded in the theatre at the Great Dionysia before they took their special seats to watch the plays. Their names and their fathers' names were announced, and they publicly took the moving oath of loyalty to the State, promising to do their military duty, and to be prepared to fight and die for the city as their fathers had done before them.

Athens, for all its cultural achievements, was a military state. It was at war almost every year of the fifth century. It had a citizen army, in which every able-bodied citizen was expected to fight. It celebrated its dead soldiers as heroes of the State. It was a fundamental principle of democracy that fighting and dying for the State was an integral commitment of citizenship. The 'parade of war orphans' dramatized this commitment in solemn ritual fashion. It showed the young Athenians, dedicating themselves to the military obligations of citizenship, before the citizens. It celebrated the military values of the city.

The Great Dionysia brought together the whole city. It ordered the citizens in the theatre according to a political map. The four rituals with which the festival opened expressed in spectacular ceremonial action the ideological values the city wished to celebrate and support. The Great Dionysia was truly an occasion on which the city put itself on display. It was in this context, so different from modern theatre, that tragedy was performed.

The Performance of Tragedy

There are many State occasions from around the ancient or modern world which could be used to parallel the Great Dionysia, as I have described it so far, from State funerals, to military parades, to such notorious events as the 1936 Berlin Olympics. What makes the Great Dionysia absolutely extraordinary, however, is the plays which were performed after such rituals and on such a grand political stage. Both tragedy and comedy produce images of the city in chaos, self-destruction or confusion. In comedy, individuals mock the State and its officials, turn the civic order upside down, and push politics into a carnival of raucous laughter. In tragedy, not only do individuals commit terrible crimes and suffer outrageous misfortunes, but also the very values of the city are challenged to breaking point.

How should we view a festival which combines such civic ceremonial with such terrible and disturbing stories? How should we understand an occasion that in the middle of its political and religious celebrations can stage the drama of a man who kills his father and sleeps with his mother?

One powerful answer to these questions is provided by scholars who see the tragic festival – the plays and the ceremonies together – offering the city a message about what a good city should be like. The vast majority of our surviving plays are set in cities other than Athens: the *Agamemnon* is set in Argos;

Oedipus Rex is set in Thebes; *Medea* in Corinth. What's more, tragedies take place in the distant past, the world of myths. *Medea* and *Oedipus Rex* are set before even the time of Homeric epic, the earliest Greek poem. The characters of tragedy are not simply like the audience, either. Rather than good citizens, tragedy gives us heroic kings like Agamemnon, heroes like Oedipus, or barbarian witches like Medea. Tragedy is peopled by others. Tragedy, in short, takes place 'at the scene of the other' – other places, other times, other people.

Consequently, tragedy's stories of disaster can be seen as the grim warnings of what happens if things do go wrong in a city – something depicted as happening in other places to other people. The ceremonials, which open the festival, show the glory of Athens as democracy, as military power, as the home of true social and political value. The plays that follow, set elsewhere, show what happens if the city is *not* properly ordered and controlled. The positive and negative images together construct a strong sense of what matters and should matter to an Athenian. Aristotle, in his *Poetics*, sees a crucial educational benefit coming from tragedy for the individual citizen in this process. By watching the reasoning of tragic heroes, reasoning which leads them into disaster, we can learn better to control our own lives. Tragedy warns the city; and the pity and fear which the audience experiences can lead to a cleansed moral awareness of what is at stake in being a citizen.

This is a very strong model for understanding the power of tragedy both emotionally and intellectually. It helps us see why tragedy might be something that the city could think it was important for the citizen to attend. We can appreciate why the searing emotions which tragedy stages and produces in its audience can be supported and even valued in the city.

But I do not think this idea of tragedy's teaching reaches to the very heart of the tragic experience. The difficulty with the model can be expressed simply by the example of Oedipus. For Oedipus is not merely a negative model, for all that he kills his father and sleeps with his mother. It is not the case that Oedipus is just an 'other', who inhabits a different, negative world. Oedipus is also an intelligent, admired and successful figure who, like us, wants to control his life. He is desperate to avoid the grim fate an oracle predicts for him, and he is desperate to find out who he really is. This makes him a model *for* all of us. As Freud recognized from his rather different perspective, there is an Oedipus inside everyone. The emotional and intellectual power of tragedy comes from the *difficulty* of its examples. Its figures are not black-and-white villains and heroes, but complex characters locked in horrific conflicts that do not allow simple solutions. It is the way in which Oedipus turns out to be like us which makes the play so affecting. Tragedy leads to *self-questioning* through the pain of others.

Let us look briefly at how the three tragedies in this volume engage their audience in such a process of self-questioning.

The *Agamemnon* is the first play in a trilogy, the *Oresteia*, which is the only surviving trilogy from ancient Athenian tragedy. The three plays are intricately linked in theme and imagery as well as in plot. The *Oresteia* is one of the greatest works of the Western imagination, and the *Agamemnon* is the first, grounding masterpiece of the whole edifice. In the *Agamemnon* the central act is the killing of Agamemnon by his wife, Clytemnestra. In the *Libation Bearers*, the second play of the trilogy, the central act is the killing of Clytemnestra by her own son Orestes, to avenge his father. In the *Eumenides*, the third play, the central act is the trial in which Orestes is judged for this crime, accused by the avenging Furies, defended by Apollo and exonerated by an equal vote of Athenian jurors. The trilogy begins in the house of Agamemnon and ends in the court in Athens and, finally, with a celebration of the city itself, led by the city's own goddess, Athena. The play moves from violent revenge to institutionalized justice and, ultimately, to the order of the State itself.

There are two overarching points that are crucial to understanding the sweep of this massive trilogy and how the *Agamemnon* opens it. The first is this. Homer's epic, the *Odyssey*, is one of the founding texts of Greek culture, which, like the Bible in Victorian society, provided for Greeks the images of how to be, moral lessons for life and a way to understand the world. In the *Odyssey*, Orestes is repeatedly held up as a paradigm of manhood. 'Be like Orestes!' is a refrain used repeatedly to encourage Odysseus' son to grow up and be a man. Orestes can play such a role in the *Odyssey* because, although the story of the house of Agamemnon is told many times, *how* Clytemnestra died is never once mentioned. Aeschylus takes that silence and makes it scream. Centre stage, in the central play of the trilogy, mother and son face each other in murderous conflict. After Aeschylus, no one ever again said 'Be like Orestes!' He had become the archetypal matricide. In the court that decides Orestes' fate, the jury's votes are equal. The jury cannot decide how to evaluate him. Where in Homer Orestes was the example of how to be a good man, for Aeschylus' tragic vision he has become an example of how impossible it is to judge, and how tortured he is by his own experience. Orestes has become a *problem* – for himself and for us. Orestes is the perfect test-case of how tragedy can turn the exemplary good man from the exemplary world of Homer into a tormented question.

The second overarching point concerns the city. The *Oresteia* finds whatever answers it does offer in the institutions and social order of the city. The trilogy is obsessed with the problematic differences between punishment, revenge, justice and the good of society. It turns punishers into victims of revenge, and shows how such violence destroys the bonds of society. Yet it ends with a grand procession of the whole city towards the Acropolis to offer sacrifice, a procession like the religious procession that opens the Great Dionysia. Tragedy takes the myths of the past, the privileged stories of Homer, and retells them within the context of the democratic city. Tragedy makes myth part of the politics of the city.

Thus the *Oresteia* brilliantly shows two essential points about tragedy. First, tragedy puts problematic, provocative and irreducible problems before the city; second, tragedy makes inherited myth a new story for the democratic city.

There are many ways in which the *Agamemnon* establishes the thematic structures of the trilogy and, indeed, sets an agenda for the genre of tragedy. I want to focus on one set of ideas here, the connection between language and gender. Although the play is called the *Agamemnon*, and Agamemnon's death is its central act, there can be no doubt that the play is dominated by Clytemnestra and that the figure with the longest scene is Cassandra: two powerful female characters. Why does Aeschylus structure his drama like this?

Clytemnestra is a woman out of place by virtue of her pursuit of power. She is a woman who has in her heart 'a man-like will'. That is the first description we hear of her in the mouth of the Watchman who opens the play. When she enters, the chorus immediately point out the oddity of her position: 'Our king and leader absent, and his throne unmanned, we pay his due observance to his wife.' It is only because there is no male for the 'unmanned' throne that Clytemnestra can act as a ruler. For the chorus, when she persuades them, her 'words are like a man's'. Indeed, the conflict of the play is seen by Cassandra, who always tells the truth, as a clash of *gender*: 'female shall murder male', she screams. Clytemnestra is a woman opposed to a man, and who becomes man-like to those around her even before she takes an axe to kill her husband. By the same token, Aegisthus, her lover, who in Aeschylus takes no part in the murder he planned and executed in Homer, is despised by the chorus as not man enough: 'You woman!', they hiss at him. There is throughout the *Agamemnon* an intense focus on gender conflict.

This opposition of male and female, however, also draws on an opposition of family or blood ties and state or social ties. Agamemnon's dilemma at Aulis is described in the first choral ode. The fleet bound for Troy is becalmed and a sacrifice is required. Agamemnon is forced to choose: either he must desert the expedition of all Greece to avenge the rape of Helen, or he must sacrifice his daughter, 'my home's delight'. He decides to kill his daughter, his own blood, treasure of the household, rather than give up his role as leader of the collective army of Greece. The *Agamemnon* sets up a tension between male and female and between household tie and social obligation, which remain unresolved in the trilogy – and a constant theme of tragedy as a genre. The trilogy's interest in social order and its final celebration of the city is a struggle to find a place for the dangerous and threatening female in the city, and to find a place for the competing obligations of family and State. How can the threat posed by Clytemnestra's power and transgressiveness be exorcized from the city? Tragedy remains obsessed with gender conflict, with the threat of the female and, above all, with the conflicting obligations of family and State.

Clytemnestra's power depends on her manipulation of communication and, especially, her persuasive way with words. The first scene of the play is the Beacon Speeches scene. Clytemnestra gives two long speeches to explain the beacon which had flared up in the prologue. The first speech tells of how she has organized an international system of beacon lights; the second tells the meaning of the fire – the capture of Troy. We see the queen dominating the stage, talking about a system of communication and persuading the chorus that Troy has fallen. The second scene is the Messenger scene, a scene where a messenger comes to announce the storm at sea, but where Clytemnestra persuades him to take back a deceptive message to Agamemnon, which will lure him to his death – more tricky language. When Agamemnon does return, in one of the most spectacular scenes of any drama, he is persuaded to enter the house by walking across crimson tapestries the queen has spread for him. We see the queen greet him with lying words, and then persuade him, against his will, to step on the precious cloths. We watch the power of her persuasion at work.

When Clytemnestra appears over the dead bodies of Agamemnon and Cassandra, she declares:

> Before now I said many things to suit the time;
> All of which, without shame, I now unsay.

Clytemnestra is threatening, dominant and transgressive because of the power of her language.

Cassandra, the prophetess, has the longest scene of the play, and she is of corresponding importance. The scene comes between the entrance of the king into the palace and his death cries. It is a scene which looks back into the history of the cursed house and forward to the other plays of the trilogy, and so gives a remarkable depth to our sense of how actions are interlinked in this tragic world. But Cassandra has a special 'gift' from Apollo. While she always knows and tells the truth, she cannot persuade anyone of it.

This makes the clash of Cassandra and Clytemnestra all the more telling. It juxtaposes the woman who lies and persuades everyone to the woman who tells the truth and persuades no one. What's more, Clytemnestra seems to take control of all around her by her manipulative words. But Cassandra, because she knows exactly what will happen, can do nothing about it. She has no control. As she says, 'there's no use trying to escape'. There is a deep irony here. So many characters in Greek tragedy imagine that if only they had knowledge, they could affect what is going to happen. Cassandra shows that absolute knowledge actually leads to a sense of total helplessness.

The *Agamemnon* reflects profoundly on the power and danger of words. This worry about language goes to the heart of democracy. The Athenian Assembly created the policy of the State and its business depended on citizens giving and inter-preting speeches. In the court-room, a citizen spoke his case to defend himself or prosecute another. Juries of citizens judged such speeches. Democracy, as Demosthenes the politician and orator put it, is 'a constitution of speech-making'. Speech-making is the route to power and the exercise of authority in Athenian democracy. The *Agamemnon* reveals the violent dangers inherent in humans' powerful use of language. It poses a stark question to every citizen's engagement in the democratic process.

The *Agamemnon* sets up central issues not just for the *Ores-teia* but for Greek tragedy in general. Its particular concerns with the political order of the city, with competing obligations of State and family, with gender, with language, with a man's control over life and with justice and revenge provide the funda-mental themes of Greek tragedy. Both the *Oedipus Rex* and the *Medea*, written a generation later, continue, in different ways, the questions raised by Aeschylus' great trilogy.

Oedipus, king of Thebes, tries to save the city, only to discover that it is his own family history which is destroying the city from within. He prides himself on being the man who solved the riddle of the Sphinx, but he cannot read the oracles and prophecies that surround him. *Oedipus Rex* shows a man desperate to find out who he is, and the horror of the play is watching this search for identity grimly and ironically revealing that Oedipus, the man asked to solve the problems of the city and find the murderer of its former king Laius, is himself the source of the plague and not just the killer of the king, but also of his own father. Oedipus, who seemed to be so in control of things, is revealed by the end to have always been disastrously out of control. As the chorus sing in one of the most famous odes of all tragedy, 'show me the man whose happiness was anything more than hopes followed by disillusion'. The very first word which Oedipus utters, the first word of the play, is 'children' – addressed to the citizens of Thebes, by a king who is like a father to his people. His last words are a plea that Creon, the new ruler and Jocasta's brother, does not take his children from him, but taken away they are. The play traces Oedipus losing his position as king, father, husband – his disillusionment. But that first word, 'children', in the mouth of Oedipus, is already no more than a sign of his false hope, a marker of his polluted life as child and father.

Creon, who delivers the final lines of dialogue in the play, sums up: 'Command no more,' he declares to Oedipus. 'Your rule is over.' The blind and crushed Oedipus is indeed a figure no more in command. But the grimmest irony of all is that Creon here is, in turn, trying to take command, to sum up, to rule: and we know that this is just one more step in this doomed family's history. The seer Tiresias' words are a motto for all who try to rule in this tragic world: 'You have eyes and yet you cannot see.' The horror of Oedipus is not just watching one man's awful fate, but the more worrying suggestion that none of us can fully know what we are doing, that our lives are running on tracks over which we have no control, and that none of us can adequately answer the question of our own identity.

Democracy demands that each citizen take responsibility for his own life, his own decisions, and his own actions. *Oedipus Rex* suggests that this founding principle of autonomy is no more than a hope leading to disillusion.

Medea offers an image of a woman even more frightening

than Clytemnestra. She is a barbarian, a witch, whose poison slaughters her enemies in agony; a monstrous figure whose divine powers allow her to escape. Her rage is violent. But, like Clytemnestra, her words are her prime weapons. Every scene in the play involves Medea persuading someone. Even her famous monologue is an attempt to persuade herself to go through with the killing of her own children.

Medea kills her children because she knows that their death will hurt Jason, her husband who has betrayed her, more than any other act she could contrive. She loves her children and has no doubt that she will suffer unbearably too: 'How sweet to hold you! So soft, children's skin, and their breath pure . . .', she weeps, 'I can't look at you any longer. The pain is more than I can bear.' Yet kill them she will.

Medea poses many questions to her audience, but there is one in particular which is raised by the genre of tragedy again and again. It concerns extremism. How far is it possible to go in the pursuit of revenge or a sense of justice? When does Medea stop being sympathetic and start becoming horrific? Medea raises the issue of how society can deal with her extremism not merely because we watch her following her sense of outrage into such an horrific response, but also because at the end of the play she leaves in the chariot of the Sun drawn by winged serpents. She is unpunished. And she is coming to Athens, the home of the play's first audience. Tragedy is obsessed with society's discomfort with the great but unbearable figure. The hero is a figure who goes too far – and that going too far is both transcendence and transgression. Tragedy asks its audience to ponder the limits of human life, and what happens when they are crossed – in grandeur or great awfulness.

It is not by chance that Euripides chooses a woman through which to pose this question to his citizen audience. (Euripides is especially renowned for his portrayal of women, particularly desperate and violent women.) The Athenian citizen defined himself in a series of oppositions. He was mortal, Greek, Athenian, male, free, in control; he was *not* immortal or an animal, 'barbarian' (that is, foreign), female, a slave or out of control. These oppositions are the basic building blocks of self-definition. Medea is especially hard to fit into such a matrix. She is female but acts and speaks like a man, indeed like a hero, an Achilles wholly committed to honour and revenge. She is a barbarian and a foreigner, but it is the Greek Jason who has acted deceitfully and nastily – at first. She is a woman, but ends up in the position of the god above the stage, and being called a monster by her husband. She is under the power of a king, but takes control of the action. Yet her taking control is also a sign of a wild emotion and violent social disruptiveness. Medea as a figure just doesn't fit into the familiar pattern of Athenian self-definition. Trying to *make sense* of Medea is what every audience has to do, just like the characters on stage. The difficulty she poses is a difficulty for the system of categories by which the self is defined. Her bizarre and extreme feminine character is a problem for everyone she meets – and for every audience that faces her.

Tragedy as a genre uses its stories of others' terrible suffering, despair and search for control over life to provoke its audience into self-questioning, a questioning about the very basis of society and the nature of the individual. What is remarkable is that such questions could be asked in a public, State festival. Tragedy provides modern society with the sobering spectacle of a community prepared to explore its own deepest worries and needs in public through great literature. It is for this reason that tragedy has played such a role in the Western imagination, and continues to do so.

The Staging of Tragedy

How were these masterpieces staged? How did these dense and remarkable words of tragedy take on the physical, bodily form of drama? Now that we have looked at the festival and the power of the scripts, let us look at their realization in theatrical performance itself.

The stage itself was divided into two parts, a circular dancing area called the *orchestra*, where the chorus performed, and a raised stage from where the actors spoke. The standard backdrop to the stage had a central door, usually representing the door of the palace. This door can be used in powerfully symbolic ways: it marks the entrance of the house with the full ideological weight of that boundary. So, in the *Agamemnon*, Clytemnestra enters through it, guards it, controls it, and makes Agamemnon walk through it under her terms. There were also two long walkways, stage left and stage right, along which an actor or the chorus could enter. These easily indicate the direction of the town, say, or the countryside, giving an expanded idea of the geography in which tragedy takes place. So, Creon enters from Delphi in the first scene of the *Oedipus Rex* from one side, while Tiresias, coming from the town, enters from the other side (bringing the message of Apollo to Oedipus from both sides, as it were, as the truth closes in on the king). The longer entrance walkways contrast with the instant opening of the door to give the stagings of entrances and exits their own dynamic. The tension between the house and the city finds immediate physical expression on stage.

It was possible to open the central doors and use a rolling trolley (*ekkuklêma*) to wheel out a tableau. That is probably how Clytemnestra emerged with the dead bodies of Agamemnon and Cassandra, to the shock of the chorus. Above the house was a walkway, the *theologeion*, on which gods could appear, spatially as well as conceptually above the humans. There was also a crane (*mêchanê*) which allowed gods or others to 'fly' above the stage. The expression *deus ex machina*, which means literally 'the god from the machine', and which is used for the surprising arrival of a saviour or a resolution, comes from the frequent use of this device to end plays, especially in the later plays of Euripides. Medea in her flying chariot was almost certainly such an appearance above the stage – in the place of a god. The sense of man's fragile place in the order of things here too finds physical expression.

The actors were all male, and there were three who took all the parts in each play. In the *Medea*, the same actor may have played, for example, the Nurse, Aegeus and the Messenger. There was a separate competition for actors, who could achieve considerable acclaim for their virtuosity. In the earliest days, tragedians acted in their own plays. By the time of the great tragedians, however, acting was becoming a profession that by the fourth century had a guild and its own tradition. The costumes were generally lavish (so that Euripides was mocked by comedians when he brought on a king in rags), and all speaking actors were always masked, a crucial resource for men playing different (and female) roles in the same play. These masks were not the familiar comic smile and tragic grimace of modern theatrical decoration, but more carefully painted and far more subtle representations – including probably a blinded and bleeding mask for Oedipus. It is extremely hard to judge acting style from such a distance, but ancient sources describe a grandeur and force of expression, and also an audience moved to tears and horror. Actors could also sing solo songs, or sing with the chorus. Many of Cassandra's dense lyrics in the *Agamemnon* would have been sung to a musical accompaniment, as would Oedipus' final horrible laments.

The chorus sang and danced all its odes. It is not always easy to see from translations when the lines of tragedy were sung, but the combination of music, dance and profound poetry is what has made tragedy such a source of inspiration for opera as well as drama. The commonest structure of tragedy is to intersperse spoken scenes with sung choral odes (*stasima*). The songs were accompanied by the *aulos*, which is often translated as 'flute', but is actually closer to the oboe as it is a reed instrument. There was also percussion. The chorus was dressed in matching costumes, and although we do not have any detailed record of the dancing, the images and texts we have suggest that the dancing was a carefully choreographed collective movement that could be wild or dignified, elegant or boisterous. The choruses of the *Oresteia* show this potential vividly. The chorus of the *Agamemnon* is a group of old men, councillors of the king, who sing songs of history, fear and celebration. The chorus of the *Libation Bearers* is a chorus of slave girls, who join in the great mourning song. The chorus of the *Eumenides* are the Furies themselves, wild, violent, female, monstrous figures whose entrance became famous for its terrifying irruption onto the stage, and who sing an awful magic spell, the 'binding song'.

The variety of musical style, dancing style and form of song from this one trilogy reveal what virtuosity a chorus must have needed – and how far such performances were from the stately, toga-clad choruses of Victorian imagination.

The extras and props of tragedy varied greatly. There are non-speaking servants in various scenes, children as in *Medea*, and, as in the first scene of the *Oedipus Rex* where the citizens supplicate the king, there are scenes which call out for large groups of extras. Most strikingly, there are objects which are invested with large symbolic weight, such as the wedding gifts of Medea or, most famously, the tapestries over which Agamemnon walks. Their crimson colour hints at the blood to be spilt, as his trampling of the household wealth recalls his destruction of his own daughter, as he proceeds towards his house and his own death. Actors' bodies, too, are essential to the meaning of tragedy, in significant gestures or actions: the limping Oedipus; the foot of Agamemnon touching the tapestries; Medea embracing her children. These charged moments are some of the most breath-taking because of their very physicality, their bodily presence on stage. The sets of tragedy were painted, but otherwise scenery seems to have been minimal, which further helps invest the few charged objects like the tapestries with such pointed significance.

Each tragedy is closely focused on a particular place and time, and usually the action is localized in a single day (which means few changes of set or scenery). This led later writers, who thought they were following Aristotle, to propose a principle of 'the Unities', namely, that each play should have a 'unified' – restricted, integral and consistent – action, place, time and characters. This 'rule' is not strictly followed at all in Greek tragedy itself, but it does at least point to the different sense of concentration or focus in tragedy from comedy, epic or later genres. Even so, tragedy does not have much 'action' (in the sense that 'action films' have action). Most violence takes place off stage – the death of Agamemnon, the hanging of Jocasta, the death of Medea's enemies and children, are all reported by the vivid words of other speakers. The focus of tragedy is more on the build-up of action, its explanations and the response to it. Yet because of this, individual moments of contact or physicality can have a huge dramatic effect: Agamemnon touching the tapestry; the removal of Oedipus' children; Medea's taunting appearance, carrying her dead children, in her flying chariot.

The performance of ancient Greek tragedy is a long way from modern theatre, its descendant. The state festival of Dionysus, the plays with their three masked male actors, its singing and dancing chorus of men, the very organization of the stage with its different acting areas, are all profoundly alien to modern Western theatrical experience.

Yet this stunning combination of profound poetry, intellectual and political intensity, deep and painful emotion, with the full resources of physical theatre – music, dance, costume – have made tragedy one of the lasting legacies of Athens. It has inspired generations of artists, thinkers and writers for theatre, as well as audiences. Opera began in the sixteenth century with a performance of *Oedipus Rex* in a conscious attempt to recreate Greek tragedy, and Wagner – to move forward to the great days of nineteenth-century opera – set out to recapture the spirit and form of the *Oresteia* in his great *Ring* cycle, which he had performed at the festival of Bayreuth, his attempt to rediscover the glories of Athenian civic ideals. The great tragic theatre of Jean Baptiste Racine in France, William Shakespeare in England, and their followers in Jacobean theatre or in the twentieth-century modernism of Bertold Brecht, all consciously turn back to the theatre of Greece, to rediscover the power of tragedy for a contemporary society. The history of modern drama starts with Greek tragedy, and keeps returning to it.

It is remarkable that from Berlin to New York, London to Paris, the twentieth century witnessed an extraordinary reflowering of Greek tragedy in modern performances, which in the twenty-first century shows no sign of stopping. These performances owe nothing to a sterile antiquarianism. They are produced because of tragedy's continuing ability to address the deepest concerns of human beings. Tragedy's intense enactment of the wrenching dilemmas of human beings faced by the confusion of moral action in a complex society of competing obligations speaks with a special authority and force to modern audiences, as it has done repeatedly over the ages. Greek tragedy may come from another time and place, but it has a remarkable power to speak to today, and to speak movingly, intensely and profoundly. Let us hope that the three great masterpieces of ancient theatre in this volume will continue such inspiration.

NOTES

1. The festival was temporarily reduced to three days during the Peloponnesian War (431–404 BC). The four-day festival had three tragedies and a satyr-play on each of the first three days, and five comedies on the fourth. The three-day festival had three tragedies, a satyr-play and one comedy on each day.
2. Probably only twelve during Aeschylus' time.

Further Reading

On Tragedy in General

Easterling, P. E., *The Cambridge Companion to Greek Tragedy* (Cambridge: Cambridge University Press, 1997)

Goldhill, Simon, *Reading Greek Tragedy* (Cambridge: Cambridge University Press, 1986)

On the *Oresteia*

Goldhill, Simon, *Aeschylus: the Oresteia: Landmarks of World Literature*, 2nd edn (Cambridge: Cambridge University Press, 2003)

On *Oedipus Rex*

Segal, C. P., *Oedipus Tyrannus: Tragic Heroism and the Limits of Knowledge* (New York: Twayne's Masterwork Series, 1993)

On *Medea*

Knox, B. M. W., 'The *Medea* of Euripides', in *Word and Action. Essays on the Ancient Theatre* (Baltimore: Johns Hopkins University Press, 1979)

On Staging

Taplin, O., *Greek Tragedy in Action* (London: Methuen, 1978)
Wiles, David, *Tragedy in Athens: Performance Space and Theatrical Meaning* (Cambridge: Cambridge University Press, 1997)

On Aristophanes, Old Comedy and *Frogs*

Bowie, A., *Myth, Ritual and Comedy* (Cambridge: Cambridge University Press, 1991)
Dover, K., *Aristophanic Comedy* (London: Batsford, 1972)
McLeish, K., *The Theatre of Aristophanes* (London: Thames and Hudson, 1980)

For the Festival

Pickard-Cambridge, A., *The Dramatic Festivals of Athens*, 2nd edn edited by John Gould and D. M. Lewis (Cambridge: Cambridge University Press, 1968)

On Aristotle

Else, G., *Aristotle's Poetics: the Argument* (Cambridge, Mass.: Harvard University Press, 1957)
Halliwell, S., *Aristotle's Poetics* (London: Duckworth, 1986)

Simon Goldhill

A Note on the Texts

The translators of these plays have adopted a similar overall strategy in approaching their material but with some stylistic differences. Neither Philip Vellacott (*Agamemnon* and *Medea*) nor E. F. Watling (*Oedipus Rex*) attempt a literal translation. Instead they aim at readability and clarity of meaning at the level of phrases, ideas and sentences rather than individual words or terms; in doing so they remain reasonably close to the original Greek. In terms of metre, there is no attempt to reflect the metrical characteristics of the original directly, but there is a discernible use of the metrical forms of English verse. Vellacott renders the dialogue parts (including set speeches) predominantly in unrhymed iambic hexameters (alexandrines) – these are more or less equivalent to the iambic trimeters of the original Greek (in Greek and Latin metrics a single metrical foot is four units instead of our two) – but with some shorter iambic lines interspersed. For lyric passages he adopts a different approach in the *Agamemnon* and the *Medea* respectively. In the *Agamemnon* we find a mixture of metrical forms (including iambics of varying lengths and trochaics) with various rhyme schemes. In the *Medea* lyric passages vary metrically, as in the *Agamemnon*, but are unrhymed. Watling's *Oedipus Rex* is metrically freer than Vellacott's two translations though it does distinguish dialogue from lyric passages in formal terms. In dialogue and speeches he employs iambic lines of varying lengths (mainly hexameters and pentameters with a five-stress rhythm) throughout, but with frequent use of 'resolved' iambics (where two short or unstressed syllables occupy a single metrical position). Lyric passages frequently involve elaborate rhyme schemes.

The language of the *Medea* is less formal and more colloquial than that of the *Agamemnon*, which retains a slightly archaic feel. In this way Vellacott conveys something of the difference in the respective styles of Aeschylus and Euripides. Watling's use of a lucid and dignified style also goes some way towards reflecting the distinctive stylistic characteristics of Sophocles' original.

In revising the translations of Vellacott and Watling my primary aim has been to make the translations clearer or more reader-friendly. I have updated anachronistic or unusual language and expressions, with a view to producing a poetic idiom and style that is consistent and contemporary. At the same time, attention has been paid to retaining the relative differences between the styles of the tragedians, inasmuch as they are evident in the three translations prior to their revision. I have also sought to render terms or expressions that may involve unhelpful or misleading connotations in more neutral language. I have generally sought to avoid making any alterations in metre or rhyme, but there are a few exceptions (mainly in the *Agamemnon*).

Vellacott's translation of the *Agamemnon* is based on the edition of A. Y. Campbell (1936). The standard editions of the text, used by most other translators, are Frankel (1950) and Page (1972). A major difference between Campbell's text and those of Frankel, Page and others is that Campbell relocates one of Clytemnestra's speeches ('There is the sea . . .') so that it precedes the section of one-line dialogue (*stichomythia*) between Agamemnon and Clytemnestra that starts after line 930. While Vellacott follows Campbell, I have restored the generally accepted order. Watling's translation of *Oedipus Rex* follows Jebb's edition (1893) with one or two minor departures. Vellacott's *Medea* is based largely on Page's 1938 edition.

The translation of Aristotle's *Poetics* appears unchanged from Malcolm Heath's Penguin edition, which is based on the Oxford Classical Text edition by R. Kassel (1965).

My primary aim in translating Aristophanes' *Frogs* has been to combine readability with clarity, while retaining as much as possible of the comic and poetic qualities of the original. I have also sought to reflect the remarkable ranges of tone and style in the original, which include everything from forthright obscenity, to specialized language (e.g. of oratory or philosophy), to elevated poetry. Where the language of the original is not unusual, imported or specialized, I have tried to keep to a neutral but contemporary colloquial style and tone. The translation is largely in prose but wherever tragedy is quoted or parodied, or a general tragic mode is adopted, I have used verse (iambics in dialogue or speeches, and freer verse forms in lyric passages). For the text of the *Frogs* I have followed the Oxford Classical Text of Hall and Geldart (1901).

The line numbers for the translations of the three tragedies and the extracts from the *Frogs* correspond to those of the respective Greek originals.

AGAMEMNON
BY
AESCHYLUS

Preface to *Agamemnon*

In the fifth century the story of Agamemnon and the events of the Trojan War (as well as those leading up to and following it) were known partly through an oral tradition of storytelling and partly through various versions in narrative, dramatic and lyric poetry. While the Homeric epics were undoubtedly the most important and authoritative source, there were other epic poems which dealt with events not treated directly in the *Iliad* and *Odyssey*. In some cases, these versions differ mainly in detail, rather than in terms of major incidents. Agamemnon's return home from Troy and subsequent murder take place outside the main narratives of the two Homeric epics: the *Iliad* deals with his quarrel with Achilles during the Trojan War but stops short of the actual fall of Troy; the *Odyssey* begins after Agamemnon's son Orestes has avenged his death by murdering Clytemnestra and Aegisthus.

Aeschylus' *Oresteia* looks to Homeric epic and, in all probability, to an earlier, non-dramatic *Oresteia* by the sixth-century poet Stesichorus (of which only a handful of fragments remain), but it significantly reworks the story. This process of revision is also evident in two later tragedies – Euripides' *Electra* and Sophocles' *Electra* – which offer their own distinctive accounts of the deaths of Clytemnestra and Aegisthus at the hands of Orestes and his sister Electra (Aeschylus' play dealing with this story, *The Libation Bearers*, is the second work in the *Oresteia* trilogy). The *Oresteia* as a whole deals with the latter stages of the family history of the Pelopids (the descendants of Agamemnon's grandfather Pelops), but the action of the *Agamemnon* in particular is also closely informed by the events of the Trojan

War. Attention is drawn to background events in the play primarily through long choral passages and the varyingly cryptic, prophetic utterances of Cassandra. The general pattern of events would have been familiar to Aeschylus' audience, although not necessarily all the details. What follows here is an account of the family history of the Pelopids and of some of the background to the Trojan War that is consistent with Aeschylus' version of events.

The Pelopids may be traced back to Pelops' father Tantalus (see genealogical table on p. 303). The family history of Tantalus and his descendants is particularly gruesome. Tantalus was the son of Zeus and his sister Pluto (daughter of Cronos and Rhea; not to be confused with her brother, the underworld god Pluton, or Hades). He was king of Sipylus in Lydia and was famed for his wealth (rather like the later Lydian king Croesus). As one of the first generation of mortals, Tantalus enjoyed the company of Zeus, who admitted him to the banquets of the gods. But he abused this hospitality by stealing the gods' privileged food and drink (ambrosia and nectar respectively), and sharing it among his mortal friends. Before this crime was discovered, however, he committed a worse one: inviting the Olympian gods to a feast, he served them a dish made of the diced pieces of his own murdered son Pelops (either to test them or simply to insult them further after his theft of ambrosia and nectar). All the gods realized what had been put before them except for Demeter, who was still grieving her daughter Persephone's abduction and unthinkingly ate Pelops' shoulder.

The gods punished Tantalus by placing him in the underworld in perpetual torment. He was confined to a pool where the water receded whenever he stooped in the hope of quenching his thirst. He was also within reach of a tree whose boughs receded each time he reached to grasp their succulent fruit. It is from these two punishments that the word 'tantalize' is derived. To add to his torment, he had a rock hanging over him that always seemed about to fall. Tantalus' son Pelops was restored to life, and his eaten shoulder replaced with a prosthetic one made of ivory. While still a young man, he was driven out of Lydia by a rival king (Ilus of Troy). He therefore ventured to the south-western peninsula of Greece, which subsequently took its name from him, the Peloponnese.

Pelops sought to marry Hippodameia, the daughter of king Oenomaus of Elis. Hippodameia's father, however, fearing an oracle proclaiming that he would be killed by his son-in-law, used to challenge suitors to a chariot race in which his daughter would ride with the suitor as a distraction. If victorious, the suitor would be allowed to marry Hippodameia; if not, he was executed. Oenomaus, who had magnificent horses given to him by the god Ares, boasted that he had almost seen off enough suitors to build a temple from their skulls. Against such odds, Pelops sought the help of Poseidon (his lover in some accounts). The god gave him a winged chariot and immortal horses, but Pelops also bribed Oenomaus' charioteer Myrtilus, who tampered with the linchpins of Oenomaus' chariot. During the race, Oenomaus was thrown and killed, and Pelops took Hippodameia as his wife. But when Myrtilus demanded his reward, Pelops refused. (In some accounts Myrtilus' reward was to spend the wedding night with Hippodameia; in others it was to be given half of Oenomaus' kingdom.) Instead Pelops murdered him by throwing him off a cliff. With his dying words Myrtilus cursed Pelops' descendants.

Pelops ruled happily and fathered several sons, but the curse upon his house afflicted two of his sons, Atreus and Thyestes. Atreus became king of Mycenae but was envied by Thyestes, who seduced Atreus' wife Aerope (the mother of Agamemnon and Menelaus). Atreus discovered the adultery and banished Thyestes. To punish him further, however, he feigned a reconciliation and invited Thyestes to a banquet, at which Atreus served him the flesh of Thyestes' own murdered children, repeating the crime of his grandfather Tantalus. When Thyestes realized what he had eaten, he fled, pronouncing a curse upon the house of Atreus.

Thyestes was informed by an oracle that he should gain his revenge by fathering a child upon his own daughter, Pelopia. He therefore accosted her in disguise, but in departing the scene he left his sword, which Pelopia kept. The son born from this union, Aegisthus, was abandoned by his mother but later

rescued by Atreus and brought up as his own. (In Aeschylus'
version of events, Aegisthus is born just before Atreus' murder
of Thyestes' children.) Some time later, Atreus sent the young
Aegisthus to kill Thyestes. Aegisthus was on the point of fulfil-
ling this task when Thyestes recognized his own sword, and
asked the boy how he had come by it. Aegisthus replied that his
mother had given it to him, whereupon Thyestes explained that
the two of them were, in fact, father and son. They then contrived the death of Atreus. This they achieved with relative ease,
since Atreus was under the misapprehension that Thyestes was
dead and that Aegisthus, whom he did not know to be Thyestes'
son, was loyal to him.

After the death of Atreus, Thyestes ruled for a time until
he was defeated and killed by the brothers Agamemnon and
Menelaus, with the help of king Tyndareus of Sparta. Agamemnon, who married Tyndareus' daughter Clytemnestra, then
became king of Argos and Mycenae. Tyndareus' other daughter
was Helen (although she was generally believed to be the daughter of Zeus, who had visited Tyndareus' wife Leda in the form of
a swan). Helen had become widely known for her unparalleled
beauty. Accordingly, she was sought by a number of leading
Greek princes and kings. Before she (or, in some versions, her
father) selected a husband, the suitors swore that they would
abide by the decision and support her future husband's marital
rights. Menelaus was chosen as Helen's husband.

Some time after this, Paris, a son of king Priam of Troy, came
to Menelaus' house as a guest. When he left he took Helen
with him. In some accounts he seduced her, in others she was
abducted. Either way, Paris' action amounted to a breach of the
laws of hospitality (of which Zeus was the guardian). This
transgression was the event that sparked the Trojan War. Agamemnon, as the senior king in Greece and brother of Menelaus,
commanded the Greek forces; the Greek princes were bound by
the oath they had taken as Helen's suitors to assist in retrieving
her. The curse on the house of Atreus resurfaced, however,
when the entire Greek fleet became stuck in the port of Aulis.
Agamemnon had offended the goddess Artemis by boasting
about his prowess during a hunt. The goddess stayed the winds

and demanded that Agamemnon sacrifice his daughter Iphigenia in exchange for favourable winds (and as atonement for the offence he had caused her). Caught between returning home in ignominy and slaughtering his own child, Agamemnon chose the latter. He sent for Iphigenia under false pretences and sacrificed her pitilessly in front of the Greek army. (In an alternative version of the myth, followed by Euripides in his *Iphigenia at Aulis*, Iphigenia is saved at the last minute by Artemis, who removes her to safety and provides a deer to be sacrificed in her place.) When Clytemnestra learnt what Agamemnon had done, she vowed to avenge her daughter's death.

Aegisthus, meanwhile, was still intent upon punishing Agamemnon for the crimes of Agamemnon's father Atreus against his own father Thyestes. Taking advantage of Agamemnon's absence, he seduced Clytemnestra and plotted with her to kill Agamemnon upon his return (both had their own motives). According to Homer, Aegisthus carried out the murder at a banquet in his own house. Aeschylus, however, makes Clytemnestra the driving force behind the planning and execution of the murder, which is carried out on the very day Agamemnon returns from the war, while he is in the bath within his own quarters in the royal palace.

While Agamemnon was in Troy, he took as a concubine Cassandra, the captive daughter of king Priam, who was doomed to prophesy the truth without ever being believed (a curse laid upon her by Apollo, whose advances she had spurned). In Aeschylus' play, Clytemnestra kills Cassandra as well as Agamemnon, describing them as lovers. Aeschylus thus gives her a double motive for her actions: as a mother, she seeks to avenge the death of Iphigenia; as a wife, she seeks to punish Agamemnon for taking a mistress (although this motive is undermined by her own prior adulterous relationship with Aegisthus).

The action of the *Agamemnon* begins before Agamemnon's return from Troy. Clytemnestra and Aegisthus have been lovers for some years, and the news of Troy's fall is imminent. So that she may be prepared for Agamemnon's return in advance, Clytemnestra has arranged a system of beacons that are set in place to relay news of Troy's fall all the way from Troy to Argos. To that end she has posted a watchman on the palace roof, whose sole task it is to inform her of the moment the final beacon proclaiming the fall of Troy is lit.

Characters

A WATCHMAN
CHORUS *of Elders of Argos*
CLYTEMNESTRA, *wife of Agamemnon*
A HERALD
AGAMEMNON, *king of Argos*
CASSANDRA, *a princess of Troy*
AEGISTHUS, *lover of Clytemnestra, cousin to Agamemnon*
Soldiers attending Agamemnon
Guards attending Aegisthus

Scene: Before the Royal Palace at Argos.
Night, a little before sunrise. A lone WATCHMAN *is*
stationed on the palace roof.

WATCHMAN

O gods! Grant me release from this long weary watch.
Release, O gods! Twelve full months now, night after night
Dog-like I lie here, keeping guard from this high roof
On Atreus' palace. The nightly gathering of stars,
Glittering rulers, bringing heat and cold in turn,
Studding the sky with beauty – I know them all, and watch
    them
Rise and set. But the only light I long to see
Is a new star, the promised sign, the beacon-flare
To speak from Troy and utter one word, 'Victory!' –
Great news for Clytemnestra, in whose woman's heart   10
A man-like will breeds hope. Now once more, drenched
    with dew,
I walk about or lie down – no dreams visit me.
Sleep's enemy, fear, stands guard beside me, forbidding
My eyes a moment's closing. If I sing some tune –
Music is the one cure prescribed for heartsickness –
Why, then I weep to think how changed this house is now
From its former splendour, ruled by its rightful lord.
So may the gods be kind and grant release from trouble,   20
And send the fire to cheer this dark night with good news.
    [*Pause. The long-awaited beacon suddenly shines out.*]

O welcome beacon, kindling night to glorious day,
Welcome! You'll make them dance in all the streets of
    Argos
When they hear your message. You there! Call
    Clytemnestra!
The queen must rise from her bed with all speed and greet
The fire with pious words and a shout of victory:
30 The city of Troy is ours – the beacon is clear enough!
I myself will be the first to start the triumphal dance.
Now I can say the gods have blessed my master's hand.
For me too that beacon's light is a piece of luck.
Now heaven bring Agamemnon safely home! May I
Hold his dear hand in mine! Of the rest, I say no more;
My tongue is held. This house itself, if walls had words,
Would tell its story plainly. I speak just to those
Who understand me; to the rest my mind is blank.
    [*The* WATCHMAN *exits.*]
    [*The* CHORUS *enter.* CLYTEMNESTRA *enters at some*
    point between the end of the WATCHMAN*'s speech and*
    the CHORUS LEADER*'s address to her* (p. 13).]

CHORUS
40 Ten years have passed since the strong sons of Atreus,
Menelaus and Agamemnon – both honoured
Alike by Zeus with throned and sceptred power –
Assembled and manned a thousand Greek ships
And, with the youth of Hellas under arms,
Sailed from these shores to settle scores with Priam.

Then loud their warlike anger cried,
As eagles cry that, wild with grief,
50 On some steep, lonely mountainside
Above their robbed nest wheel and sail,
Plying the airy waves, and bewail
Their wasted toil, their watchful pride.
Till some celestial deity –
Zeus, Pan, or Apollo – hears on high
Their screams of wordless misery,

And pitying their unhappy state
(Since air is heaven's protectorate),
Sends a swift Fury to pursue
Marauding guilt with vengeance due.

So against Paris' guilty boast   60
Zeus, protector of guest and host,
Sends Atreus' sons for harsh redress
Of his and Helen's wantonness.
Now Greece and Troy pay equal debt
Of aching limbs and wounds and sweat,
While knees sink low in bloodstained dust,
And spears are scraped as they are thrust.
Things are as they are now; their end
Shall trace a fate that none can bend.
In vain shall Priam's altars burn;   70
Vainly his rich libations flow
To gods above and powers below.
No gift or sacrificial flame
Can hope to soothe or turn
The wrath of heaven from its relentless aim.

We were too old to take our share
With those who joined the army then.
We lean on sticks – in strength not men
But children – so they left us here.
In weakness youth and age are one;
The sap is weak in unripe bones
As in the withered. The green stalk
Grows without thorns. So, in their grey   80
And brittle years, old men must walk
Three-footed, weak as babes, and stray
Like dreams lost in the light of day.
   [*The* CHORUS LEADER *now addresses*
   CLYTEMNESTRA.]
Daughter of Tyndareus, Queen Clytemnestra,
What have you heard? What has happened? Why have you
   ordered

Sacrifice throughout the city? Is there news?
Altars of all the gods who guard our state –
Gods of the sky and the powers below –
Throughout both town and country, blaze with offerings.
On all sides upward-leaping flames implore
Anger to melt in gentleness – a glare
Enriched with holy ointment, balm so rare
As issues only from a royal store!

Why is this so? Be gracious, Queen,
And tell us whatever you may.
Be healer of this haunting fear
Which now like an enemy creeps near,
And now again, when hope has seen
These altars bright with promise, slinks away.
Tell us, so hope may lift the load
Which galls our souls by night and day,
Sick with the evil that has been,
And evil that our hearts forebode.
    [CLYTEMNESTRA *stands away from the* CHORUS
    and remains silent. They continue to address the
    audience.]
I am the man to speak, if you would hear
The whole tale from its hope-filled starting-place:
That portent which amazed our marching youth.
It was ten years ago, but I was there.
The poet's grace, the singer's fire,
Grows with his years. I can still speak the truth
With the clear ring the gods inspire –
How those twin monarchs of our warlike race,
Two leaders joined in purpose, were sped forth,
Their vengeful spears in thousands pointing north
To Troy, by four wings' furious beat:
Two royal birds that seemed to bode
Great fortune to the kings of that great fleet.
Close to the palace, the spear-side of the road,
One tawny-feathered and one white of tail,

90

100

110

Perched in full view, they ravenously tear
The body of a pregnant hare
Large with her litter; now a living prey
In the last darkness of their unborn day.   120
Cry sorrow, sorrow – yet may good prevail!

The army's learned seer saw this, and knew
The devourers of the hare
For that relentless pair –
Different in nature as the birds in hue –
The sons of Atreus. In council of war
He prophesied, 'Your army, it is true,
In time shall make Priam's city their prey;
Those flocks and herds Troy's priests shall slay
With prayers for the safety of her walls
Will die in vain – Troy's violent doom shall swallow all.   130
Only, see to it, you who go
To bridle Trojan pride, that no
Anger of the gods should darken your day
And strike before your hulls are under way.
For virgin Artemis, whom all revere,
Loathes with a deadly hate
The swift-winged hounds of Zeus who swooped to assail
Their helpless victim wild with fear
Before her ripe hour came;
Who dared to violate
(So warning spoke the priest)
The awe that parenthood must claim,
As for some rite performed in Heaven's name;
Yes, Artemis abominates the eagles' feast!'
Cry sorrow, sorrow – yet may good prevail!

On it spoke, the prophet's tongue:
'Lovely child of Zeus, I pray,   140
You who love the tender whelp
Of the ravening lion, and care
For all the suckling young
Of fox and rat and hind and hare;

If ever by your heavenly help
Hope of good was brought to flower,
Bless the sign we saw today!
Ward off all its foretold ill,
All its promised good fulfil!
Next my anxious prayers entreat
Lord Apollo's healing power,
That his sister may not plan
Winds to chain the Hellene fleet;
Also, that her grievance may not crave
150   Blood to drench another grave
From a different sacrifice
Hallowed by no festive joy;
Blood that builds a store of hate,
Mad blood raging to destroy
Its own source, a ruthless fate
Warring with the flesh of man;
Bloodshed bringing in its train
Kindred blood that flows again,
Anger still unreconciled,
Poisoning a house's life
With darkness, treachery and strife,
Wreaking vengeance for a murdered child.'

So Calchas, from that parting prodigy
Auguring the royal house's destiny,
Pronounced his warning of a fatal curse,
With hope of better mixed with fear of worse.
Let us too, echoing his uncertain tale,
Cry sorrow, sorrow – yet may good prevail!

160   May good prevail!
So be it! And yet, what is good? And who
Is god? How should we name him and speak true?
If he accepts the name that men
Give him, Zeus I call him then.

Still, troubled in my mind,
I have long searched and weighed
Every hope of comfort and of aid.
Yet I can find
No creed to lift this heaviness,
This fear that haunts without excuse,
No name inviting faith, no hopeful guess –
Except for Zeus.

The first of the gods is gone –
Old Uranus, once blown
With violence and pride.
His name shall not be known;
Nor that his dynasty once lived and died.   170
His strong successor Cronos had his hour,
Then went his way, overthrown
By a yet stronger power.
Now Zeus is lord, and he
Who loyally acclaims his victory
Shall by the heart's instinct find the universal key.

Zeus, whose will has marked for man
The sole way where wisdom lies,
Orders one eternal plan:
Man must suffer to be wise.
Headwinds heavy with past ills
Stay his course and cloud his heart.   180
Sorrow takes the blind soul's part –
Man grows wise against his will.
For powers who rule seated above
By ruthlessness commend their love.

So it was then. Agamemnon, mortified,
Dared not – would not – admit his fault. He thought
Of his great Hellene fleet, and in his pride
Spread sail to the ill wind he should have fought.

Meanwhile his armed men moped along the shore,
And cursed the wind, and ate his dwindling stores;
190 Stared at the white cliffs of Chalcis day after day
Across the sea that churned in Aulis bay.
And still from Strymon came the northern blast,
While hulks and ropes grew rotten, mooring parted,
And deserters slunk away.
All ground their teeth – bored, helpless, hungry, thwarted.
The days of waiting doubled. More days passed.
The flower of warlike Hellas withered fast.

200 But Calchas spoke again. The wind, he said,
Was sent by Artemis. Then he revealed
Her remedy – a thought to crush like lead
The hearts of Atreus' sons, who wept, as weep they must,
And speechless ground their sceptres in the dust.

The elder king then spoke: 'What can I say?
Disaster follows if I disobey;
Yet surely worse disaster if I yield
And slaughter my own child, my home's delight,
In her young innocence, staining my hand
With profane and unnatural cruelty,
210 And bathing in the blood I fathered! Either way
Lies ruin! But disband the fleet, sail home, and earn
A deserter's name? Abandon my command,
Betray the alliance – now? No, the wind must turn,
There must be sacrifice, the girl must bleed!
The men's sore rage demands it – they are right!
May good prevail and justify my deed!'

So he put on
The harness of Necessity.
The doubtful tempest of his soul
220 Veered, and his prayer was turned to blasphemy,
His offering to impiety.
Hence that repentance late and long
Which, since his madness passed, pays toll

For that one reckless wrong.
Shameless self-willed infatuation
Emboldens men to dare damnation,
And starts the wheels of doom which roll
Relentless to their grievous goal.

So Agamemnon, rather than retreat,
Prepared to offer up his daughter's life
To help a war fought for a faithless wife
And pay the ransom for a storm-bound fleet.

Heedless of her tears,
Her cries of 'Father!', and her tender years
Her judges valued more
Their glory and their war.   230
A prayer was said. Her father gave the word.
Limp in her flowing dress
The priest's attendants held her high
Above the altar, as men hold a kid.
Her father spoke again, but just to bid
Them bring a gag, and press
Her soft mouth tightly with a cord,
In case his house be cursed by some ill-omened cry.

Rough hands tear at the girdle, cast
Her saffron silks to the earth. Her eyes
Search for her slaughterers, but each,   240
Seeing her beauty, which surpassed
A painter's vision, yet denies
The pity her dumb looks beseech,
Struggling for voice; though often in earlier days,
When brave men feasted in her father's halls,
With simple skill and pious praise,
In keeping with the flute's pure tone,
Her virgin voice would melt the hearts of all,
Honouring the last libation near her father's throne.

The rest I did not see,
Nor do I speak of it . . .
                              But this I know:
What Calchas prophesied will be fulfilled.
250   The scale of justice falls impartially:
The killer will be killed. — *Retributive justice*

But now, farewell foreboding! Time may show,
But cannot alter, what shall be.
What use, then, in bewailing
Troubles before they fall?
Events will wend their way
Even as the prophet's words foreshadowed all.
For what is next at hand,
May good prevail!
That is the prayer we pray –
We, who now stand
In Agamemnon's place to guard this Argive land.
     [*Day has broken.* CLYTEMNESTRA *now turns and faces
     the* CHORUS.]
CHORUS
We come obedient to your bidding, Clytemnestra.
Our king and leader absent, and his throne unmanned,
260   We pay his due observance to his wife.
Have you received some message? Do these sacrifices
Rise for good news, as thanks for long hope reassured?
I ask out of love, and will as loyally accept
An answer or silence.
CLYTEMNESTRA
Good news, if the proverb is true,
Should break with sunrise from the kindly womb of night.
But here is richer joy than you ever dared hope:
Our Greek army has captured Priam's city.
CHORUS
                                        What!
I must have heard you wrong – I don't believe it!
CLYTEMNESTRA
                                        Troy is ours!

Is that clear enough?

CHORUS

                         Happiness fills my eyes with tears.   270

CLYTEMNESTRA

Which show your loyalty.

CHORUS

                   Do you have proof of this?

CLYTEMNESTRA

I do indeed, unless a god has played me false.

CHORUS

A god? Were you persuaded by a dream?

CLYTEMNESTRA

A dream! I am not one to air drowsy imaginings.

CHORUS

Surely you feed yourself on unconfirmed report?

CLYTEMNESTRA

You criticize me as you would a foolish girl!

CHORUS

Well then, when was Troy captured?

CLYTEMNESTRA

                            On this very night

That brought to birth this glorious sun.

CHORUS

                        What messenger

Could fly so fast from Troy to here?   280

CLYTEMNESTRA

                     The god of fire!

Ida first launched his bright beam; from there to this palace
Beacon lit beacon in relays of flame. From Ida
It came to Hermes' crag on Lemnos; from there, next
To receive the towering torch was Athos, rock of Zeus;
There, as the blaze leapt the dark miles, the watch leapt too
For joy as the twin towers of light speared the sky,
Pointing across the former course; and in one stride
The resinous firebrand flew across the Aegean –
Molten gold, like a bolt of lightning – till the fish danced,
As at sunrise, enraptured with the beacon's glow,
Which shone like a second sun on Makistos' heights.

290 The watchman there – proof against sleep, surprise
Or sloth – rose faithful to the message, and his flame
Swept the wide distance to Euripus' channel, where
Its burning sign was blazoned to the Messapian guards.
They blazed in turn, kindling their pile of withered heath,
And passed the signal on. The strong beam, still undimmed,
Crossed the plain of Asopus in one bound, and like a
         brightly
Shining moon, lighted on Cithaeron's crags, and woke
Another watch to speed the flying signal on its way.
300 On still the hot torch hurtled, past Lake Gorgopis;
It made Aegiplanctus, and stirred those watchful
         mountaineers
Not to stint on their boughs and brushwood; full they fed
Their beacon, and up burst a raging beard of fire
That vaulted the proud headland fronting the Saronic Gulf,
On to high Arachneus, which neighbours our streets;
310 From there on to this palace the triumphant fire
Flashed, a direct descendant of the flame of Ida.

Such, elders, was the ritual race my torchbearers,
Each, faithful at his post, succeeding each, fulfilled;
And first and last to run share equal honours.
Such, elders, is my evidence to you,
A message sent to me from Troy by Agamemnon.

CHORUS
Lady, we will in due course offer thanks to heaven,
But now we want to savour our awe to the full,
And hear you speak at length – tell us your news again!

CLYTEMNESTRA
320 Today the Greeks hold Troy! Her walls echo with cries
That do not blend. Pour oil and vinegar into one vessel
And they will part and swirl but never mix. So too
In Troy, down narrow streets a discord grates the ear:
Cries of the conquered and shouts of the conquerors;
The desolate and the joyful. Women of Troy prostrate
Over dead husbands and brothers; aged grandfathers
Mourning dead sons and grandsons, and remembering

Their very cries are slaves' cries now. And then the victors:
After a night of fighting, roaming, plundering,   330
Hungry to breakfast, while their hosts lie silent in the dust;
No rules to keep, no pecking order; each with the luck
That fell to him, quartered in captured Trojan homes.
Tonight, at last, rolled in dry blankets, safe from frost –
No keeping watch – they'll sleep soundly from dusk to
      dawn.

If in that sacked city they reverence the gods,
Whose home it was, and do not profane holy places,
The victors will avoid being vanquished in their turn.   340
Only, may no lust of unlawful plunder tempt
Our soldiers' hearts with gain to their own cost. There still
Remains the journey home. Heaven grant we see them safe!
If the fleet sails free from sacrilege then the gods
May grant them safely to retrace their outward course –
Those whom no wakeful anger of the forgotten dead
Waits to surprise with vengeance . . .
                                 These are a woman's words.
May good prevail beyond dispute, in sight of all!
My life holds many blessings – may I enjoy them now!   350

CHORUS
Lady, your words are like a man's, both wise and kind.
Now we have trustworthy proof from your own lips,
We will prepare ourselves again to praise the gods,
Whose gracious acts call for our most devout response.

      [CLYTEMNESTRA *goes into the palace.*]

CHORUS
Zeus, supreme of heavenly powers!
Kindly night, whose fateful hours
Built for Argos' warlike name
Bright imperishable fame!
Night in which a net was laid
Fast about the Trojan towers
Such that none of mortal flesh,
Great or little, could evade
Grim annihilation's deadly mesh!   360

This is the hand of Zeus, whom we revere,
Whose lasting law both host and guest must fear.
He long since towards Paris bent
His bow with careful aim, and sent
His vengeance flying, not too near
Nor past the stars, but timed to pay
The debt of Justice on the appointed day.

'The hand of Zeus has cast
the proud from their high place!'
This we may say, and trace
That hand from first to last.
As Zeus foreknowing willed,
So was their end fulfilled.

One said, 'The gods disdain
370   To mark man's wanton way,
Who tramples in the dust
Beauty of holy things.'
Impious! The truth shows plain:
Pride now has paid its debt, and they
Who laughed at Right and put their boastful trust
In arms and the inflated wealth of kings,
Have gone their destined way.
A middle course is best,
Not poor nor proud. But this,
By no clear rule defined,
380   Eludes the unstable, undiscerning mind,
Whose aim will surely miss.
Thenceforth there is no way to turn aside;
When man has once transgressed,
And in his wealth and pride
Spurned the high shrine of justice, nevermore
May his wrongs hope to hide
In that safe obscurity he enjoyed before.

With no retreat, the fiend Temptation
Forces him onwards, the unseen
Effective agent of damnation.
Once his fair freshness has been
Blotched and defiled with grime, and he,
Like worthless bronze which testing blows   390
Have blackened, lies tarnished and shows
His baseness plain for all to see,
Then every cure renews despair.
He on his race and land must bring –
A boy chasing a bird on the wing –
A deeper doom than flesh can bear;
The gods are deaf to every prayer,
And if some pity lights a human eye
Then pity must, by the law of justice, share
The wrongdoer's guilt, and with the wrongdoer die.
So, doomed, deluded, Paris came
To sit at his host's table, and seduce   400
Another's wife, and shame
The house of Atreus and the law of Zeus.

Bequeathing us in Argos
The ring of shields and spears,
The din of forge and dockyard,
She crossed the threshold lightly
And left her palace, fearless
Of what should wake her fears;
And took to Troy as dowry
Destruction, blood, and tears.
Here, in her home deserted,
The voice of guard and groom
With love and grief lamented:
'O house, O king! O pity!   410
O pillow softly printed
Where her dear head had rested!'
There lies her husband fasting,

Stricken dumb in his room.
His thoughts reach over the sea
With longing, not reproaches;
A ghost will rule the palace,
A home become a tomb!
Now statues' sweet proportions
Augment his desolation.
His hungry eye still searches –
But living grace is hardened
And lost that beauty's bloom.

420   Visions of her beset him
With false and fleeting pleasure
When dreams are dark and deep.
He sees her, runs to hold her;
But slipping through his fingers,
Lightly departs his treasure,
The dream he cannot keep,
Wafted on wings that follow
The shadowy paths of sleep.

Such are the searching sorrows
This royal palace knows,
While through the streets of Argos
Grief yet more grievous grows,
With all our manhood gathered
430   So far from the soil of Greece;
As in each home unfathered,
Each widowed bed, the whetted
Sword of despair assails
Hearts where all hope has withered
And angry hate prevails.
They sent forth men to battle,
But no such men return;
And home, to claim their welcome,
Come ashes in an urn.

War is a banker, flesh his gold.
There by the furnace of Troy's fields,   440
Where thrust meets thrust, he sits to hold
His scales, and watch the spear-points sway.
Then back to waiting homes he sends
Slag from the ore, a little dust
To drain hot tears from hearts of friends;
Good measure safely stored and sealed
In a convenient jar – the just
Prize for the man they sent away.
They praise him through their tears, and say,
'He was a soldier!' or 'He died
Nobly, with death on every side!'
And fierce resentment mutters low,
'For someone else's wife!' And so
From grief springs gall, which fear must hide –   450
Let kings and their vendettas go!
But under Trojan walls the dead,
In their youthful bloom, lie chambered deep,
While soil, whose living blood they shed,
Covers its conquerors in sleep.

A nation's voice inflamed by anger
Strikes deadly as a public curse.
I wait for word of hidden danger,
Fearing bad may give place to worse.   460
God marks that man with watchful eyes
Who counts his kills by companies;
And when his luck, his proud success,
Ignores the law of righteousness,
Then the dark Furies launch at length
A counterblow to crush his strength
And cloud his lustre, till the dim
Pit of oblivion swallows him.
In fame unmeasured, praise too high,
Lies danger: Zeus' sharp lightning flies   470

To stagger mountains. So I choose
Such wealth as stirs no rankling hate,
And not to lay towns desolate,
Nor wear the chains of those who lose
Freedom and life to war and fate.

[*The* CHORUS *now turn their attention once more to the
news conveyed by the beacon. The following remarks are
made severally by chorus members.*]

Since the beacon's news was heard
Rumour flies through every street.
Ought we to believe a word?
Is it some inspired deceit?
Foolish, crackbrained fantasy!
480   Arm your hopes with such a tale,
And you'll soon find fire can lie,
Facts can change, and trust can fail.
Women are all hasty-headed:
Beacons blaze, belief rejoices –
All too easily persuaded.
Rumour fired by women's voices,
As we know, is quickly spread;
As we know, is quickly dead.

[*Exit* CHORUS. *At this point there is a gap in the action
of several days – the time taken for* AGAMEMNON *and
his men to reach Argos from Troy – after which the*
CHORUS *re-enter excited.*]

CHORUS

We shall soon see whether this relay-race of flame,
490   This midnight torch-parade, this beacon-telegraph,
Told us the truth, or if the fire made fools of us –
All a fanciful dream. But look! Here comes a herald
Up from the shore, wearing a crown of olive-leaves!
And, further off, a marching column of armed men,
Sheathed in hot dust, suggests this herald won't stand dumb
Or light a pinewood fire to announce the smoke of Troy!
Either his news doubles our happiness, or else –
The gods forbid all else! Good shows at first appearance.

Now may the proof be good! He who prays otherwise
For Argos, let him reap the folly of his soul!   500
   [*Enter a* HERALD.]

HERALD
Argos! Dear earth my fathers trod! After ten years
Today I have come home! All other hopes were false,
But this proves true! I dared not think my own land would
Receive me in death to my due and cherished rest.
Now blest be Argos, and the sun's sweet light, and Zeus,
God of this realm, and Pythian Apollo, who no more
Aims against us the shafts of his immortal bow.   510
You fought us, Phoebus, by Scamander long enough.
Be saviour now, and healer – once, not twice, our death.
Gods of the city's gathering, hear my prayer; and thou,
Hermes, dear guardian, herald – every herald's god.
And you, heroes of old, whose blessing sent us forth,
Bless the returning remnant that the sword has spared!
O house of kings! Beloved walls! O noble thrones!
You deities who watch the rising sun, watch now!
Welcome with shining eyes the royal architect   520
Of towering glories to adorn his ancient throne.
To you and every Argive citizen Agamemnon
Brings light from darkness. Come, then, and greet him
   royally,
As fits one in whose hand Zeus the Avenger's plough
Passed over Troy, to crack her towers, scar and subdue
Her fields, and from her fair soil extirpate her seed.
So harsh a halter has the elder son of Atreus thrown
Around Troy's neck, and now comes home victorious   530
To claim the utmost honours among mortal men.
For neither Paris now, nor his complicit city,
Can boast their deed was greater than their punishment.
Found guilty of theft and robbery, he has forfeited
His treasured spoil, destroyed his father's house and realm,
And made his people pay twice over for his crime.

CHORUS
Greetings, herald of the Greek army! Welcome home!

HERALD
I thank you. For ten years I've prayed for life; now I can die.
CHORUS
540   Did thoughts of Argos, of your home torment you?
HERALD
Terribly; and now my cloak is wet with tears of joy.
CHORUS
Your suffering has its positive side.
HERALD

                          What do you mean?

CHORUS
Your love was requited. Is that not good?
HERALD
You mean that Argos longed for us, as we for her?
CHORUS
Our hearts were sick with worry. We missed and needed
    you.
HERALD
What is it that caused you concern? An enemy?
CHORUS
I learnt long ago that silence is the safest course.
HERALD
Was Argos under threat during the king's absence?
CHORUS
550   You said just now that death was most welcome; we feel the
    same.
HERALD
Yes, I could die now war is over, and all's well.
Time blurs the memory: some things one recalls as good,
Others as hateful. We're not gods, so why expect
To reap a lifetime of unbroken happiness?
To think what we went through! If I described it all,
The holes we camped in, dirt and weariness and sweat;
Or out at sea, with storms all night, trying to sleep
On a narrow board, with half a blanket; and all day,
Miserable and sick, we suffered but put up with it.
Then, when we landed, things got worse. We had to camp
560   Close to enemy walls, in the wet river meadows,

Soaked with the dew and mist, ill from damp clothes, our
   hair
Matted like savages. If I described the winter, when
In cruel snow-winds from Ida birds froze on the trees;
Or if I told of the fierce heat, when Ocean dropped
Waveless and windless to his noonday bed, and slept . . .
Well, it's no time for moaning; all that's over now.
And those who died out there – it's over for them too.
No need to jump to orders; they can take their rest.
Why call the roll of those who were expendable,   570
And make the living wince from old wounds probed again?
Nor much rejoicing either, if we're sensible.
For us who've come home safe the good weighs heaviest,
And what we've suffered counts for less. The praise that's
   due
Proudly inscribed, will show these words to the bright sun:
   The Argive army conquered Troy,
   And brought home over land and sea
   These hard-won spoils, the pride and joy
   Of ancient palaces, to be
   Trophies of victory, and grace
   The temples of the Hellene Race.
Let Argos hear this, and receive her general home   580
With thanks and praise. Let Zeus, who gave us victory,
Be blest for his great mercy. I have no more to say.

CHORUS
Well, I was wrong, I admit. Old and keen to learn
Is ever young. But this great news is for the palace,
Most of all Clytemnestra, whose wealth of joy we share.
   [*Enter* CLYTEMNESTRA.]

CLYTEMNESTRA
I sang for joy to hail this victory long ago,
When first the fiery midnight message told that Troy
Was sacked and ravaged. Then someone took me to task: 590
'Beacons! And you believe them? You think Troy is taken?
Typical female wishful thinking.' Gibes like these
Alleged my folly. Yet I made grateful sacrifice,
And throughout Argos women gathered to celebrate

Victory with songs of praise in the temples of all the gods,
And feed their scented fires with rich flesh-offerings.
I have no need to hear your full account;
600   I'll hear all from the king's own lips. But first, to greet
My honoured husband promptly on his homecoming –
What day is sweeter to a wife than when she
Receives her lord by heaven's mercy safely home from war,
And flings open the gates in welcome? Take him this
      message:
Let him come quickly; Argos longs for him. And he
Will find at home a wife as faithful as he left,
A watchdog at his door, knowing one loyalty:
Implacable to enemies, and in all ways unchanged.
610   No seal of his have I unsealed in these ten years.
Of pleasure found with other men, or any breath
Of scandal, I know no more than how to dip hot steel.

[*Exit* CLYTEMNESTRA *into the palace.*]

HERALD
Such a boast as this, if it is full of truth,
Is fitting for a royal wife to make.

CHORUS
She spoke as she did for your benefit;
To those who know she showed her true intentions.
But, herald, tell us of our beloved Menelaus.
Has he come back? Did he sail with you? Is he safely home?

HERALD
620   The good news you ask for I cannot give you.
My friends, delusion would not comfort you for long.

CHORUS
Telling a fair tale falsely cannot hide the truth;
When truth and good news differ the rift is plain enough.

HERALD
Then here it is: Menelaus has vanished, ship and all!

CHORUS
You mean he sailed with you from Troy, but then the fleet
Was struck by a storm, and parted his ship from the rest?

HERALD
You've hit the mark. His whole misfortune in a nutshell.

CHORUS
    But what is thought to have become of him?
    Is he given up for lost? Or could he still be alive?   ·   630
HERALD
    No one can tell. Nobody knows except, perhaps,
    The sun, who fosters every earthly creature's life.
CHORUS
    Do you mean that when this storm struck our fleet
    Some anger of the heavenly powers was satisfied?
HERALD
    Can it be right to foul this fair and holy day
    By blurting bad news? After our thanksgiving to the gods
    Such a speech is out of place. When a man stands
        recounting,
    With bloodshot stare, disaster and horror, an army dead,
    The state staggered and gored, homes emptied, men   640
    Blasted, their lives taken by fire and sword, war's scourges –
    If such was my tale, this triumph-song of disaster
    I bring would suit well. But my news is victory,
    Brought to a jubilant city. How can I counter
    Such good with sorrow, and tell of the deadly armed
        alliance
    Fate forged with angry gods to pursue and harass us?
    For fire and water, age-old enemies, joined forces   650
    And pledged good faith in combined slaughter of the
        Greeks.
    One night a vicious storm rose with a gale from Thrace.
    The sky was like a mad shepherd tearing his own flock;
    Ship butted against ship like rutting rams; mountains
    Of wind and water leapt, the sea swallowed and rain
        thrashed.
    At dawn – where were the ships? The bright sun beamed.
        We saw
    The Aegean teeming with faces of dead Greeks
    And scraps of wreckage . . .   660
                    Our hull had held, and we came
        through.
    It was no mortal hand that gripped our helm that night:

Some god, by guile or intervention, saved our lives.
Fortune sat smiling on our prow; we sprang no leak,
Nor ran aground on rocks. In the next morning's light,
Stunned, sickened, still unbelieving of our own luck,
670　We brooded, dwelling on our bruised and battered fleet.
And they, if any still draw breath, now speak of us
As caught in the same fate we picture theirs. But still,
May best prove truest! For Menelaus, more than the others
Expect him home. If any searching ray of light
Sees him alive and well, by the providence of Zeus
Not yet resolved to exterminate this house – there's hope
That Menelaus will yet come safely to his own home.
680　And every word that you have heard me speak is the plain
　　　truth.
　　　[*Exit* HERALD.]

CHORUS
Who was the unknown seer whose voice –
Uttered at the outset, but stamped
With foresight of what fate decreed –
Guessed infallibly in the choice
Of a child's name, and deftly linked
Symbol with truth and name with deed?
Naming, inspired, the glittering bride
Of spears, for whom men killed and died,
Helen, the Wrecker. On whose lips
Was born that fit and fatal name,
To grant the sea a wreck of ships,
690　Wreck lives, and wreck a city with flames?
The curtained softness of her bed
She left, to hear the Zephyr breathe
Gigantic in tall sails; and soon
Comes hue and cry – armed thousands fly
Tracing her trackless oar, and sheathe
Their keels in Simois' shingly bank,
Near fields where grass today grows rank
In soil that war's rich rain has turned red.

And anger – roused, relentless, sure –
Taught Troy that words are double-edged,   700
That men and gods use 'bond' and 'pledge'
For love past limit, doom past cure:
Love seals the hearts of bride and groom;
And seal of love is seal of doom.
Loud rings the holy marriage-song
As kinsmen honour prince and bride;
The hour is theirs – but not for long.
Wrath, borne on Time's unhurrying tide,
Claims payment due for double wrong:
The outraged hearth; the god defied.
And songs are drowned in tears, and soon
Troy of old must learn a new tune.   710
On Paris, once her joy and pride,
She calls reproach, that his proud wooing
Has won his own and her undoing:
Her sons beset on every side,
Her life-blood mercilessly spilt –
Hers is the loss, and his the guilt.

There was a shepherd once who reared at home
A lion's cub. It shared with sucking lambs
Their milk – gentle, while bones and blood were young.   720
The children loved it; the old watched and smiled.
Often the shepherd held it like a child
High in his arms; and often it would seek
His hands with soft eyes and caressing tongue,
Tense with the force of hunger. But in time
It revealed its proper nature. Repaying
Its debt for food and shelter, it prepared
A feast unbidden. Soon the nauseous reek   730
Of torn flesh filled the house; a bloody slime
Drenched all the ground from that unholy slaying,
While helpless weeping servants stood and stared.
The whelp once reared with lambs, now grown a beast,
Fulfils his nature as Destruction's priest!

And so to Troy there came
One in whose presence shone
Beauty no words can name:
740   A still enchantment of sweet summer calm;
A rarity for wealth to dote upon;
Glances whose gentle fire
Bestowed both wound and balm;
A flower to melt man's heart with wonder and desire.
But time grew ripe, and love's fulfilment ran
Aside from that sweet course where it began.
She, once their summer joy,
Transmuted, now like a swift curse descended
On every home, on every life
Whose welcome once befriended
The outlaw wife;
A fiend sent by the god of host and guest,
Whose law her lover had transgressed,
To break his heart, and break the pride of Troy.

750   When Earth and Time were young,
A simple ancient saw
Phrased on the common tongue
Declared that man's good fortune, once mature,
Does not die childless, but begets its heir;
That from life's goodness grows, by nature's law,
Calamity past cure
And ultimate despair.
I disagree; my mind
Rejects this general belief.
Crime, not prosperity, engenders grief;
For impious acts breed their own kind,
760   And evil's nature is to multiply.
The house whose ways are just in word and deed
Still as the years go by
Sees lasting wealth and noble sons succeed.

So, by the law of consequence,
Pride or Fault the Elder will,
In the man who chooses ill,
Breed a Younger Insolence.
Pride the Younger breeds again
Yet another unseen power
Like the powers that gave it birth:
Recklessness, whose force defies
War and violence, heaven and earth;
Whose menace like a black cloud lies
On the doomed house hour by hour,   770
Fatal with fear, remorse, and pain.

But Justice with her shining eyes
Lights the smoke-begrimed and mean
Dwelling; honours those who prize
Honour; searches far to find
All whose hearts and hands are clean;
Passes with averted gaze
Golden palaces which hide
Evil armed in insolence.
Powers and riches close combined,
Falsely stamped with all men's praise,
Win from her no reverence.   780
Good and evil she will guide
To their sure end by their appointed ways.
    [*Enter* AGAMEMNON *and* CASSANDRA.]
King! Heir of Atreus! Conqueror of Troy!
What greetings shall we bring? What shall we say
To voice our hearts' devotion,
Observe both truth and measure,
Be neither scant nor fulsome in our love?
Many, whose conscience is not innocent,
Attach high value to a show of praise.
As ill-luck finds on all sides   790
Eyes brimming with condolence
Where no true sting of sorrow pricks the heart,

So now some harsh embittered faces, forced
Into a seemly smile, will welcome you,
And hide the hearts of traitors
Beneath their feigned rejoicing.
Well, a wise shepherd knows his flock by face;
And a wise king can tell the flatterer's eye –
Moist, unctuous, and fawning –
The expressive sign of loyalty unfelt.
Now this I will not hide: ten years ago
800   When you led Greece to war for Helen's sake
You were set down as sailing
Far off the course of wisdom.
We thought you wrong, misguided, when you tried
To keep morale from sagging
In superstitious soldiers
By offering sacrifice to calm the storm.
Those times are past. You have come home victorious.
Now from our open hearts we wish you well.
Time and your own enquiries
Will show, among your people,
Who has been loyal, who has played you false.

AGAMEMNON
810   First, Argos and her native gods, receive from me
The conqueror's greeting on my safe return, for which,
As for the just revenge I wrought on Priam's Troy,
Heaven shares my glory. Supplications without end
Won heaven's ear. Troy stood her trial. Unfaltering,
The immortals cast their votes into the urn of guilt,
Dooming Troy's walls to dust and her men to the sword.
The urn for acquittal saw hope alone come near, and pass,
Vanishing in each empty hand. Smoke, rising still,
Marks Troy's downfall. Flames of destruction's sacrifice
Live yet, and, as they die, the wind-borne incense
820   Of dead wealth and luxury stirs from settled ash.
Now for this victory let our pious thanksgiving
Tell and retell heaven's favour. We have made Troy pay
For her proud theft a woman's price. The Argive beast,
The lion rampant on all our shields, at dead of night

Sprang from the womb of the horse to grind that city's
    bones;
A ranked and ravening litter, that over wall and tower
Leaping, licked royal blood till lust was surfeited.
Thus to the gods I pay my first full salutation.
For your advice, I note it. I am of your mind   830
And respect your judgement. There are few whose inborn
    love
Warms without envy to a friend's prosperity.
Poisonous jealousy pricks the disappointed heart,
Doubling its grievance: pain at its own losses match
The pain at neighbours' wealth. Life and long observation
    have
Taught me the look of men whose show of love, when
    examined,
Proves but a shadow's shadow: I speak of what I know.   840
Only Odysseus, who set sail unwillingly, once
Enlisted, shared my troubles with good will – I say
This whether he is alive or dead. For affairs of State,
And this feared disaffection, I will set a day
For assembly and debate among our citizens,
And take wise counsel; where disease wants remedy,
Fire or the knife shall purge this body for its own good.   850
Now to my home, to stand at my own household altar
And give heaven my first greeting, whose protecting power
Sent forth, and brought me home again. May victory,
My guardian up till now, walk constant at my side!
    [*Enter* CLYTEMNESTRA *with attendants holding crimson
    silks.*]
CLYTEMNESTRA
Elders and citizens of Argos! In your presence now
I will tell, without shame, a wife's love for her husband.
With time diffidence dies. What I shall say I learnt
Untaught, from my own long endurance, these ten years
My husband spent under the walls of Troy.   860
First, that a woman should sit forlorn at home, unmanned,
Is a crying shame. Then, travellers, one after the other,
Dismayed the palace, each with worse news than the last.

Why, if my lord received as many wounds as Rumour,
Plying from Troy to Argos, gave him, he is a net –
All holes! Or had he died each time report repeated
News of his death – see him, a second Geryon,
Boasting his monstrous right, his triple quilt of earth,
One for each death, each body! Many times despair
At a cruel message noosed my throat in a suspended cord,
Which force against my will untied. These fears explain
Why our child is not here to give you fitting welcome,
Our true love's pledge, Orestes. Do not be uneasy.
He is in Phocis, a guest of Strophius, your trusted friend,
Who warned me of peril from two sources: first, the risk
Threatening your life at Troy; then, if conspiracy
Spiralled into widespread revolt in Argos, fear
Of man's instinct to trample on his former masters.
Such was his reasoning – surely free from all suspicion.
For me the springing torrents of my tears are all
Dried up, not one drop left; what's more, my sleepless eyes
     are sore
With weeping by the lamp long lit for you in vain.
In dreams, the tenuous tremors of droning gnats
Roused me to dreadful visions of more deaths for you
Than could be envisaged in the hour that I slept.
There is no dearer sight than shelter after storm;
No escape sweeter than from siege of circumstance.
Now, after siege and storm have been endured, my happy
     heart
Welcomes my husband as the faithful watchdog of his home,
Our ship's firm anchor, towering pillar that upholds
This royal roof – as dear as is his longed-for son
To a father's hope, a spring to thirsty travellers,
Or sight of land unlooked-for to men long at sea.
Such praise I hold his due, and may heaven's jealousy
Acquit us; our past suffering has been quite enough.
Now, dearest husband, come, step from your chariot.
But do not set to earth, my lord, the conquering foot
That trod down Troy. Servants, do as you have been
     bidden.

870

880

890

900

Make haste, carpet his way with crimson tapestries,
Spread silks before your master's feet. Justice herself   910
Shall lead him to a home he never hoped to see.
All other matters forethought, never lulled by sleep,
Shall order justly as the will of heaven decrees.
    [CLYTEMNESTRA's *maids spread a path of crimson cloth
    from the chariot to the palace door.*]
AGAMEMNON
Daughter of Leda, guardian of my house, your speech
Matches my absence – its theme – as both were prolonged.
Praise aptly spoken should be heard on other lips.
And do not feminize me with these soft attentions,
Nor greet me like a fawning Persian with loud   920
Addresses; and don't, with your outspread cloths, invite
The gods' envy for honours due to them alone.
I deem it dangerous, being mortal, to set foot
On rich embroidered silks. I would sooner be reverenced
As man, not god. The praise of fame rings clear without
These frills and fancy foot-rugs. And the gods' best gift
Is a mind free of folly. Call him fortunate
Whom the end of life finds harboured in tranquillity.   930
I have said how I would enter with an easy mind.
CLYTEMNESTRA
Tell me one thing – not contrary to your resolve.
AGAMEMNON
Rest assured that I shall do nothing against my resolve.
CLYTEMNESTRA
Would you not, if in danger, vow such an act to the gods?
AGAMEMNON
Yes, if someone with knowledge had prescribed it.
CLYTEMNESTRA
Imagine Priam as conqueror – what would he have done?
AGAMEMNON
Walked on embroidered satin, I have little doubt.
CLYTEMNESTRA
Then why humble your heart to men's critical tongues?
AGAMEMNON
Why indeed? Yet the people's voice has great influence.

CLYTEMNESTRA
    Greatness incurs hatred. Unenvied is unenviable.
AGAMEMNON
940   It does not suit a woman to be combative.
CLYTEMNESTRA
    Yet it suits greatness also to accept defeat.
AGAMEMNON
    Why here's a contest! What would you not give to win?
CLYTEMNESTRA
    Yield! You are victor: give me too my victory.
AGAMEMNON
    Since you're determined –
        [*to an attendant*]
                              Come, kneel, untie my shoes, remove
    This slave-like leather that serves my feet. And as I tread
    This deep-sea treasure, may no watchful envious god
    Glance from afar. It offends modesty, that I
    Should dare with unwashed feet to soil these costly rugs,
    Worth weight for weight of silver, spoiling my own house!
    But let that pass.
        [*to* CLYTEMNESTRA]
950   Take in this girl and treat her well.
    God will reward from heaven a gentle conqueror.
    Slavery is a yoke no one bears willingly; and she
    Came to me as the army's gift, choice prize of all Troy's
        wealth.
    Now, since I have been won round in this matter,
    Treading on purple I will go into my house.
CLYTEMNESTRA
    There is a sea – who shall exhaust the sea? – which teems
    With purple dye costly as silver, a dark stream
960   For the staining of fine clothes, unceasingly renewed.
    This house has its store of crimson, by heaven's grace,
        enough
    For one outpouring – you are no king of beggary!
    Had oracles prescribed it, I would have dedicated
    Twenty such cloths to trampling, if by care and cost
    I might ensure a safe return for this one life.

Now you have come to your dear home, your altar-hearth.
The tree, its roots refreshed, spreads leaf to the high beams
To veil us from the Dog Star's heat. Your awaited return
Shines now like spring warmth after winter; but when Zeus
Presses his wine from the unripe grape, then   970
Straightaway heat departs, and coolness comes,
As into his halls the rightful lord enters.
Eleleleleu!

[AGAMEMNON *walks alone along the crimson path and
enters the palace.* CLYTEMNESTRA, *the* CHORUS *and*
CASSANDRA *remain on stage.*]

CLYTEMNESTRA
Zeus, Zeus, Fulfiller! Now fulfil these prayers of mine!
And let your care accomplish all that is your will!

[CLYTEMNESTRA *goes into the palace, leaving the*
CHORUS *and* CASSANDRA *on stage.*]

CHORUS
What is this persistent dread
Haunting, hovering to show
Signs to my foreboding soul,
While unbidden and unwelcome
Throbs the prophet in my veins,
While persuasive confidence,   980
Which should rule the heart and scorn
Fantasies and cloudy dreams,
Trembles and resigns her throne?
Once before, though far away,
My heart knew the ominous hour,
When at Troy our sailors' shouts,
As they coiled their sheets astern,
Chimed with my triumphal song;
And the fleet set sail for home.

Then was guesswork; now I see
With these eyes the fleet returned.
Yet my spirit knows again   990
The foreboding hour; again
Sings, by untaught instinct, that

Sad, familiar, fateful dirge;
Yields her kingdom in the flesh,
Daunted with surmise, and feels
Pang and pulse of loin and gut,
Blood in riot, brain in chaos,
Nerve and tissue taut, and knows
Truth must hurt where flesh is sore.
Yet I pray, may time and truth
Scotch my fears, may prophecy
1000   Vanish, and fulfilment fail!

When fortune flowers too lushly,
Decay, her envious neighbour,
Stands eager to invade;
Glory's brief hours are numbered,
And what has flowered must fade.
Bold in success, ambition
Sails on, where rocks lie hidden,
Strikes, and her debt is paid.
Yet, debts may be compounded:
When Thracian storm-winds threaten,
The merchant, for his silver,
With pious prayers devotes
1010   A tithe in ample measure;
Into the sea he slings it,
And safe his vessel floats.

The house that offers to the envious powers
Its wealthy surplus will not fail and die.
Zeus to their prayers will bounteously reply,
Bless each year's furrowed fields with sun and showers,
Bid harvests teem, and fear of famine fly.
But when, from flesh born mortal,
Man's blood on earth lies fallen –
1020   A dark, unfading stain –
Who then by incantations
Can bid blood live again?

Zeus in pure wisdom ended
That sage's skill who summoned
Dead flesh to rise from darkness
And live a second time;
In case murder cheaply mended
Should invite men's hands to crime.
Were I not sure that always
Events and causes follow
A divinely ordered sequence,
With next by last controlled,
Speech would subdue reluctance,
Voice thoughts I dare not fathom,
And leave no fear untold.

But now my tongue mutters in darkness, sharing   1030
The heart's distress, tormented with desire
To produce some timely word, and yet despairing,
While my dumb spirit smoulders with deep fire.
    [CLYTEMNESTRA *re-enters from the palace.*]
CLYTEMNESTRA
You too, Cassandra, do you hear me? Come indoors.
You may thank Zeus this palace bears you no ill-will.
You shall stand near our sovereign altar and partake,
With many other slaves, the cleansing ritual.
So leave that chariot. Do not be proud. They say
Heracles once was sold and learnt to eat slaves' bread.   1040
If such misfortune falls, and cannot be avoided,
A house of long-established wealth is generous;
Where meagre hopes reap riches, they are hard on slaves.
Here you shall have your due – what custom requires, and
        more.
CHORUS
It was to you she spoke. She waits. Was it not clear?
As you are a captive in the toils of destiny,
Obey, if you understand. Or do you choose defiance?
CLYTEMNESTRA
If she's not mad, she will obey; unless she speaks   1050
Some weird, unheard-of language like twittering swallows.

CHORUS

Come, now; her bidding is the best course possible.
Leave your seat in that chariot. Obey, go in.

CLYTEMNESTRA

I have no time to waste standing out here. Already
Victims for sacrifice are waiting at the central hearth.
If you understand what I have said, come in at once;
1060 If not, as she's a foreigner, someone explain by signs.

[*An attendant makes signs to* CASSANDRA *to enter the palace.*]

CHORUS

It's clear to us that she needs an interpreter.
She has the look of a wild creature newly caught.

CLYTEMNESTRA

She is mad and hears only her own frenzied thoughts.
Has she not left her own city razed to the ground?
Still she lacks the sense to accept her owner's bit
Till she has frothed her rage out from a bloody mouth.
I will waste words no longer, just to be ignored.

[CLYTEMNESTRA *goes into the palace.*]

CHORUS

1070 I feel pity, not anger. Come, poor girl, step down;
Yield to this harsh necessity; wear your new yoke.

[CASSANDRA *steps down.*]

CASSANDRA

O Apollo! Oh, no, no, no! O earth! O Apollo!

CHORUS

Why name Apollo with this wail of agony?
He is no god of mourning, to be so invoked.

CASSANDRA

Oh ! Oh, horror! O earth! O Apollo, Apollo!

CHORUS

Again she utters blasphemy, calling Apollo,
Whose godhead may not stand in the same house as grief.

CASSANDRA

1080 Apollo, Apollo! Leader of journeys, my destroyer!
All this way you have led me, to destroy me again!

CHORUS
    She is inspired to speak of her own sufferings.
    Her prophetic powers remain even in slavery.

CASSANDRA
    Apollo, Apollo! Leader of journeys, my destroyer!
    Where have you led me? Oh, what fearful house is this?

CHORUS
    Does prophecy not tell you this is Atreus' palace?
    Well, I can tell you – call it so, and you will not be wrong.

CASSANDRA
    No! It is a house that abhors   1090
    The gods; whose very stones
    Bear guilty witness to a bloody act;
    That hides within these gates
    Remnants of bodies hacked,
    And murdered children's bones!

CHORUS
    This prophetess goes to work like a keen-scented hound.
    We know the trail she follows and it leads to blood.

CASSANDRA
    To blood, I know. See there,
    The witness that they bear –
    Those children weeping for their blood shed,
    For their tender flesh,
    That cruel, nameless dish
    On which their father fed!

CHORUS
    We had all heard of your prophecy, but this
    Requires no prophecy to tell us of –

CASSANDRA
                         Ah, ah!

    Oh, shame! Conspiracy!   1100
    A heart obsessed with hate,
    And lurking to betray,
    Pollutes this house anew,
    With deadly injury
    Where deepest love is due!

Surprised, unarmed, how can he fight with fate?
And help is far away.

CHORUS

The first we understand – all Argos speaks of it.
But I know nothing of this second prophecy.

CASSANDRA

Shame on her! She will stand –
Would there were room for doubt! –
To cleanse her lawful lord
From guilt of war, and then –
How can I speak the words?
This cleansing ritual
Shall serve his burial!
1110   Despairing hands reach out,
Snared by a stronger hand!

CHORUS

Still I am baffled by her cryptic utterance.
What can one make of prophecy so obscure?

CASSANDRA

There, there! O terror! What is this new sight?
A hunting-net, Death's method of attack!
And she who hunts is she who shared his bed.
Howl, Furies, you bloody, ravening pack,
Gorged with a house's blood, yet thirsting still.
The victim bleeds – come, fiends, and drink your fill!

CHORUS

What fiends are these you call to bay at Death?
1120   Your ghastly hymn brings me no joy. My pale
Blood shrinks back to my heart, as when men die
Sword-struck in battle; pulse and vision fail,
And Life's warm colours fly.
See how her utterance chokes her laboured breath!

CASSANDRA

Help! Look! Oh, nightmare! What, will the cow gore the
    bull,
The black-horned monarch? Save him, drag him away!
The treacherous water is poured, the lustral bath is full.

She holds him in a trap made like a gown –
She strikes! He plunges down!
Listen! It is treachery, treachery, I say!

CHORUS

Although I claim no special skill in oracles,   1130
Her words, I feel, augur no good. Yet, in the end,
What good news ever comes to men through oracles?
Prophets find bad news useful. The primary aim
Of all their wordy wisdom is to make men gape.

CASSANDRA

O fear, and fear again!
O pity! Not alone
Does he suffer; with his pain
I also mourn my own!
Cruel Apollo! Why,
Why have you led me here?
Only that I may share
The death that he must die!

CHORUS

She is insane, poor girl, or else possessed,   1140
And for herself alone she makes this wail,
Unwearied in her tuneless song
As the shrill nightingale
Unburdens her distracted breast,
Crying, 'Itys, Itys', and remembering her wrongs.

CASSANDRA

Bitter was her ordeal;
Yet by the kind gods' wish
The lovely robe she wears
Is feathered wings; and even
The lament she pours to heaven,
Note answering note with tears,
Rings sweet. But I must feel
The parting of the flesh
Before the whetted steel.

CHORUS

Where do these violent miseries come from,   1150

Inspired by god and yet devoid of meaning?
Why do you chant these horrors in heart-rending words
With a doom-laden voice? Who marked the path
Of prophecy whose evil terms you trace?

CASSANDRA

O Paris and his passion!
O marriage-bed that slew
His family and city!
O sweet river Scamander
Our thirsting fathers knew,
By whose dear banks I grew!
But soon the dark Cocytus
1160   And Acheron shall echo
My prophecies, and witness
Whether my words are true.

CHORUS

Paris' marriage! This, at last, is clear
To any child. Yet in her muttered fears
Lies more than is visible at first sight:
With stunning pain, like a wild serpent's bite,
Her murmuring cries grate upon my ear.

CASSANDRA

O Troy and her destruction!
O city burnt and razed!
O fires my father kindled
To keep his towers defiant!
O blood of beasts he offered
From every herd that grazed!
1170   Yet no propitiation
Could save her sons from dying,
As I foretold they would.
And I will join my brothers,
And soon the ground will welcome
My warm and flowing blood.

CHORUS

Once more her utterance adds like to like.
Tell us what god he is, so merciless,
Whose grievous hand can strike

Such deathly music from your mournful soul,
Arrows of prophecy whose course and goal
I seek, but cannot guess?

CASSANDRA

Then listen. Now my prophecy shall no more peep
From under shy veils like a new-made bride, but blow
A raging gale towards the sunrise, on whose surge   1180
A crime more fearful than my murder shall at once
Sweep into blazing light. No more by riddles
Will I instruct you; but first take note of how close
I scent the trail of bloody guilt incurred long since.
Under this roof live day and night a ghastly choir
Venting their evil chant in hideous harmony;
Drunk with men's blood, boldly established here, they hold
Unbroken revel, fiends of royal blood, whom none   1190
Can exorcize. They sit drinking, and with their songs
Drive folly first to crime. The crime performed, in turn
They spew out the defiler of his brother's bed!
Do I miss? Or has my arrow found a mark you know?
Or am I 'lying prophet', 'gipsy', 'spinner of tales'?
Come, on your oath, bear witness: the foul history
Of Atreus' palace, sin for sin, is known to me!

CHORUS

The holiest oath could help but little. Yet I marvel
That you, bred overseas in a foreign tongue, unfold   1200
Our city's past as truly as if you had been here.

CASSANDRA

Apollo, god of prophecy, gave me this power.

CHORUS

Did he, a god, lust for your mortal body?

CASSANDRA

Yes. Until now I was ashamed to speak of it.

CHORUS

We are all more reserved when we are prosperous.

CASSANDRA

He urged me hard, warmly declared his love.

CHORUS

And did you lie together? Did you have his child?

CASSANDRA
I gave my word, and broke it – to the God of Words.
CHORUS
Already possessed of the prophetic art?
CASSANDRA
1210 I had foretold already the whole doom of Troy.
CHORUS
Surely the god was angry? Did he punish you?
CASSANDRA
Since my mistake, no one believed a word I spoke.
CHORUS
To us your prophecies seem all too credible.
CASSANDRA
Oh! Oh!
Horror and crime! Again the anguish of true vision –
Yes, crime and horror! – racks and ravages my mind.
Look! See them sit, there on the wall, like forms from
        dreams,
Children butchered like lambs by their own kindred. See,
1220 What do they carry in their hands? O pitiful sight!
It is their own flesh – guts and organs – that they hold,
Clear yet hideous, the food their father ate!
I tell you, for this crime revenge grows hot: there lurks
At home, as regent, a cowardly lion
Who plots against the master absent in the war.
While the lion-like commander who uprooted Troy,
Met by the fawning tongue and the spry, obsequious ear
Of the evil-scheming she-hound, does not know what
1230 Wounds laced with hidden vengeance she prepares for him.
Female shall murder male. What kind of outrage
Is that? What loathsome beast lends apt comparison?
A basilisk? Or Scylla's breed, living in the rocks
To drown men in their ships – a raging shark of hell,
Dreaming of steel thrust in her husband's unarmed flesh?
You heard her assured bluff, that cry of triumph, raised
As if for a hard battle won, disguised as joy
At his safe homecoming? You are incredulous.

No matter, I say, no matter. What will be will be.
Soon you will see with your own eyes, and pity me,   1240
And wish my prophecy had not been half so true.

CHORUS
Thyestes' feast of children's flesh we understand.
Horror gives place to wonder at your true account.
The rest exceeds our comprehension; we give up.

CASSANDRA
I say Agamemnon shall lie dead before your eyes.

CHORUS
Silence, you wretched outcast, or speak wholesome words!

CASSANDRA
No wholesome words can purge the poison of that fact.

CHORUS
None, if it is to be; but may the gods forbid!

CASSANDRA
You turn to prayer; others meanwhile prepare to kill.   1250

CHORUS
What man can be the source of such polluting crime?

CASSANDRA
What *man*? You miss the main point of my prophecies.

CHORUS
How could such murder be contrived? This baffles me.

CASSANDRA
Yet I speak good Greek – all too good.

CHORUS
                                        The oracles
Of Delphi are good Greek, but hard to understand.

CASSANDRA
Oh, for pity! Apollo, where can I escape?
This death you send me is impatient, merciless!
She, this lioness in human form, who when her lord
Was absent paired with a wolf, will take my wretched life.   1260
Like one who mixes medicine for her enemies,
Now, while she whets the dagger for her husband's heart,
She vows to drug his dose with a memory of me,
And makes him pledge my safe arrival – in my blood.

This robe – why should I wear what mocks me? Why still
    keep
This sceptre, these prophetic garlands round my neck?
Before I die I'll make an end of you . . . and you . . .
Go, with my curse, go! So I pay my debt to you!
Go, make some other woman rich in misery!
And let Apollo see, and witness what I do –
1270   He who once saw me in the same insignia
Scorned, jeered at like some gipsy quack, by enemies
And friends alike, called starveling, beggar, conjuror,
Pitiable wretch. All this I bore, and now Apollo,
Who gave a portion of his own prescience to me,
Brings me from Troy, to this porch that reeks of death,
Where I shall never court crass disbelief again,
Where not my father's hearthstone but the slaughterer's
    block
Awaits me, warm already with a victim's blood.
Yet we shall not die unregarded by the gods.
1280   A third shall come to take up our cause, a son resolved
To kill his mother, honouring his father's blood.
He, now a wandering exile, shall return to set
The apex on this tower of crime his race has built.
A great oath, sealed before the gods, binds him to exact
Full penance for his father's outstretched corpse.

Why then should I lament? Am I so pitiable?
I have watched Fate unfold her pattern. Troy endured
What she endured; her captor now, by Heaven's decree,
1290   Ends like this. I have done with tears. I will accept my death.
O gates of the dark world, I greet you as I come!
Let me receive, I pray, a single deadly blow,
Sink without spasm, feel the warm blood's gentle ebb,
Embrace death for my comfort, and so close my eyes.
CHORUS
O woman deep in wisdom as in suffering,
You have told us much. Yet, if you have true foreknowledge
Of your own death, why, like an ox for sacrifice,
Do you move towards the altar with intrepid steps?

CASSANDRA
  Friends, there is no escape – not once the hour has come.
CHORUS
  Still, they who go last gain the longest time.   1300
CASSANDRA
  This is the day. There's no use trying to escape.
CHORUS
  Courage and destiny are proudly matched in you.
CASSANDRA
  The happy never hear such praise.
CHORUS
  Yet a brave death lends dignity to man.
CASSANDRA
  O father! O my brothers!
  I go now. Within this palace I will mourn
  My end and Agamemnon's. I have lived enough . . .
CHORUS
  What is it? What do you see? What terror turns you back?
      [CASSANDRA *chokes in horror.*]
  You gasp, as if some nausea chokes your very soul.
CASSANDRA
  There is a smell of murder! The walls drip with blood!
CHORUS
  The altar is ready. It is the smell of sacrifice.   1310
CASSANDRA
  It is just like the air that rises from a grave.
CHORUS
  You mean the Syrian perfume sprinkled for the feast?
CASSANDRA
  I am not like a bird scared at an empty bush,
  Trembling for nothing. Wait. When you shall see my
      death
  Atoned with death, woman for woman, when in place
  Of him whom marriage cursed another man shall fall,
  Then witness for me – these and all my prophecies
  Were utter truth. This I request before I die.   1320
CHORUS
  To die is sad; sadder to know death pre-ordained.

CASSANDRA

Yet one word more, a prophecy – or, if a dirge,
At least not mine alone. In this sun's light – my last –
I pray: when the sword's edge requites my captor's blood,
Then may his murderers, dying, with that debt pay too
For her they killed in chains, their unresisting prey!

Alas for human destiny! Man's happiest hours
Are pictures drawn in shadow. Then ill fortune comes,
And with two strokes the wet sponge wipes the image out.
1330   And grief itself is hardly more pitiable than joy.
        [*She goes into the palace.*]

CHORUS

Of fortune no man tastes his fill.
While pointing envy notes his store,
And tongues proclaim his happiness,
Man satisfied will hunger still.
For who grows weary of success,
Or turns good fortune from his door
Bidding her trouble him no more?

Our king, whom Fortune loves to bless,
By the gods' will has taken Troy,
And honour crowns his safe return.
If now, for blood shed long ago,
In penance due his blood must flow,
And if his murderers must earn
1340   Death upon death, and fate stands so,
I ask, what mortal man can claim
That he alone was born to enjoy
A quiet life, and an untarnished name?
        [AGAMEMNON's *voice is heard from inside the palace.*]

AGAMEMNON

Ah! Help, help! I'm being attacked! Here, inside!

CHORUS

Listen! Who was that crying they've been attacked?

AGAMEMNON

Ah! Help! I'm struck again!

CHORUS

1. It was the king! From that groan it sounds like the deed is
      done!
   We must decide together on the safest plan.
2. Here is what I think: let us send a herald round
   Bidding the citizens assemble here with arms.
3. Too slow. I say we should burst in at once, and catch   1350
   The murder in the act, before the blood dries on the sword.
4. I agree. That is what we ought to do –
   Or something along those lines. Now is the time to act.
5. It's obvious what this act points to: the murderers
   Mean to establish a tyrannical regime.
6. And meanwhile we waste time. Action spurns sleep,
   And stamps the gentle face of caution in the dust.
7. I can't think of a plan that might prove useful.
   I say, let those who did this make their next move.
8. I'm of the same opinion. If the king is dead,   1360
   We cannot bring him back to life through argument.
9. Then should we patiently drag out our servile lives,
   Governed by these disgracers of our royal house?
10. That would be intolerable! Who would not rather die –
    A milder fate than living under tyranny!
11. Wait! Not so fast. What is our evidence? Those groans?
    Are we to assume from them that the king is dead?
12. We must be certain. Our anxieties are premature;
    Guesswork and certain knowledge are two different things.

CHORUS

   I think this is the general consensus: that we   1370
   Make full enquiry into what has happened to the king.
        [*The palace doors open, revealing* CLYTEMNESTRA *with
        the dead bodies of* AGAMEMNON *and* CASSANDRA *beside
        her.*]

CLYTEMNESTRA

   Before now I said many things to suit the time,
   All of which, without shame, I here unsay.
   How else, when one prepares death for an enemy
   Who seems a friend, can one set a deadly trap
   High enough to prevent the victim's highest leap?

A great while I have pondered on this trial of strength.
At long last the pitched battle came, and victory:
Here where I struck, I stand and see my task achieved.
1380   Yes, this is my work, and I lay claim to it. To prevent
Him foiling death by flight or resistance, I cast on him,
As one who catches fish, a broad, capacious net
That walled him in with endless woven folds.
And then I struck him, twice. Twice he cried out and groaned;
Then he fell, limp. And as he lay, I gave a third
And final blow, my thanks for prayers fulfilled, to Zeus,
Lord of the nether region, Saviour . . . of dead men!
So falling he belched forth his life. With coughs and retching
There spurted from him bloody foam in a fierce jet.
1390   It spread, and spattered me with drops of crimson rain;
While I exulted as sown cornfields do when drenched
With the dew of heaven when buds burst forth in spring.

So stands the case, elders of Argos. You may be
As you choose, glad or sorry; I am jubilant.
And, were it seemly over a *dead* man to pour
The thank-offering for safe journey, surely Justice here
Allows it, here demands it; so enriched a draught
Of evil did this man store in his house, and now
Returned, he drains his own cursed cup to the last dregs.

CHORUS
The sheer audacity of your speech astounds us.
1400   To boast so shamelessly over your husband's corpse!

CLYTEMNESTRA
You speak as to some thoughtless woman: you are wrong.
My pulse beats firm. I tell what you already know:
Praise or blame, as you will – it's all the same to me.
This is my husband, Agamemnon, now stone dead;
His death the work of my right hand, whose craftsmanship
Justice acknowledges. There lies the simple truth.

CHORUS
Evil woman! What unnatural food or drink,
Malignant root, brine from the restless sea,
Transformed you, that your nature did not shrink

From gravest guilt? Argos will execrate
Your nameless murder with a common voice of hate,
Revoke your rights among the just and free,   1410
And drive you outlawed from the city gates.

CLYTEMNESTRA

Yes, now you self-righteously threaten me with exile,
Award me public curses, roars of civic hate.
Why, once before, did you not dare oppose this man,
Who with no more compunction than men butcher sheep,
When his own fields were white with flocks, sacrificed
His child – my own daughter, whom my pains brought forth?
He killed her for a charm to stop the Thracian wind!
He was the one you should have driven from Argos; he,
Marked with his daughter's blood, was ripe for punishment.
But *my* act shocks your ears, stirs your judicial wrath!   1420
Your threats doubtless rely on force. You have your men
And weapons: try your strength in a fair fight against mine.
Win, and you may command me. If – god willing – you lose,
Old as you are, you shall be taught some wisdom yet.

CHORUS

Such boasts show folly in a cunning mind.
So surely as your robe blazons your crime
In those red drops, shall your own head bow low
Under a bloody stroke. Just wait and see:
Friendless, dishonoured, outcast, you shall find
Your debt called in, and suffer blow for blow.   1430

CLYTEMNESTRA

Is that so? Then hear the righteous oath I swear:
By Justice, guardian of my child – now accomplished –
By her avenging Fury, at whose feet I poured his blood:
I have no fear that *his* avenger's tread shall shake
This house, while my staunch ally now as then,
Aegisthus, kindles on my hearth the ancestral fire.
With such a shield, strength marches boldly on. Meanwhile,
He who was sweet to every Trojan Chryseis,
And soured my life, lies here; and with him lies his prisoner,
His faithful soothsayer, who shared his berth and knew   1440
The wantonness of sailors. Their ends were richly deserved.

He died as you see him; she first, like a dying swan,
Sang her death-song, and now lies in her lover's clasp.
Brought as a variant to the pleasures of my bed,
She lends an added relish now to victory.

CHORUS
Come, look on him, and weep.
O that some merciful swift fate,
Free from wasting sickness or harsh pains,
1450   Would bid me share his never-ending sleep.
Low lies the kindly guardian of our state,
Who fought ten years to win
Redress for a woman's sin;
By a woman's hand slain.

Helen! Distracted Helen! You who spilt
Beneath Troy's walls lives beyond counting! You
Now on your house have fixed a lasting guilt
Which every age will tell anew.
Surely, that day you fled beyond recall,
1460   A curse of grief already grew
Deep-rooted in this royal hall.

CLYTEMNESTRA
Is fact so great a burden?
Put up no prayers for death;
Nor vent your spleen on Helen,
As if her act had ordered
The fate of fighting thousands
And robbed their souls of breath,
Or as if from her fault alone
Sure cureless grief had grown.

CHORUS
Spirit of hate, whose strong curse weighs
Hard on the house and heirs of Tantalus,
1470   It is your power that engenders thus
In women's brains such evil art,
And darkens all my bitter days.

It is your hateful form I see rejoice,
Standing like a crow on carrion; your voice
Whose execrable song affronts both ear and heart.

CLYTEMNESTRA

You speak now more in wisdom,
Naming the Fury, fed three times,
That hates and haunts our race.
Hers is the thirst of slaughter,
Still slaked with feud and vengeance,
Till, with each wrong requited,
A new thirst takes its place.   1480

CHORUS

This grievous power whose wrath you celebrate
With cursed truth, no royal house's fall,
No grim catastrophe, can ever sate.
O pitiful mystery! Is Zeus not lord?
Zeus, Zeus, alas! Maker and source of all?
Could horror such as this occur, without his sovereign
    word?

Sad, silent king! How shall I mourn your death?   1490
How shall I find the heart's true word, to prove me
    friend?
Here where you spent your dying breath,
Caught by the ruthless falsehood of a wife,
In the foul spider's web bound fast you lie.
Unholy rest, and most ignoble end –
That man like beast should die
Pierced by a two-edged knife!

CLYTEMNESTRA

This murder is mine, you clamour.
I was his wife; but henceforth
My name from his be freed!
Dressed in my form, a bitter   1500
Avenger from long ago
On that gruesome host Atreus,

For his abhorrent deed,
Has poured this blood in payment,
That here on Justice' altar
A man for children should bleed.

CHORUS

And are you guiltless? Some avenging power
Stood, maybe, at your side. But of this blood
Who will – who could – absolve you? Hour by hour
On his unyielding course the black-robed king,
Pressing to slaughter, swells the endless flood
Of crimson life by pride and hate released
1510   From brothers' veins – till the due reckoning,
When the dried gore shall melt, and Ares bring
Justice at last for that unnatural feast.

Sad, silent king! How shall I mourn your death?
How shall I find the heart's true word, to prove me
        friend?
Here where you spent your dying breath,
Caught by the ruthless falsehood of a wife,
In the foul spider's web bound fast you lie.
Unholy rest, and most ignoble end –
That man like beast should die
1520   Pierced by a two-edged knife!

CLYTEMNESTRA

The guile I used to kill him –
He used it himself first,
When by guile he uprooted
The tender flower he gave me,
And made this house accursed.
When on my virgin daughter
His brutal sword descended,
My tears in rivers ran;
If now by brutal sword-thrust
His adult days are ended,
Let shame and conscience ban
His boasts, where he pays forfeit
For wrong his guile began.

CHORUS

Where, where lies Right? Reason despairs her powers,   1530
Mind numbly gropes, her quick resources spent.
Our throne endangered, and disaster near,
Where can I turn? I fear
Thunder that cracks foundations, blood-red showers.
The light rain slacks – the deluge is in store.
Justice, in harmony with Fate's intent,
Hardens her hold to shake the earth once more.

O Earth! O Earth! Would that some timely chance
Had laid me in your lap, before my eyes
Had seen him laid so low,
Lord of this silver-walled inheritance!   1540
Who will inter him? Who lament the dead?
Will *you* wear mourning for disguise?
Bewail the husband whom your own hand killed?
For his high glories offer gifts of lies?
Since Justice answers, 'No!'
By whom shall tears of honest love be shed,
His graveside ritual of praise fulfilled?   1550

CLYTEMNESTRA

That question is not your concern.
I felled him; I despatched him;
I will inter his bones.
No troops from the palace or city
Shall beat their breasts and lay him
In vaults of bronze and marble
With seemly civic groans.
But, as is fit, his daughter
Shall meet him near the porchway
Of those who perish young;
His dear Iphigenia
With loving arms shall greet him,
With gagged and silent tongue.

CHORUS

Reproach answers reproach; truth recedes still.   1560
She strikes the striker; he who dared to kill

Pays the full forfeit. While Zeus holds his throne,
This maxim holds on earth: the wrongdoer dies.
That is heaven's law. Oh, who can exorcize
This breeding curse, this cancer that has grown
Into these walls, to plague them at its will?

CLYTEMNESTRA

The wrongdoer dies: you have reached the truth at last.
Now to the powers that persecute
1570   Our race I offer a sworn pact:
With this harsh deed and bitter fact
I am content; let *them* forget the past,
Leave us forever, and oppress
Some other house, with murderous foulness.
I ask no store of wealth;
For me it will suffice
To purchase, at this price,
For our long sickness, health.

        [*Enter* AEGISTHUS.]

AEGISTHUS

O happy day, when Justice comes into her own!
Now I believe that gods, who dwell above the earth,
See what men suffer, and award a recompense:
1580   Here, tangled in a net the avenging Furies wove,
He lies, a sight to warm my heart; and pays his blood
In full atonement for his father's treacherous crime.

The events were as follows. There was a dispute between
Atreus, Agamemnon's father, who ruled Argos then,
And my father Thyestes, his own brother, whom
Atreus drove out from home and city. He came back,
Sat as a pitiful suppliant at Atreus' hearth,
Gained his request in part – his own blood did not stain
1590   His childhood's home. But Atreus, this man's father, gave
His guest, my father, a welcoming gift more full
Of recklessness than love. He feigned a feasting-day,
And amid the lavish meats served him his own sons' flesh.
The feet and splayed fingers he concealed, putting
The other parts, minced unrecognizably small,

Over them. Each guest had his table, and this dish
Was set before my father. He, in ignorance,
At once took that which prompted no close scrutiny,
And tasted food from which, as you now see, this house
Has not recovered. Then he realized, in all
Its gruesomeness, what had been done. With one deep
    groan,
He fell back from his chair, vomiting murdered flesh,
Cursed the race of Pelops with an inexorable curse,   1600
Sending the table crashing with his foot, and screamed,
'May the whole house of Tantalus so crash to ruin!'

That deed gave birth to what you see here now, this death.
I planned the killing, as was just. I was the third
Child of Thyestes, then a brat in baby-clothes;
Spared and sent off with my distracted father, till,
Full-grown, Justice restored me to my native land.
I, from a distance, cunningly devised this plan,
And caught my man. Thus satisfied, I could die now,   1610
Seeing Agamemnon in the clutch of Justice, dead.

CHORUS
Aegisthus, we acquit you of the insults to the dead.
But since you claim that you alone laid this whole plot,
And so, though absent, took his blood upon your hands,
I tell you plainly, your own life is forfeited:
Justice will curse you; Argive hands will stone you dead.

AEGISTHUS
So, this is how you lecture, from the lower deck,
The master on the bridge? Then you shall learn, though old,
How harsh a thing discipline is, when reverend years   1620
Lack wisdom. Chains and distress of hunger are
A marvellous tonic with great power to school the mind.
Does this sight not bid you reflect? Then do not kick
Against the goad, in case you stumble and get hurt.

CHORUS
You woman! While he went out to fight, you stayed at home,
Seduced his wife meanwhile, and then, against a man
Who led an army, you schemed such a murder!

AEGISTHUS
   You still use words that have in them the seeds of tears.
   Your voice is most unlike the voice of Orpheus,
1630 Who bound all that heard him with delight. Your childish
   Yelps annoy us, and will fasten bonds on you yourselves.
   With strict control you will prove more amenable.

CHORUS
   Control! Are we to see *you* king of Argos – you
   Who, after plotting the king's murder, did not dare
   To lift the sword yourself?

AEGISTHUS
                                        To lure him to the trap
   Was plainly woman's work; I, an old enemy,
   Was suspect. Now, helped by his wealth, I will attempt
   To rule in Argos. And those who complain shall not
1640 Be fed fat like show-ponies, but shall feel the yoke –
   A heavy one. Hunger and darkness together will soon
   Soften resistance.

CHORUS
                           If you were so bold, why not
   Yourself with your own hands plunder your enemy?
   Instead, a woman, whose life makes this earth unclean,
   Who flouts the gods of Argos, helped you murder him!
   If Orestes lives, may kind fortune bring him home
   To set against these two his invincible sword!

AEGISTHUS
   Since you think so, you shall soon learn
   That it is foolish to insult the powers that be.
1650 Ready there! Guards, forward!
      [*Armed soldiers rush in.*]
                                        Right then. Each man
   Take up his sword.

CHORUS
   Our swords are ready. We are prepared to die.

AEGISTHUS
   'Die'! We take you at your word. Fortune holds the stakes!

CLYTEMNESTRA
   Stop, stop, dearest Aegisthus! No more violence!

When this first harvest ripens we'll reap grief enough.
Crime and despair are fed to bursting. Let us not
Plunge deeper still into bloodshed. Elders, I beg you,
Yield in good time to destiny. Go home, before
You come to harm. What we have done was pre-ordained.
If our long agony finds fulfilment here, we,
Twice gored by Fate's long talons, welcome it. I speak   1660
With a woman's wisdom, if you choose to understand.

AEGISTHUS
But are these foul-mouthed men to aim their pointed gibes
At will, and defy the fate they richly deserve?

CHORUS
No man of Argos grovels at a coward's feet.

AEGISTHUS
Enough! Some other day I'll settle scores with you.

CHORUS
Not if Fate sets Orestes on the road to Argos.

AEGISTHUS
For men in exile hopes are meat and drink; I know.

CHORUS
Rule on, grow fat defiling justice – while you can.

AEGISTHUS
You are unwise. In time you will pay for those words.   1670

CHORUS
Brag wildly on – a cock that struts behind his hen!

CLYTEMNESTRA
Pay no attention to their empty whining. You and I,
As joint rulers, will put this house in order.

OEDIPUS REX
BY
SOPHOCLES

Preface to *Oedipus Rex*

Myths about Oedipus and the royal house to which he belonged (the Labdacids, or the descendants of Labdacus; see genealogical table, p. 304) were well known to Sophocles' fifth-century Athenian audience. They were treated in two lost epics, the *Oedipodeia* and the *Thebais*, which were roughly contemporary with the Homeric epics. The *Iliad* refers to Oedipus as a well-known figure of myth, and the *Odyssey* briefly describes his murder of his father Laius and his marriage to his mother (who is called Epicasta rather than the more usual Jocasta). Aeschylus also wrote a trilogy dealing with various parts of the Oedipus story. The first play of this trilogy covers Oedipus' killing of his father; the second jumps forward to the part of the story treated in *Oedipus Rex*; and the last play of the trilogy moves on again to the fate of Oedipus' two sons, Eteocles and Polyneices, who kill one another in a duel arising from a quarrel over who should rule the city. Only this last play, *Seven Against Thebes*, is extant. The satyr-play accompanying Aeschylus' trilogy deals with Oedipus' encounter with the Sphinx.

Sophocles' version of events probably tallies in a number of respects with that of Aeschylus and with versions of the myth in epic. Nevertheless, it almost certainly involves significant departures. One major difference is Oedipus' having children by Jocasta: in most versions Oedipus' children are by another wife. Another is the way in which Jocasta and Oedipus learn of their true relationship. In other accounts of the myth the truth is simply revealed publicly either by Tiresias, the unerring blind prophet of Thebes, or by the Delphic oracle, or by a message from Oedipus' adoptive mother, queen Merope of Corinth. In *Oedipus Rex*, Oedipus discovers his identity through his own stubborn determination to solve the mystery of his birth. The account that follows is consistent with Sophocles' play, which, judging by Aristotle's admiration for it, came to be regarded as the canonical version of this part of the Oedipus story.

The origins of the house of Labdacus may be traced back to Cadmus, the legendary founder of Thebes. In his old age, Cadmus abdicated in favour of Pentheus, his grandson. Pentheus rejected Dionysus' attempts to introduce his rites in Thebes and was duly punished. In Euripides' macabre version of the story, the *Bacchae*, Pentheus' mother Agave decapitates him while under the influence of the god. Thebes was subsequently ruled by Cadmus' son Polydorus, and then by Polydorus' son Labdacus.

Little is known of Labdacus but he was succeeded in turn by his son Laius. Laius was married but childless. He consulted the Delphic oracle, who told him that any child he had by his wife Jocasta would murder him. He therefore sought to avoid marital relations with her. Some time later, however, they came to have a son (either through Laius' laxity or by Jocasta's design). Fearing the prophecy, Laius decided to dispose of the child, but he did not wish to incur divine wrath for the murder of one of his kin (a crime punishable by the Furies, as seen in their pursuit of Orestes for the murder of his mother in Aeschylus' *Oresteia*). He therefore ordered a shepherd to expose the child on Mount Cithaeron with an iron rivet driven through its ankles so that, ultimately, wild beasts would be responsible for killing the child (according to Jocasta, in Sophocles' play, this action was taken by herself and Laius in concert). The shepherd to whom the task was entrusted lacked the heart to leave the child pinned to the mountainside in this way. Instead he released it and gave it to a fellow shepherd, who happened to be leaving Thebes, telling him to give the child away; no mention was made of this to Laius or Jocasta. The second shepherd made his way to Corinth, where king Polybus and queen Merope happily accepted the boy as their own on account of being childless themselves. They named him Oedipus ('Swollen-foot') because of the injury to his ankles from the rivet that had been driven through them.

One day, when Oedipus had reached adulthood, he was

taunted at the court of Corinth about his lack of resemblance to his supposed parents. Though assured (falsely) by Polybus and Merope that he was their son, Oedipus remained troubled, and resolved to consult the Delphic oracle about his future. The oracle informed him that he would murder his father and marry his mother. Appalled at such a prospect he decided not to return to Corinth, in the misguided belief that he might thereby avoid the oracle. On his journey, however, in a narrow section of the road between Delphi and Daulia, he encountered Laius, who was on an excursion from Thebes. Laius and his men refused Oedipus right of way and, in the altercation that followed, Oedipus killed Laius (and some or all of his men), without realizing that Laius was king of Thebes; needless to say, neither Laius nor Oedipus recognized that the two of them were, in fact, father and son.

Oedipus now ventured to Thebes, which was under the curse of the Sphinx. The Sphinx, half-woman and half-lion, was perched on a rock by the entrance to the city and would ask all who wished to enter a riddle: what has four legs in the morning, two during the daytime, and three in the evening? If a traveller was unable to answer the riddle the Sphinx would devour them. Oedipus, using his native wit, offered the correct answer – man (who crawls on all fours as a baby, stands on two legs as an adult, and leans on a stick, a third leg, in old age) – whereupon the Sphinx threw herself from her rocky perch to her death. The citizens were grateful to Oedipus, the stranger who had rid the city of its monstrous tormentor; moreover, in the event of their former king having been murdered by an unknown assailant, they invited him to become their new king and marry their widowed queen, Jocasta.

For a time Oedipus and Jocasta lived happily – in ignorance of their true relationship. They had two daughters, Antigone and Ismene, and twin sons, Eteocles and Polyneices. But some years after the death of Laius, while the children of Oedipus and Jocasta were still young, Thebes was stricken by a terrible plague affecting crops and livestock as well as the city's inhabitants. Sophocles' play begins as the Theban elders prepare to petition Oedipus to save the city from the ravaging plague. Oedipus meanwhile eagerly awaits the return of his brother-in-law (and uncle) Creon – Creon shares power with Oedipus and Jocasta, although ultimate royal authority resides with Oedipus – whom he has sent to consult the Delphic oracle. The action takes place on the day of Creon's return.

Characters

OEDIPUS, *king of Thebes*
JOCASTA, *queen of Thebes*
CREON, *brother of Jocasta*
TIRESIAS, *a blind prophet*
PRIEST
FIRST MESSENGER
SHEPHERD
ATTENDANT
CHORUS *of Theban Elders*
King's Attendants
Queen's Attendants
Citizens of Thebes

Scene: Before the Royal Palace at Thebes.
A crowd of citizens, led by a PRIEST, *is seated in*
supplication on steps by the altars in front of the palace.
Enter OEDIPUS.

OEDIPUS

Children, new blood of Cadmus' ancient line,
What is the meaning of this supplication,
These branches and garlands, the incense filling the city,
These prayers for the healing of pain, these lamentations?
I have not thought it fit to rely on my messengers,
But am here to learn for myself – I, Oedipus,
Whose name is known afar. (*To the* PRIEST) You, sir,
By virtue of your age should speak for all.
What is the matter? Some fear? Something you desire?   10
I would willingly do anything to help you;
Indeed, I should be heartless if I were
Unmoved by a petition such as this.

PRIEST

My lord Oedipus, we are gathered by your altars,
As you see, from fledglings to aged elders;
Priests – I of Zeus – and the pick of our young manhood.
More sit in the market-place, carrying boughs like these,
And around Athena's twin altars and the embers   20
Of divination, beside the river Ismenus.
You too have seen our city's affliction, caught
In a tide of death from which there is no escape:
Death in the fruitful flowering of her soil;

Death in the pastures; death in the womb of woman.
Hateful plague, a fiery demon, has gripped the city,
Stripping the house of Cadmus, to fatten hell
30   With a profusion of lamentation.
We come to you now as suppliants, I
And these young people, not supposing you
The equal of gods but the first of men,
Whether in the ordinary business of mortal life,
Or in the encounters of man with more than man.
It was you, we remember, a newcomer to Thebes,
Who broke our bondage to that cruel enchantress.
With no foreknowledge or guidance from us,
But, as we truly believe, with the help of God,
You gave us back our lives.
40   Now, great and glorious Oedipus, we seek
Your help again. Find some deliverance for us
By any way that god or man can show.
We know that past experience gives strength
To present counsel. Therefore, O greatest of men,
Restore our city to life. See that this land calls you
Its saviour as it did before. Let it not be said
50   That under your rule we were raised up only
To fall; no, restore our city to safety.
Under the same bright star that gave us then
Good fortune, guide us into good today.
If you are to be our king, as now you are,
Be king of living men, not emptiness.
Surely there is no strength in walls or ships
Where men are lacking and no life breathes within them.

OEDIPUS

I grieve for you, my children. Believe me, I know
60   All that you desire of me and all that you suffer.
But while you suffer, none suffers more than I.
You have your several griefs, each for himself;
My heart bears the weight of my own, and yours,
And all my people's sorrows. I am not sleeping;
I weep, and sift through endless trains of thought.
But I have not been idle. One thing I have done already –

The only thing that promises hope. I have sent
My kinsman, Creon the son of Menoeceus,   70
To the Pythian shrine of Apollo to learn what act
Or word of mine may help you. This is the day
I reckon he should return. It troubles me
That he is not already here. But when he comes,
Whatever the god commands, upon my honour,
It shall be done.

PRIEST

Well said.
And look, they are making signs
That Creon is on his way back right now.

OEDIPUS

He has a bright expression, by Apollo –   80
I hope his news is good!

PRIEST

It must be good. His head is crowned with bay
Full of berries; that is a sign.

OEDIPUS

We shall soon know.
He can hear us now . . . Royal brother, what news?
What message for us from the mouth of the god?
    [*Enter* CREON.]

CREON

Good news. As far as good may come
Even out of painful matters, if all goes well.

OEDIPUS

And the answer? You hold us between fear and hope.   90

CREON

I will tell you, if you wish me to speak in the presence of
        all;
If not, let us go in.

OEDIPUS

Speak before all.
Their plight concerns me now, more than my life.

CREON

This, then, is the answer, the plain command
Of lord Apollo: there is an unclean thing,

Born and nursed in this land, polluting our soil,
Which must be driven away, not kept to destroy us.

OEDIPUS

What unclean thing? And what purification is required?

CREON

100   The banishment of a man, or payment of blood for
       blood –
The shedding of blood is the cause of our city's peril.

OEDIPUS

What blood does he mean? Did he say who it was that
       died?

CREON

We had a king before you came to rule us.
His name was Laius.

OEDIPUS

So I have heard. I never saw him.

CREON

He was killed. Clearly the meaning of the god's command
Is that we bring the unknown killer to justice.

OEDIPUS

And where might he be? How can we hope to uncover
The faded traces of that distant crime?

CREON

110   Here, the god said: seek, and you shall find.
He that is not sought out goes undetected.

OEDIPUS

Was it at home, or out of doors, or abroad
On foreign soil that Laius was murdered?

CREON

He left the country on a pilgrimage, or so he said,
And from that day forth we never saw him again.

OEDIPUS

Was there no word, no fellow traveller who saw
What happened, whose evidence could have been used?

CREON

All died except for one, who fled the scene in terror,
And had nothing to tell for certain – except one thing.

OEDIPUS

What was it? One thing might point the way to others,   120
If we could just lay our hands on the smallest clue.

CREON

His story was that robbers – not one but many –
Fell in with the king's party and put them to death.

OEDIPUS

Robbers would hardly dare commit such an act,
Unless they were paid to do it by someone here.

CREON

That too was suggested. But in the troubles
That followed no avenger came forward.

OEDIPUS

What troubles? Surely none great enough to hinder
A full inquiry into a royal death?

CREON

The Sphinx's cunning forced us to turn our attention   130
From such mysteries to more immediate matters.

OEDIPUS

I will start afresh and bring everything to light.
All praise to Phoebus, and thanks, for your part,
To you for pointing out our duty to the dead.
You will find me as willing an ally as you could wish
In the god's cause and that of our country. My own cause
    too –
Not merely from another will I clear this taint,
But from myself. The killer of Laius,
Whoever he is, may try to turn his hand   140
Against *me*. So in serving Laius, I serve myself.
Now, up from your seats, my children! Away with these
    boughs!
Bring all the people of Cadmus here, and tell them
There is nothing I will not do. But it is certain
That by the help of god we stand – or fall.

    [*Exeunt* OEDIPUS *and* CREON.]

PRIEST
    Up, children. The king has promised us
    All that we came to ask for. Let us pray that Phoebus,
    From whom the answer came, may come himself
150   To save and deliver us from our grave afflictions.
       [*The* PRIEST *and the crowd of suppliants depart.*]
       [*Enter the* CHORUS *of Theban Elders.*]

CHORUS
    In glittering Thebes from the Pythian House of Gold
    The gracious voice of Zeus is heard.
    My heart is stricken with fear of what shall be told.
    O Healer of Delos, hear!
    Fear is upon us. What will you do?
    Things new, or old as the circling year?
    Speak to us, child of golden Hope! Come, deathless
       Word!

    Deathless Athena, daughter of Zeus, first of all we
160   Call on you, then your sister Queen
    Artemis, over our city enthroned in majesty;
    And finally Phoebus, Lord of the Bow.
    Show us again your threefold strength
    This hour, as in ages long ago.
    Save us from the fire and pain of plague, and make us
       clean.

    Sorrows beyond all telling:
    Sickness rife in our ranks, outstripping
170   Invention of remedy; blight
    On barren earth,
    And barren agonies of birth;
    Life after life from the wildfire winging
    Swiftly into the night.

    Beyond all telling, the city
180   Reeks with death in her streets, death-bringing.
    None weep, and her children die,
    None by to pity.

Mothers at every altar kneel.
Golden Athena, listen to our cries!
Apollo, hear us and heal!

Not with the rattle of bronze, but loud around us   190
The battle is raging, swift the death-fiend flies.
Fling to the farthest corners of the sea,
Or to some bleak northerly bay,
The onset of his armoury!
Night's agony grows into tortured day.   200
Zeus, let your thunder crush and lightning slay.

Slay him with your golden bow, Lycean, slay him,
Artemis, resplendent over the Lycian hills!
Bacchus, our native god, golden in the dance   210
Of maenad revelry,
Euoe! The fiery torch advance
To slay the Death-god, the grim enemy,
God whom all other gods abhor to see.
    [*Enter* OEDIPUS.]

OEDIPUS
You ask, and your request shall be met with release
From plague, if you will obey me, and are willing to take
The remedy your distress requires. I speak
As a stranger, except by hearsay, to what has passed
And the story that has been told. Without this clue   220
I would make little headway in my search.
Therefore, Thebans, as a citizen recently
Received among you, I make this proclamation:
If any one of you knows whose hand it was
That killed Laius, the son of Labdacus,
Let him declare it fully to me now.
    [*Silence.*]
Or if any man's conscience is guilty, let him give himself up.
He will suffer the less. His fate will be nothing worse
Than banishment. No other harm will come to him.
    [*Still silence.*]
Or, if some foreigner is known to have been the assassin,   230

Speak up. The informer shall have his reward of me,
As well as the thanks he will earn from all of you.
 [*Silence once again.*]
But if you will not speak, and any man
Is found to be screening himself or another, in fear,
I here pronounce my sentence upon his head:
No matter who he may be, he is forbidden
Shelter or association with any man
In all this country over which I rule;
From communal prayers and sacrifice
240   And lustral rites he is prohibited; and he
Is barred from every house, unclean and accursed,
According to the word of the Pythian oracle.
This way I shall have done my duty to the god
And to the dead. And it is my solemn prayer
That the unknown murderer, and his accomplices,
If such there be, may live in shame for their
Shameful act, unfriended, to their life's end.

And if, with my knowledge, house or hearth of mine
250   Should receive the guilty man, may all the curses
I have laid on others fall upon my own head.
It is for you to see this faithfully carried out,
As you are duty-bound to me, to the god,
And to our barren plague-tormented country.
Indeed, I am surprised that no purification was made,
Even without the express command of heaven.
The death of a man so worthy – your king –
Should surely have been probed to the utmost.
Still, now that I hold the place that he once held –
260   His bed and his wife, whose children, had fate so willed,
Would have grown to be another bond of blood between
        us –
And upon him, alas, has this disaster fallen,
I mean to fight for him now, as I would fight
For my own father, leaving no way untried
By which to bring to light the killer of Laius,

Son of Labdacus, son of Polydorus, son of Cadmus, son of
   Agenor.
The gods curse all that disobey this charge!
For them may the earth be barren of harvest, may   270
Women be childless, and may this present calamity,
And worse than this, pursue them to their deaths!
For the rest, you sons of Cadmus who are on my side,
May Justice, and all the gods, be with you for ever.

CHORUS

Under your curse, my king, I make bold to answer:
I am not the man, nor can I point him out.
The question came from Phoebus, and he, if anyone,
Could surely tell us who the offender is.

OEDIPUS

No doubt, but to compel a god to speak   280
Against his will, is not in mortal power.

CHORUS

I have another thing to say.

OEDIPUS

Go on. Second or third thoughts, we will hear them all.

CHORUS

Next to lord Apollo, lord Tiresias
Stands nearest, I would say, in divination.
He is the one who could help us most in our search.

OEDIPUS

I have not overlooked that. I have sent for him –
It was Creon's advice – on two occasions.
I am surprised he is not already here.

CHORUS

There were rumours, of course, but mostly old wives'   290
   tales.

OEDIPUS

Rumours? What rumours? I must hear them all.

CHORUS

He was said to have been killed by travellers on the road.

OEDIPUS

So I have heard. But where are the witnesses?

CHORUS
   He'd be a bold man, sir, that would pay no heed
   To such a curse as yours, once he had heard it.
OEDIPUS
   Will he that did not shrink from the deed fear words?
CHORUS
   There is one who can find him. They are bringing him –
   The prophet in whom, of all men, lives truth incarnate.
     [*Enter* TIRESIAS *led by an attendant.*]
OEDIPUS
300   Tiresias, you who know all lore, sacred and profane,
   And all heavenly and earthly knowledge,
   In your heart, if not with your eyes,
   You see our city's condition. We look to you
   As our only help and protection. We have sent
   To Phoebus – they may have told you – and he has
      answered.
   The only means of deliverance from this plague
   Is for us to discover the killers of Laius
   And kill or banish them.
   Do not begrudge us now your skill
310   In bird-lore or whatever other arts
   Of prophecy you possess. It is for yourself,
   It is for Thebes, it is for me. Come, save us all,
   Save all that is polluted by this death.
   We look to you. To help his fellow-men
   With all his power is a man's most noble calling.
TIRESIAS
   Wise words; but then, when wisdom brings no profit,
   To be wise is to suffer. And why did I forget this,
   Who knew it well? I never should have come.
OEDIPUS
   It seems you bring us little encouragement.
TIRESIAS
320   Let me go home. It will be easier this way
   For you to bear your burden, and me mine.
OEDIPUS
   Take care, sir. You show yourself no friend to Thebes,

Whose son you are, if you refuse to answer.

TIRESIAS

It is because I can see your words tending
To no good end; therefore I guard my own.

OEDIPUS

By the gods! If you know, do not refuse to speak!
We all beseech you; we are all your suppliants.

TIRESIAS

You are all deluded. I refuse to utter
The heavy secrets of my soul – and yours.

OEDIPUS

What? Something you know, and will not tell? Do you   330
   mean
To fail us and to see your city perish?

TIRESIAS

I mean to spare us both great pain. Ask me
No more. It is useless. I will tell you nothing.

OEDIPUS

Nothing? You despicable man, you would rouse
A stone to fury! Will you not speak up?
Are you set on being obstinate to the end?

TIRESIAS

Do not blame me; put your own house in order.

OEDIPUS

Hear him! Such words, such insults to the State!
What man would not be moved to anger?   340

TIRESIAS

What will be
Will be, though I should never speak again.

OEDIPUS

It is your trade to tell what is to be.

TIRESIAS

I tell no more. Rage with what wrath you will.

OEDIPUS

I shall, and speak my mind unflinchingly.
I tell you I believe *you* had a hand
In plotting, and all but doing, this very act.
If you had eyes to see with, I would have said

Your hand, and yours alone, had done it all.

TIRESIAS

350   Would you now? Then hear this: upon your head
Is the ban your lips have uttered. From this day forth
Never speak to me or any here –
You are the cursed polluter of this land.

OEDIPUS

You dare to say such a thing! Have you no shame at all?
And do you expect to escape the consequences?

TIRESIAS

I am immune. The truth is my defence.

OEDIPUS

Whose work is this? This is no soothsaying.

TIRESIAS

You taught me. You made me say it against my will.

OEDIPUS

Say it again. Let there be no mistake.

TIRESIAS

360   Was it not plain? Or will you push me further?

OEDIPUS

I would have it said beyond all doubt. Say it again.

TIRESIAS

I say that the killer you are seeking is yourself.

OEDIPUS

A second time! You will be sorry for this.

TIRESIAS

Will you have more, to feed your anger?

OEDIPUS

Yes!
More, and more madness. Tell us all you know.

TIRESIAS

I know, as you do not, that you are living
In shameful union with the ones you love –
Living in ignorance of your own undoing.

OEDIPUS

Do you think you can say such things with impunity?

TIRESIAS

I do, if the truth has any power to protect.

OEDIPUS

It has, but not for you; no, not for you,   370
You shameless, brainless, sightless man!

TIRESIAS

You are to be pitied, uttering such taunts
As all men's mouths will one day cast at *you*.

OEDIPUS

Living in perpetual night, you cannot harm
Me, or anyone else that sees the light.

TIRESIAS

No, it is not for me to bring you down;
That is in Apollo's hands, and he will do it.

OEDIPUS

Creon! Was this trick his, then, if not yours?

TIRESIAS

Not Creon either. You are your own enemy.

OEDIPUS

Ah, riches and royalty, and wit matched against wit   380
In the race of life, must they always be coupled with envy?
Must Creon, so long my friend, my most trusted friend,
Stalk me by stealth, and seek to dispossess me
Of the power this city has given me – freely given –
Not of my asking – setting this schemer on me,
This peddler of fraudulent con tricks, with his eyes
Wide open for profit, but blind in prophecy?
What was your vaunted divination ever worth?   390
And where were you when the Riddling Bitch was here?
Had you any word of deliverance for our people then?
There was a riddle too deep for common wits.
A seer should have answered it; but no answer came
From you; bird-lore and divination were all silent.
Until, that is, *I* came – I, ignorant Oedipus –
And stopped the riddler's mouth, guessing the truth
By native wit, not bird-lore. This is the man
Whom you would dispossess, hoping to stand
Nearest to Creon's throne. You will regret,   400
You and your fellow-plotter, your zeal
For scapegoat-hunting. Were you not as old

As you appear to be, sharp punishment
Would soon convince you of your evil ways.

CHORUS

Sir, to our thinking, both of you have spoken
In the heat of anger. Surely this is not well,
When all our thoughts should be how to discharge
The god's command.

TIRESIAS

King though you are, one right –
To reply – makes us equal, and I claim it.
It is not for you, but Loxias, whom I serve;
Nor am I bound to Creon's patronage.
You are pleased to mock my blindness. You have eyes
And yet you cannot see your own damnation,
Nor do you see what company you keep.
Whose son are you? I tell you, you have sinned –
And do not know it – against your own earth
And in the grave. A swift and two-edged sword,
Your mother's and your father's curse, shall sweep you
Out of this land. Those now clear-seeing eyes
Shall then be darkened. No place will be deaf,
No corner of Cithaeron echoless,
To your loud crying, when you learn the truth
Of that sweet marriage-song that hailed you home
To the fair-seeming haven of your hopes –
With greater misery than you can guess,
To show you what you are, and who they are
That call you father. Rail as you will at Creon,
And at my speaking. You shall be trodden down
With fouler scorn than ever fell on man.

OEDIPUS

I shall bear no more of this! Out of my sight!
Go! Quickly, go! Back where you came from! Go!

TIRESIAS

I will. It was your wish brought me here, not mine.

OEDIPUS

Had I known what madness I was to listen to,
I would have spared myself the trouble.

TIRESIAS
  Mad as I may seem to you,
  Your parents would not think me so.
OEDIPUS
  What's that? My parents? Who then . . . gave me birth?
TIRESIAS
  This day brings you your birth, and brings you death.
OEDIPUS
  Must you still wrap your words in riddles?
TIRESIAS
  Are you not famed for skill at solving riddles?   440
OEDIPUS
  You taunt me with the gift that is my greatness?
TIRESIAS
  Your great misfortune, and your ruin.
OEDIPUS
  No matter!
  I have saved this land from ruin. I am content.
TIRESIAS
  Well, I will go. Your hand, boy. Take me home.
OEDIPUS
  Let him take you home. You've been nothing but
  A nuisance here. We can well do without you.
TIRESIAS
  I have said my all, thus to your face,
  Fearful of nothing you can do to me. And I add this:
  The man for whom you have ordered hue and cry,   450
  The killer of Laius, that man is *here*,
  Passing for a foreigner, a sojourner here among us,
  But, as presently shall appear, a Theban born –
  To his cost. He that came seeing, blind shall he go;
  Rich now, then a beggar; stick-in-hand, groping his way
  To a land of exile; brother, as it shall be shown,
  And father at once, to the children he cherishes; son,
  And husband, to the woman who bore him; father-killer
  And father-supplanter. Go in and think on this.   460
  When you can prove me wrong, then call me blind.
    [*Exeunt* TIRESIAS *and* OEDIPUS.]

CHORUS
From the Delphian rock the heavenly voice denounces
The shedder of blood, the doer of deeds unnamed.
Who is the man?
Let him fly with the speed of horses racing the wind.
470   The son of Zeus, armed with his fire and lightning,
Leaps to destroy,
And the fates, sure-footed, close around him.

Out of the snowy dawn on high Parnassus
The order flashed, to hunt a man from his hiding.
But where is he?
In forest or cave, a wild ox roaming the mountains,
480   Treading a friendless path; but the deathless voices
Ring in his ear,
From the earth's core they cry against him.

Terrible things indeed has the prophet spoken.
We cannot believe, we cannot deny; all is dark.
We fear, but we cannot see, what is before us.
490   Was there a quarrel between the house of Labdacus
And the son of Polybus? None that we ever knew,
For which to impugn the name of Oedipus,
Or seek to avenge the house of Labdacus
For the undiscovered death.

All of earth's secrets are known to Zeus and Apollo,
500   But of mortal prophets, that one knows more than
        another
No man can surely say. Wisdom is given
To all in their several degrees. I impute no blame
Till blame is proven. Oedipus faced the Winged
        Enchantress,
And stood the test, winning glittering renown.
510   Never, therefore, will I consent
To think other than good of him.
        [*Enter* CREON.]

CREON
　　Citizens, they tell me that King Oedipus
　　Has laid a slanderous accusation upon me.
　　I will not bear it! If he thinks that I
　　Have done him any harm, by word or deed,
　　In this desperate hour, I will not live –
　　Life is too long – to hear such scandal. Why, it
　　Is more than scandal, a grievous allegation,　　　　520
　　If you, my friends – my country – call me traitor.
CHORUS
　　The words, I think, were spoken in the heat
　　Of anger, ill-considered.
CREON
　　　　　　　　But did he not say
　　The prophet had lied at my instigation?
CHORUS
　　He did; though with what intention I cannot tell.
CREON
　　Said with an unflinching look, was it? On purpose –
　　This accusation that he made against me?
CHORUS
　　I do not scrutinize my master's actions.　　　　530
　　But here he comes.
　　　　[*Enter* OEDIPUS.]
OEDIPUS
　　Well? What brings you here?
　　Have you the gall to stand before my door,
　　Proven plotter against my life and seeker of my
　　　　crown?
　　Do you take me for a coward, or a fool?
　　Did you suppose I lacked the eyes to see
　　The plot being prepared, or the wits to counter it?
　　And what a foolish plot! You, without backing　　　　540
　　Of friends or means, to go in quest of kingship!
　　Kingdoms are won by men and moneybags.
CREON
　　Hear my reply. And when you know, then judge.

OEDIPUS

    I doubt your eloquence will teach me much.

    You are my bitterest enemy, that I know.

CREON

    First, let me tell you—

OEDIPUS

    Tell me anything,

    Except that you are honest.

CREON

    Do you really believe

550   This obstinacy does you any good?

OEDIPUS

    Do *you* believe that you can carry on

    Scheming against your house and go unpunished?

CREON

    I should be a fool to believe it. But tell me

    What wrong you think I have done you.

OEDIPUS

    Was it not you

    That made me bring that ranting prophet here?

CREON

    It was; and I would do the same again.

OEDIPUS

    Tell me . . . how long ago did Laius . . .

CREON

    Did Laius – what? I don't quite understand.

OEDIPUS

560   How long is it since Laius . . . disappeared?

CREON

    A long time now; longer than I can say.

OEDIPUS

    And was this old prophet at his business then?

CREON

    Yes he was – held in equal honour then as now.

OEDIPUS

    In those days, did he ever mention me?

CREON

    Not to my knowledge.

OEDIPUS
  Was there no inquest made
  Into this death?

CREON
  Of course there was. But in vain.

OEDIPUS
  And the man of wisdom – why was he silent then?

CREON
  I cannot tell you any more than I know.

OEDIPUS
  You know one thing, and would be wise to confess it.   570

CREON
  What I know I will freely confess. What do I know?

OEDIPUS
  That without your prompting the fortune-teller
  Would never have dared to name *me* as Laius' killer.

CREON
  If he did so, you know best. But give me leave
  To question you as you have questioned me.

OEDIPUS
  Ask away. You cannot prove me guilty of blood.

CREON
  Are you my sister's husband?

OEDIPUS
  That I am.

CREON
  And is she your equal partner in power?

OEDIPUS
  All that she desires is hers by right.   580

CREON
  Have I a third and equal share of honour?

OEDIPUS
  You have – so much the more your proven falseness.

CREON
  But I deny it. Reason with yourself,
  And ask whether any man would exchange
  A quiet life, with royal rank assured,
  For an uneasy throne? To be a king

In name was never part of my ambition.
Enough for me to lead a kingly life.
What more could any moderate man desire?
590   I have your ear for all my fair requests;
But, in your place, I would have much to do
That riled me. How could kingship please me more
Than royalty and rule with no drawbacks?
I am not yet so besotted as to seek
More honours than are good for me. I stand
In all men's favour, I am all men's friend.
Why, those who seek your ear, ask for me first,
Knowing that way to be the best chance of success.
And would I change this life for the other? No.
600   None but a fool would be so faithless. Treason?
That is neither my policy, nor, as far as I know,
The policy of any friend of mine.
To test me, first, go to the Pythian shrine;
Ask if the message I brought back was true.
Second, prove me guilty of any dealing
With the soothsayer. Then take me and condemn me
To death. My voice will join yours in pronouncing
        sentence.
But charged behind my back on blind suspicion
I will not be. To slur a good man's name
With baseless slander is a crime; and so too
610   Is rashly mistaking bad men for good.
Cast out an honest friend, and you cast out
Your life, your dearest treasure. Time will teach
The truth of this. Time alone can prove
The honest man; a single day proclaims the criminal.

CHORUS
Good words, and fitting for a prudent man
To hear and heed. First thoughts are seldom wisest.

OEDIPUS
When a sly thinker is on the move, my friend,
It's safest to be quick in counter-thinking.
620   Am I to sit and wait for him, and lose
My opportunity while he takes his?

CREON
    What do you want then? Will you banish me?
OEDIPUS
    Not at all. I would have you dead, not banished.
CREON
    If you can show in what way I have wronged you—
OEDIPUS
    Still clinging stubbornly to your arguments?
CREON
    Because I know you are wrong.
OEDIPUS
    I know I am right.
CREON
    In your own eyes perhaps, not in mine.
OEDIPUS
    You're a traitor.
CREON
    And what if you are mistaken?
OEDIPUS
    Kings must rule!
CREON
    Not when they rule unjustly.
OEDIPUS
    Hear him, Thebes,
    My City!
CREON
    Yours? Is she not also mine?   630
CHORUS
    Gentlemen, enough! Here comes the queen, Jocasta.
    She should be able to settle this quarrel.
        [Enter JOCASTA (from the palace).]
JOCASTA
    What is the meaning of this loud argument,
    You quarrelsome pair? I wonder you're not ashamed,
    Airing your private troubles in this time of distress.
    Come in, dear husband; and you, Creon, go home.
    You're making too much of some unimportant
        grievance.

CREON

Not so, sister. Your husband Oedipus
640   Condemns me out of hand with a terrible sentence,
A choice of death or banishment.

OEDIPUS

It's true.
I have found him secretly plotting against my person.

CREON

May the curse of heaven rest on me forever,
If I am guilty of any such designs!

JOCASTA

For the love of god, believe it Oedipus!
For his oath's sake, please believe it – and for mine
And theirs who are here to witness!

CHORUS

Consent, my lord, consent!
650   Be merciful, and learn to yield.

OEDIPUS

And why should I repent?

CHORUS

His oath should be his shield.
He never played you false before.

OEDIPUS

Do you know for what you pray?

CHORUS

We do.

OEDIPUS

Say more.

CHORUS

He swore
His friendship; is it right to cast away
A friend, condemned, unheard,
Upon an idle word?

OEDIPUS

660   In seeking this you ask *my* death or banishment.

CHORUS

Forbid the thought! O by the Lord of Life,
The Sun, forbid! Lost may I be

To god and man, if it was ever mine!
But while our people pine,
My heart is racked anew
If you,
My princes, add your strife
To our old misery.

OEDIPUS

Then let him go; even if it means my death
Or exile in disgrace. Your voice, not his,   670
Has won my mercy; him I hate forever.

CREON

In mercy unflinching, and harsh in anger –
Such natures earn self-torture.

OEDIPUS

Will you be gone?

CREON

I will; unjustly judged by you alone.
    [*Exit* CREON.]

CHORUS

Madam, persuade the king
To spend some time apart.

JOCASTA

How did this trouble start?   680

CHORUS

Wild suspicion; and the sting
Of baseless accusations grown sore.

JOCASTA

Each holding each to blame?

CHORUS

Why yes.

JOCASTA

What for?

CHORUS

Ask no more.
Enough our stricken country's shame.
To let this other matter rest
Where it is, seems best.

OEDIPUS
You see what you have done, though you meant well?
And all because you tried to quell my anger.

CHORUS
690   Listen, my lord, what we say is true.
Could we show such simplicity
As rashly from your sheltering arms to stray?
You whose wisdom in the days
Of strife upheld our land,
Whose hand
Again will lead us through
This storm into tranquillity?

JOCASTA
Will you not tell me too? Tell me, I implore you,
Why you have conceived this terrible hatred against him.

OEDIPUS
700   I will. You are more to me than these good men.
The fault is Creon's, and his this plot against me.

JOCASTA
How is it his? What is the accusation?

OEDIPUS
He says the murder of Laius was my doing.

JOCASTA
From what he knows himself or what others have told him?

OEDIPUS
Ah, that's where he's clever; he shields himself
By using a devious soothsayer as his tool.

JOCASTA
Then absolve yourself at once. I can tell you,
No man possesses the secret of divination.
710   And I have proof. An oracle was given to Laius –
Not from Phoebus, but from his ministers –
That he would die at the hands of his own child,
His child and mine. And what came of it? Laius,
As is common knowledge, was killed by outland robbers
At a place where three roads meet. As for the child,
It was not yet three days old, when he cast it out –
By others' hands, not his – with ankles riveted

To perish on an empty mountainside.
There, then, Apollo did not so contrive it.   720
The child did not kill the father; the father,
For all his fears, was killed – by someone else.
Yet such were the prophet's warnings. Why should you,
Then, heed them for a moment? What he intends,
The god will show us in his own good time.

OEDIPUS
Dear wife, what you have said has troubled me.
My mind goes back . . . and something in me stirs . . .

JOCASTA
Why? What is the matter? How you turn and shake!

OEDIPUS
Did you not just say that Laius was killed
At a place where three roads meet?   730

JOCASTA
That was the story;
And is the story still.

OEDIPUS
Where? In what region?

JOCASTA
The land of Phocis – where the road divides,
Leading to Delphi one way and Daulia the other.

OEDIPUS
How long ago did it happen?

JOCASTA
It became known . . .
A little while before your reign began.

OEDIPUS
God, what will you do to me?

JOCASTA
Why, Oedipus,
What weighs upon your mind?

OEDIPUS
Don't ask!   740
But tell me what Laius was like. How old?

JOCASTA
Tall, silvery-grey hair, about your build.

OEDIPUS
Oh god! Am I unwittingly self-cursed?
JOCASTA
What, my lord? What is it? You frighten me.
OEDIPUS
Could the prophet see after all? Is it possible?
To prove it for sure, tell me one thing more.
JOCASTA
You frighten me. I'll tell you all I know.
OEDIPUS
750   How was the king attended? By a few men,
Or in full state with all his bodyguards?
JOCASTA
Five men in all, a herald leading them;
One carriage only, in which Laius rode.
OEDIPUS
Oh god, it's all too clear! Who told you this?
JOCASTA
A servant, the only survivor that returned.
OEDIPUS
Is he still in the household?
JOCASTA
No. When he came back,
And found you king, in his late master's place,
760   He earnestly begged me to let him go away
Into the country to become a shepherd,
Far from the city's reach. I let him go.
Poor fellow, he could have asked a greater favour;
He was a good slave.
OEDIPUS
Could we have him here
Without delay?
JOCASTA
We could. But why?
OEDIPUS
Dear wife, I fear . . . I fear that I have said
Too much, which is why I must see this man.

JOCASTA

  Well, you shall see him. Meanwhile, may I not hear
  What weighs so heavily on your heart?   770

OEDIPUS

  You may.
  If things are as I see them, you are the first
  To whom I should tell my story. Listen then.
  My father was a Corinthian, Polybus;
  My mother a Dorian, Merope. At home
  I rose to be a person of some pre-eminence, until,
  That is, a strange thing happened – a curious thing –
  Though perhaps I took it to heart more than it deserved.
  One day at supper, a man who had been drinking
      heavily
  Boldly exclaimed that I was not my father's son.   780
  It hurt me, but for the time being I suffered in silence
  As well as I could. The next day I asked my parents
  To tell me the truth. They were bitterly annoyed
  That anyone should dare put such a story about,
  And I was relieved. Yet somehow the smart remained,
  And a thing like that soon passes from hand to hand.
  So without my parents' knowledge I went to Delphi,
  But I came back without a proper answer
  To the question I'd asked. Instead I heard a tale   790
  Of horror and misery: how I must marry my mother,
  Become the parent of misbegotten children –
  An offence to all mankind – and kill my father.
  On hearing this I ran away, putting some distance
  Between me and Corinth, never to see home again,
  So that no such horror should ever come to pass.
  My journey brought me to the region where
  Your last king met his end. Now listen: this is the truth.
  When I came to the place where the three roads meet, 800
     I saw
  A herald followed by a horse-drawn carriage, and a man
  Seated within, just as you have described.
  The driver rudely ordered me out of the way,

And his master joined in with a surly command.
The driver then thrust me aside, and I struck him
In anger. The old man saw this leaning out of the
    carriage.
He waited till I passed, then, seizing as a weapon
The driver's two-pronged goad, he struck me on the head.
810   He paid with interest for his rash behaviour.
With lightning speed, the staff in my right hand
Did its work. He tumbled headlong out of the carriage,
And every one of them I killed right there. But now,
If the blood of Laius ran in this stranger's veins,
Is there anyone more wretched than I, more hated
By god or man? It is I whom no stranger or citizen
Must take into his house; I to whom none may speak.
820   On me is the curse that I myself have laid.
His wife! These hands that killed him have touched *her*!
Is this my sin? Am I not utterly foul?
Banished from here, and in my banishment
Debarred from home and from my fatherland,
Which I must shun forever, for fear of living
To make my mother my wife, and killing my father . . .
My father . . . Polybus, to whom I owe my life.
Can it be anyone but a monstrous god
Of evil that has sent this doom upon me?
830   O never, never, holy powers above,
May that day come! May I sooner be dead,
And wiped off the face of the earth, than live
To bear the scars of such an awful fate!

CHORUS

Sir, these are terrible words. But remain hopeful,
Until you learn the whole truth from our witness.

OEDIPUS

That is my only hope, to await the shepherd.

JOCASTA

But why? What help do you expect from him?

OEDIPUS

If the man's story fits with yours,

I am absolved. 840

JOCASTA
On what particular grounds?
What did I say?

OEDIPUS
You said he spoke of robbers – that robbers
Killed him. If he maintains that it was robbers,
I didn't kill him; one man can't be several.
But if he says it was a solo traveller,
There's no escape; the finger points to me.

JOCASTA
But I assure you that was what he said;
He cannot go back on it now. Everyone heard,
Not I alone. And even if he changes his story 850
In some small point, he cannot, in any event,
Pretend that Laius died as was foretold:
Loxias said a child of mine would kill him.
It was not to be. Poor child, it was he that died.
So much for divination! After this
I wouldn't even cross the road for it.

OEDIPUS
You're right. Still, let us have the shepherd here.
Send someone off to fetch him. 860

JOCASTA
I will at once.
Come in. I'll do exactly as you wish.
  [*Exeunt.*]

CHORUS
I only ask to live with pure faith, keeping
In word and deed that Law which spans the sky,
Made of no mortal mould, undimmed, unsleeping
Whose living godhead does not age or die. 870

Pride breeds the tyrant. Swollen with ill-found booty,
From castled height Pride tumbles to the pit,
All footing lost. Zeal, stripped for civic duty,
No law forbids; may god still foster it. 880

He who travels his own high-handed way, disdaining
True reverence for divine sanctuaries;
Who falsely wins, all sacred things profaning;
890   Shall he escape his doomed pride's penalties?

Shall he by any armour be defended
From heaven's sharp wrath, who casts out right for
        wrong?
If wickedness for virtue be commended,
Farewell, sweet harmonies of sacred song;

Farewell Abaean and Olympian altars;
900   Farewell, O Heart of Earth, inviolate shrine,
If at this time your omens fail or falter,
And man no longer owns your voice divine.

Zeus! If you live, all-powerful, all-pervading,
Awake! Old oracles are out of mind.
Apollo's name denied, his glory fading.
910   There is no godliness in all mankind.
        [*Enter* JOCASTA *from the palace.*]
JOCASTA
        Gentlemen, I am minded to visit the holy temples,
        Bringing in my hands these tokens of supplication
        And gifts of incense. The king makes up figments of
        His own imagination, and can no longer sanely judge
        The present by the past, dwelling on every word
        That feeds his apprehension. I can do nothing
        To comfort him.
        To you, bright shining Apollo,
920   Who are nearest to my door, is my first prayer.
        Save us from the curse of this pollution.
        I am afraid, seeing our sovereign ruler so distraught.
        [*Enter a* MESSENGER *from Corinth.*]
MESSENGER
        Excuse me, strangers, I seek the palace of Oedipus.
        Can you guide me to it – or him, if you know where he is?

CHORUS
> This is the palace; and he is inside. This lady
> Is the man's wife and mother to his children.

MESSENGER [*to* JOCASTA]
> My blessings on you,
> And all your house, true consort of such a man.   930

JOCASTA
> Blessings on you, sir, and thanks for your kindly greeting.
> Is it a request or a message that you bring?

MESSENGER
> Good news
> For your husband, madam, and for his house.

JOCASTA
> What news? And from whom?

MESSENGER
> From Corinth. You cannot but be happy
> At the message, though you may also be distressed.

JOCASTA
> What is it that can have such power to please and grieve?

MESSENGER
> Our people say he will be king of all the Isthmus.   940

JOCASTA
> Is Polybus no longer king?

MESSENGER
> King Polybus, madam, is dead and in his grave.

JOCASTA
> What? Dead? The father of Oedipus?

MESSENGER
> On my life.

JOCASTA [*to an attendant*]
> Go to your master quickly!
> Tell him this news.
>   [*The attendant goes.*]
> Where are you now, divine prognostications?
> The man whom Oedipus avoided all these years,
> In case he should kill him is dead – by natural causes,
> And no act of his!
>   [*Enter* OEDIPUS.]

OEDIPUS

950   My dear Jocasta,
Why have you called me out of doors again?

JOCASTA

Hear this man's news, and when you've heard it, say
What has become of those famous oracles.

OEDIPUS

Who is this man? What news has he for me?

JOCASTA

He comes from Corinth. Your father Polybus
Is dead – dead!

OEDIPUS

What?
    [*To the* MESSENGER]
Tell me yourself.

MESSENGER

I assure you – if you must have this first –
He has gone the way of all mortality.

OEDIPUS

960   By foul play, or because of natural causes?

MESSENGER

Such natural cause as puts the old to sleep.

OEDIPUS

You mean he died of illness, the poor man.

MESSENGER

That, and the tally of years he had fulfilled.

OEDIPUS

Well, well . . . So, wife, what of the Pythian fire;
The oracles, the prophesying birds
That scream above us? I was to kill my father;
Now he lies in his grave, and here am I
Who never raised a finger . . . unless it could be said
970   Grief at my absence killed him – and so *I* did it.
But no, the letter of the oracle
Is unfulfilled and lies, like Polybus, dead.

JOCASTA

Have I not said so all along?

OEDIPUS
You have.
My fear misled me.
JOCASTA
Think no more of it.
OEDIPUS
There is still this other fear . . . my mother.
JOCASTA
Fear? What does a man have to do with fear?
Chance rules our lives, and the future is all unknown.
Better to live as best we may, from day to day.
Nor need this mother-marrying frighten you;   980
Many a man has dreamt as much. Such things
Must be forgotten, if life is to be endured.
OEDIPUS
If she were dead, you might have said so with
Good reason. But she lives; and while she lives,
Say what you will, I still cannot rest easy.
JOCASTA
At least your father's death is a relief.
OEDIPUS
Agreed. But while my mother lives, I am not safe.
MESSENGER
But, sir, who is the woman you still fear?
OEDIPUS
Queen Merope, the wife of Polybus.   990
MESSENGER
In what way does her life endanger yours?
OEDIPUS
We have an oracle of deadly tenor.
MESSENGER
Is it one that may rightly be uttered to a stranger?
OEDIPUS
Why, yes. Loxias said I was predestined
To make my mother my wife and kill my father,
Shedding his blood with my own hands. This is the reason
For my long estrangement from Corinth. And I have fared
     well,

Though nothing can fill the place of absent parents.

MESSENGER

1000   Was that the fear that banished you all this time?

OEDIPUS

Yes. I was determined not to kill my father.

MESSENGER

Then let me rid you of this other fear.
I came to do you good—

OEDIPUS

My gratitude
Shall not be stinted.

MESSENGER

And, if truth be told,
To do myself good on your return home.

OEDIPUS

Home, never! Never under my parents' roof.

MESSENGER

My dear young man, you're mistaken.

OEDIPUS

How so?
For god's sake, tell me.

MESSENGER

1010   This fear that bars you from your home—

OEDIPUS

Yes, that.
Apollo's word may yet come true for me.

MESSENGER

That story of pollution through your parents?

OEDIPUS

The very same, my ever-present torment.

MESSENGER

All idle, sir; your fears are without grounds.

OEDIPUS

But how can that be, if I am their son?

MESSENGER

You're not. Polybus is no kin of yours.

OEDIPUS

No kin?

You mean he's not my father?

MESSENGER

No more than I am.

OEDIPUS

Come now; no more than you? Explain yourself.

MESSENGER

I am not your father; neither is Polybus.   1020

OEDIPUS

How is it, then, that I was called his son?

MESSENGER

I will tell you. You were given to him – by me.

OEDIPUS

Given? And yet he loved me as a son.

MESSENGER

He had no other.

OEDIPUS

Was I . . . found? Or bought?

MESSENGER

Found, in a wooded hollow on Cithaeron.

OEDIPUS

What brought you there?

MESSENGER

Tending sheep on the mountain.

OEDIPUS

Were you a hireling shepherd then?

MESSENGER

I was;
And, by that happy chance, your rescuer.   1030

OEDIPUS

Why? Was I in pain or danger when you took me?

MESSENGER

The weakness in your ankles tells the tale.

OEDIPUS

Oh god, please don't mention that old complaint!

MESSENGER

Your ankles were riveted, and I set you free.

OEDIPUS

It's true; I've carried that stigma from the cradle.

MESSENGER
  It is to that you owe your present name.
OEDIPUS
  O gods!
  Was it my father or mother that named me?
MESSENGER
  I couldn't say. Ask the man who gave you to me.
OEDIPUS
  Gave me? So did you not find me yourself?
MESSENGER
1040 Another shepherd put you in my care.
OEDIPUS
  And who was he? Can you tell us who he was?
MESSENGER
  I think he was said to be one of Laius' men.
OEDIPUS
  Laius? Our former king?
MESSENGER
  Why, yes; king Laius.
  The man was one of his servants.
OEDIPUS
  Is he alive?
  And could I see him?
MESSENGER
  Your people here should know.
OEDIPUS
  Good men, do any of you know this fellow –
  This shepherd of whom he speaks? Has anyone seen
      him
  In the fields or the city? Speak up if you know.
1050 This is our chance to get to the bottom of this mystery.
CHORUS
  I think that he will prove to be the same man
  That you have already asked to see. The queen
  Is the one best placed to tell you if this is so.
OEDIPUS [to JOCASTA]
  Well? Do you know the man that we have sent for?

Is that the man he means?

JOCASTA [*terrified*]

What does it matter
What man he means? It makes no difference now.
Forget what he has told you. It makes no difference.

OEDIPUS

Nonsense! I must pursue this trail to the end,
Till I have unravelled the mystery of my birth.

JOCASTA

No! in god's name – if you want to survive, this quest   1060
Must not go on. Have I not suffered enough?

OEDIPUS

There is nothing to fear. Even if I am proved a slave
To the third generation, *your* honour is not affected.

JOCASTA

All the same, I beg you, do not do this.

OEDIPUS

I must. I cannot leave the truth unknown.

JOCASTA

I know I am right. I warn you – for your own good.

OEDIPUS

My 'good' has been my bugbear long enough.

JOCASTA

Doomed man! May you never live to learn the truth!

OEDIPUS

Go, someone; fetch the shepherd. Leave the lady
To enjoy the pride of her birth.   1070

JOCASTA

O lost and damned!
This is my last and only word to you – forevermore!
    [*Exit.*]

CHORUS

Why has the queen left us in such a state?
I fear some grave catastrophe will out
From what she dare not tell.

OEDIPUS

Let all come out,

However bad! However base it be,
I must unlock the secret of my birth.
My wife, with more than a woman's pride is ashamed

1080 At my low origins. I am the child of Fortune,
The giver of good, and I shall not be shamed;
She is my mother, my sisters are the Seasons;
My rising and falling march with theirs.
Born so, I ask to be no other man
Than that I am – and will know *who* I am.

CHORUS
If my prophetic eye fails not, tomorrow's moon
Makes known to all earth
The secret of our master's birth.

1090 Cithaeron's name shall fill
Our song; his father, mother, nurse was she,
And for this boon
To our great king, praised shall Cithaeron be.
Phoebus our lord, be this according to your will.

Was this offspring born of some primeval sprite
With amorous glances beguiled

1100 By mountain-haunting Pan? Or child
Of Loxias, the very son
Of our bright god who walks the high grasslands?
Did he delight
Cyllene's lord? Did Dionysus' hands
Receive him from a nymph he loved on Helicon?

OEDIPUS
1110 Gentlemen, I think I see our shepherd approaching.
I guess this is the man, though I never set eyes on him.
He and our Corinthian friend are of similar ages.
And those are my men that bring him in. It must be so.
But you could tell more surely, if you know him.

CHORUS
This is the man. I know him. Laius' shepherd –
As good a man as any in his service.
[*Enter an elderly* SHEPHERD, *escorted by
attendants.*]

OEDIPUS
    Now, good Corinthian, your evidence first –
    Is this the man you spoke of?   1120
MESSENGER
    This is the man.
OEDIPUS
    Come now, old shepherd. Please look at me
    And answer my questions. Were you in Laius' service?
SHEPHERD
    Indeed I was, sir; born and bred, not bought.
OEDIPUS
    What trade or occupation did you follow?
SHEPHERD
    For most of my life, sir, I was a shepherd.
OEDIPUS
    What part of the country did you mainly work?
SHEPHERD
    Below Mount Cithaeron or thereabouts.
OEDIPUS
    Do you remember having seen this man before?
SHEPHERD
    What man is that, sir? Where would I have seen him?
OEDIPUS [*pointing to the* MESSENGER]
    This man. Have you ever met him anywhere?   1130
SHEPHERD
    I can't say I have, sir – not that I remember.
MESSENGER
    I'm not surprised. I'll jog his memory.
    He won't forget the days when he and I
    Were neighbours on Cithaeron – he with two flocks
    And I with one. Three seasons we were there
    From spring to autumn. And I would drive my flock
    Back towards Corinth for winter, and he to Thebes –
    To Laius' folds. Wasn't that how it was?   1140
SHEPHERD
    Yes, that's how it was. But that was many years ago.
MESSENGER
    Well then, maybe you remember a baby boy

You gave me, and asked me to raise as my own?

SHEPHERD [*suddenly alarmed*]

What do you mean? What are you asking me to say?

MESSENGER

Why, my old friend, *here* stands your baby boy!

SHEPHERD

Damn you, man, hold your tongue!

OEDIPUS

Come, come, old fellow.
He speaks more honestly than you, I think.

SHEPHERD

Why, how have I offended, honourable master?

OEDIPUS

1150   By not replying straight to his question about that child.

SHEPHERD

He doesn't know what he's saying. He's making a
        mistake.

OEDIPUS

If you won't speak willingly, we must make you speak.

SHEPHERD

Don't hurt an old man, sir, for the love of god.

OEDIPUS

Pin back his arms!

SHEPHERD

No, sir, what is this?
What more do you want to know?

OEDIPUS

The child he speaks of –
Was it you that gave it to him?

SHEPHERD

Yes, it was.
I wish I might have died that very day.

OEDIPUS

As you shall now, unless you tell the truth.

SHEPHERD

It'll be the death of me to tell it.

OEDIPUS

1160   Still stalling?

SHEPHERD
    Did I not say I gave it to him? What more?
OEDIPUS
    Where did it come from? Your home or another's?
SHEPHERD
    Not mine. Another man's.
OEDIPUS
    What man? What house?
SHEPHERD
    By all the gods, master, ask me no more!
OEDIPUS
    Answer! If I have to ask again, you die!
SHEPHERD
    It was . . . a child of Laius' house.
OEDIPUS
    A slave's?
    Or was it a child of his own?
SHEPHERD
    Must I say?
OEDIPUS
    You must. And I must hear.   1170
SHEPHERD
    It was his child,
    They said. Your wife could tell the truth of it.
OEDIPUS
    She gave it to you?
SHEPHERD
    Yes, master.
OEDIPUS
    To what end?
SHEPHERD
    To be destroyed.
OEDIPUS
    The child she bore!
SHEPHERD
    Yes, master.
    They said that it was because of some evil curse.

OEDIPUS
   What curse?

SHEPHERD
   One that foretold the child would kill its father.

OEDIPUS
   What, in god's name, made you give it to this man?

SHEPHERD
   I hadn't the heart to destroy it, master. I thought
   He would take it away to another country, his home.
1180   He took it and saved its life – to come to this!
   If you are the man then your life is lost!

OEDIPUS
   Oh god! All out! All known, no more concealment!
   O light! May I never look on you again,
   Revealed as I am, wrongful in my begetting,
   Wrongful in marriage, wrongful in the shedding of blood!
     [*Exit.*]
     [*The* MESSENGER *and* SHEPHERD *depart.*]

CHORUS
   All the generations of mortal men add up to nothing!
1190   Show me the man whose happiness was anything more
       than hopes
   Followed by disillusion.
   Here is the instance, here is Oedipus, here is the reason
   Why I will call no mortal creature happy.
   With what supreme sureness of aim he hit his marks;
   Grasped every prize, by Zeus, once he had drowned the
       she-devil,
1200   The Taloned Lady.
   He was our bastion against disaster, our honoured king;
   All Thebes was proud of the majesty of his name.
   And now, where is there a more heart-rending story of
       affliction?
   Where a more awful turn into the arms of torment?
   O glorious Oedipus!
1210   When the same bosom enfolded the son and father,

Could not the engendering clay have declared its
    indignation?
Time sees all; and now he has found you, when you least
    expected it;
Has found you and judged that marriage-mockery,
    bridegroom-son!
I wish I had never seen you, offspring of Laius,
Yesterday my morning of light, now my night of endless   1220
    darkness!
    [*Enter an* ATTENDANT *from the Palace.*]

ATTENDANT
O you most honourable lords of Thebes,
Weep for the things you shall hear, and must see,
If you are true sons and loyal to the house of Labdacus.
Not all the waters of Ister and Phasis
Can wash this dwelling clean of the foulness within,
Clean of deliberate acts that soon shall be known,   1230
Of all horrific acts most horrific, wilfully chosen.

CHORUS
Already we have wept enough for the things we have learnt,
The things we have seen. What more will your story add?

ATTENDANT
First, to be brief, the queen is dead.

CHORUS
Poor soul! What brought her to this end?

ATTENDANT
Her own hand it was. You that have not seen,
And shall not see, this worst shall suffer the less.
But I that saw, remember, and will tell what I know
Of her last agony. You saw her cross the threshold   1240
In desperate unease. Straight to her bridal-bed
She hurried, fastening her fingers in her hair.
There in her chamber, flinging the doors sharply to,
She cried aloud to Laius long since dead,
Remembering the son she bore back then, the son
By whom the sire was slain, the son to whom
The mother bore yet other children, fruit

Of hapless misbegetting. There she bewailed
The doubly confused issue of her unions –
1250   Husband born of husband and children born of child.
So much we heard. Her death was hidden from us.
Before we had the chance to witness it,
The king broke in with piercing cries, and all
Eyes turned to him. This way and that
He ranged among us. 'A sword, a sword!' he cried,
'Where is that wife, no wife of mine – that soil
Where I was sown, and where I reaped my harvest!'
While he raved in this way some demon guided him –
None of us dared to speak – to where she was.
1260   As if in answer to some leader's call,
With wild bellowing cries he hurled himself
Upon the locked doors, bending by sheer force
The bolts out of their sockets, and stumbled in.
We saw a knotted pendulum, a noose,
A strangled woman swinging before our eyes.
The king saw too, and with heart-rending groans
Untied the rope, and laid her on the ground.
But worse was yet to come. Her dress was pinned
With golden brooches, which the king snatched out
1270   And plunged, from full arm's length, into his eyes –
Eyes that will see no longer his shame, his guilt,
No longer see those they should never have seen,
Nor see, unseeing, those he had longed to see,
Henceforth seeing nothing but night. To this wild tune
He pierced his eyeballs, time and time again,
Till bloody tears ran down his beard – not drops,
But in full spate, a whole cascade descending
In drenching cataracts of scarlet rain.
1280   Two have done wrong, and on two heads, not one –
On man and wife – falls mingled punishment.
Their age-old happiness of former times
Was happiness earned with justice; but today
Calamity, death, ruin, tears and shame –
All ills that there are names for – are all here.

CHORUS
    And he – how is he now? Does he still suffer?
ATTENDANT
    He shouts for someone to unbar the doors
    And show all Thebes the father-murderer,
    The mother- . . . shame forbids the unholy word!
    He means to cast himself out of this land   1290
    To rid his house of the curse of his own lips.
    But he scarcely has the strength, poor suffering man,
    And none to guide him. He cannot bear the pain,
    As you shall see. The doors are opening.
    Yes, you will see a sorry spectacle
    That even loathing cannot choose but pity.
        [*Enter the blind* OEDIPUS.]
CHORUS
    Ah!
    Horror beyond all bearing!
    Foulest disfigurement
    That ever I saw! O cruel,
    Insensate agony!
    What demon of destiny   1300
    With swift assault outstriding
    Has ridden you down?
    O wretched soul!
    I dare not see, I am hiding
    My eyes, I cannot bear
    What I most long to see;
    And what I long to hear,
    That I most dread.
OEDIPUS
    O agony!
    Where am I? Is this my voice
    That is borne on the air?
    What fate has come to me?   1310
CHORUS
    Unspeakable to mortal ears,
    Too terrible for eyes to see.

OEDIPUS

O dark intolerable inescapable night
That knows no day!
Cloud that no air can take away!
Ah! And again
That piercing pain,
Torture in the flesh and in the soul's dark memory.

CHORUS

It must be so. Such suffering has to be borne
1320   Twice: once in the body and once in the soul.

OEDIPUS

Is that my true and ever-faithful friend
Still at my side?
Your hand shall be the blind man's guide.
Are you still near?
That voice I hear
Is yours, although your face I cannot see.

CHORUS

Those eyes – how could you have done what you have
        done?
What evil power has driven you to this end?

OEDIPUS

Apollo, friends, Apollo
1330   Has laid this agony upon me.
But not by his hand; I did it.
What should I do with eyes
Where all is ugliness?

CHORUS

It cannot be denied.

OEDIPUS

Where is there any beauty
For me to see? Where loveliness
1340   Of sight or sound? Away!
Lead me quickly away
Out of this land. I am lost,
Hated by gods, no man so damned.

CHORUS

Twice-tormented, in the spirit as in the flesh.

If only you had never lived to solve this riddle.
OEDIPUS
Cursed be the benefactor
That loosed my feet and gave me life   1350
For death; a poor exchange.
Death would have been a boon
To me and all of mine.
CHORUS
We could have wished it so.
OEDIPUS
Now I am known as shedder of my
Father's blood, husband to my mother.
I am godless and a child of shame,   1360
Begetter of sibling-children.
What infamy remains
That is not spoken of Oedipus?
CHORUS
Yet to my thinking this act was ill-advised;
It would have been better to die than live in blindness.
OEDIPUS
I will not accept that this is not the best
That could have been done. Teach me no other lesson.   1370
How could I meet my father beyond the grave
With eyes that see – or my unhappy mother,
Against whom I have committed such heinous wrong
As no mere death could pay for? Could I still love
To look at my children, begotten as they were?
Could I want eyes to see that pretty sight?
To see the towers of Thebes, her holy images,
Which I, her noblest, most unhappy son   1380
Have forbidden myself to see – having commanded
All men to cast away the offence, the unclean,
Whom the gods have declared accursed, the son of Laius,
And, having proved myself that branded man,
Could I want sight to face our people's stares?
No! Hearing neither! Had I any way
To block that channel too, I would not rest
Till I had prisoned up this body of shame

In total blankness. For the mind to dwell
1390   Beyond the reach of pain, would be peace indeed.
Cithaeron! Foster-mother! Did you shelter me
For this? Could you not let me die that instant,
Instead of saving me to tell the world
How I was begotten? Corinth, and Polybus,
My seeming home and parent, did you think
What foul corruption festered under the bloom
Of your adopted son's young loveliness –
Now found entirely evil and of evil born.
That silent crossroad in the forest clearing,
That copse beside the place where three roads met,
1400   Whose soil I watered with my father's blood,
My blood – will they remember what they saw,
And what I came that way to Thebes to do?
The crime of incest! Breeding where I was bred!
Father, brother and son; bride, wife and mother;
United in one monstrous matrimony!
All human filth compounded in one crime!
Unspeakable acts – I speak no more of them.
1410   Hide me at once, for the love of god, hide me away,
Away! Kill me! Drown me in the depths of the sea!
Take me!
For pity, hold me, and take me away!
You can touch me. Don't be afraid. On no one else,
Just me alone, is the scourge of my punishment.
CHORUS
Creon is coming. The answer to your desires
Will now depend on him, in word and deed.
He stands as our sole protector in your stead.
OEDIPUS
What can I say to him? What plea of mine
1420   Can now have any justice in his eyes,
Whom I, as now is clear, have wronged so utterly?
        [*Enter* CREON.]
CREON
Oedipus, I am not here to jeer at your fall,
Nor to reproach you for your past misdeeds.

But, friends, remember your respect for the Sun-God,
Helios, if not for the children of men.
What is unclean must not remain in the light of day;
Neither earth nor air nor water may receive it.
Take him within. Piety at least demands
That none but kinsmen should hear and see such suffering.   1430

OEDIPUS
I ask only one thing, my gentle friend,
Whose gentleness to such a one as me
Was more than could be hoped for. One thing only,
For the love of god – for your good, not mine—

CREON
What thing, so humbly begged?

OEDIPUS
Cast me away this instant
Out of this land, out of the sight of man.

CREON
Be sure it would have been done without delay,
But for my awaiting instruction from the god.

OEDIPUS
Isn't his instruction already plain? The father-killer,   1440
The unclean one, was to die; and here he stands.

CREON
It was so. Yet in the present turn of events
We need more certain guidance.

OEDIPUS
For my lost life?
Will you ask the god's direction for one so damned?

CREON
Have you not found good cause to trust him?

OEDIPUS
Yes.
Then I have only this to ask, of your goodness:
The funeral rites of her that lies within,
Provide as you think fit. She is your sister,
And you will do rightly by her. As for me,
No longer let my living presence curse   1450
This fatherland of mine, but let me go

And live upon the mountains – and die there.
Cithaeron! Name forever linked with mine –
On Mount Cithaeron, which my parents chose
To be my deathbed, I will go and die
Obedient to their desires. And yet I know,
Not age, nor sickness, nor any common accident
Can end my life; I was not snatched from death
That once, unless to be preserved
For some more awful destiny. So be it.

1460 And the children . . . Don't trouble yourself about the boys,
Creon; they will be able to fend for themselves
Wherever they go. But the girls, poor little things,
Have never known a meal without their father;
Everything was shared between us. Take care of them . . .
Creon, if I could touch them once, and weep . . .
Once more . . .
If you would permit it,
Gracious and generous . . .

1470 Just touch them once, and I could think I had them
Once more before my eyes . . .

   [*The children*, ISMENE *and* ANTIGONE, *have already
   been led in, and stand before* OEDIPUS.]

What! Do I hear my darlings sobbing?
Has Creon had the heart to send them to me?
My darlings,
Are they here?

CREON
They are here. I had them brought to you. I knew
How much you loved them – how much you love them still.

OEDIPUS
Heaven bless you, Creon, for this, and make your way
Smoother than mine has been.

1480 Where are you, children?
Come, feel your brother's hands. It was their work
That darkened these bright eyes – your father's eyes
As once you knew them, though he never saw
Nor knew what he did when he became your father.
They cannot see you; but they weep for you.

I think of your sorrowful life in days to come,
When you must face the world: the holy days,
High days and days of state, joyless for you, 1490
Returning sadly home while others play.
And when you look for marriage, will there be men,
Will there be one man brave enough to outface
The scandal that will cling to all my children
And children's childen? Is there a name of ill
That is not ours? A father that killed his father,
Despoiled his birth-bed, begetting where he was begot –
So they will brand you. Where, then, will you find 1500
    husbands?
There will be none, my children, for you; your days
Can only end in fruitless maidenhood.
Menoeceus' son, you are their kinsman still;
You are their only father – I am no more,
Who gave them life. These lost waifs must not wander
Homeless and husbandless. They must not see
Such days as I will see. Take care of them,
So young, so poor, so lost to all but you.
Will you do it? Give me your hand to pledge and promise.
    [CREON *gives his hand*]
Friend! 1510
Children, there is much that you will understand
When you are older, though you cannot bear it now.
But in your prayers ask this: that you may live
Not more nor less well, and so live better,
Than your father did.

CREON
    That's enough. Will you go in?

OEDIPUS
    I must; against my will.

CREON
    There is a measure in all things.

OEDIPUS
    I have your promise, then?

CREON
    What promise?

OEDIPUS
  To send me away.
CREON
  The gods will decide, not I.
OEDIPUS
  No god will speak for me.
CREON
  Then you will have your wish.
OEDIPUS
  And your consent?
CREON
1520 I do not speak beyond my knowledge.
OEDIPUS [*satisfied, but reluctantly, to attendants*]
  Take me in.
CREON
  Go then.
    [OEDIPUS *moves towards the palace, his arms still*
    around the children]
        But leave the children!
OEDIPUS
  No! Never take them from me!
CREON
  Command no more. Obey. Your rule is over.
    [OEDIPUS *is led away.*]
CHORUS
  Sons and daughters of Thebes, behold: this was Oedipus,
  Greatest of men. He held the key to the deepest mysteries,
  Was envied by all his fellow men for his great prosperity.
  Behold, what a tide of misfortune swept over his head.
  Learn, then, that mortal man must look to his own end,
  And none can be called happy till the day they carry
1530 Their happiness down to the grave in peace.

MEDEA
BY
EURIPIDES

Preface to *Medea*

The myths concerning Medea are not limited to her relationship with Jason. There are a number of stories – and several versions of each – about Medea's life subsequent to her departure from Corinth, concerning among other things her marriage to Aegeus and her enmity with Theseus. Still, largely as a result of the Euripides' play, it is her marital strife with Jason over his plans to remarry and her subsequent murder of her children that have remained the focus of most later treatments of the Medea story. To understand the background to the action of Euripides' play we must take account of Jason's quest for the golden fleece, Medea's role in that quest, and the events after Jason and Medea returned to Jason's homeland. It is upon this prior history that the nurse reflects in the opening speech of the play. While Euripides manipulates events in Corinth to a significant degree, in referring to background events he does not depart significantly from the narrative of the myth as it is commonly known.

Jason was the son of Aeson, the king of Iolchus, a city on the east coast of the Greek mainland close to Mount Pelion and not far from Mount Olympus. Before Jason's birth his uncle Pelias, Aeson's half-brother and the son of Poseidon, usurped the throne (see genealogical table, p. 305). Pelias was warned by an oracle that he would be killed by a descendant of the wind god Aeolus (the royal house of Iolchus were all decendants of Aeolus). He therefore put to death all prominent Aeolians except Aeson, whom he spared for the sake of his and Aeson's mother Tyro. When Jason was born Aeson had him smuggled out of the city and educated in the wild by the centaur Chiron (who later taught the young Achilles).

Pelias had also been warned by a second oracle to beware a person wearing only one sandal. One day he came across a stranger, Jason, who had lost a sandal while carrying an elderly woman – the goddess Hera in disguise – across a river. After he and Pelias revealed their respective identities to one another, Jason laid claim to the throne. Pelias was not well placed to refuse Jason's claim since Jason was backed by another uncle, king Pheres of neighbouring Pherae. Pelias, however, insisted that he would only hand over the throne if Jason could bring back the golden fleece. Jason accepted this challenge. He enlisted a craftsman named Argus to build a large ship, the Argo, and summoned fifty heroes from all over Greece, the Argonauts, to accompany him.

The Argonauts underwent numerous adventures before reaching their final destination, Colchis, which lay at the far shore of the Black Sea. Colchis was ruled by king Aeëtes, who was the brother of the witch Circe and a descendant of the sun-god Helios (see genealogical table, p. 305). When he first heard that Jason was on a quest for the golden fleece, which was in his possession, he refused to give it up and threatened the Argonauts with violence. He reconsidered, however, and said that Jason was free to try to remove the fleece, which resided in the grove of Ares and was guarded by a large dragon, if he could fulfil three tasks. Aeëtes' plan was to set tasks so difficult that Jason would perish in the attempt, thus avoiding the need for open conflict between himself and the Argonauts. These tasks were, first, to yoke two fire-breathing bulls, second, to plough a large field (called the field of Ares) using the bulls, and third, to sow the field with the teeth of a dragon.

At this point in events the gods intervened. Aphrodite made Medea, Aeëtes' daughter, fall hopelessly in love with Jason (in Euripides' play, Jason mentions Aphrodite as his chief helper during their first encounter). She decided to betray her father and assist Jason, provided that he took her back with him to Greece as his spouse. Jason agreed to this condition, and swore a solemn oath by all the gods to remain faithful to Medea. She gave him a potion to protect him from the flames of the fire-breathing bulls. After subduing the bulls and ploughing the field, Jason sowed the dragon's teeth, from which there sprang armed men. He defeated them by making them fight among themselves – he threw a single object of value among the group – and despatching those who survived. Aeëtes intended to renege on his offer and slaughter the Argonauts, but he unwisely confided in Medea, who warned Jason of her father's plan. Leading him in secret to the grove of Ares, she helped him, with her knowledge of magic, to sedate the ever-wakeful dragon that guarded the fleece. Jason removed the fleece and he and Medea tried to make their escape, but the alarm was raised and the Colchians pursued them. As the Argonauts sought to leave the Black Sea, Medea slowed the Colchians' pursuit through a macabre stratagem. She murdered her own half-brother Aspyrtus and scattered his dismembered body into the sea (according to some versions of the myth he was brought on board the Argo at the outset; according to others he was in one of the vessels sent to pursue the ship). Aeëtes was forced to search for and retrieve all of the pieces in order to give Aspyrtus a proper burial; otherwise, his ghost would not rest in peace.

There are various accounts of the return of the Argonauts, involving some adventures that closely resemble those of the returning Odysseus, in terms both of their location and incidents. There is, however, broad agreement among most accounts of the myth on the events that took place once Jason and Medea returned to Iolchus. It had been supposed in Iolchus that the Argonauts had perished, or had decided never to return. Upon arriving home, Jason was unsure whether to endeavour to defeat Pelias openly or through subterfuge. Medea, however, took matters into her own hands. She entered the city in disguise and persuaded Pelias' daughters that it was possible to rejuvenate their now aged father. She did this by cutting an old ram into pieces and boiling it in a cauldron with special herbs while uttering spells. The diced ram emerged from this treatment reconstituted as a young lamb. Pelias' daughters, persuaded by this display, attempted the same thing with their father. Medea, however, omitted a crucial ingredient, and Pelias perished pitiably. For this deed both Medea and Jason were banished from Iolcus and sought refuge in Corinth.

Euripides' treatment of the events with which the play is directly concerned involves selective handling of, and departure from, available versions of the story. In earlier literature – for instance, the *Corinthiaca* by Eumelos (an early epic of which only fragments remain) and certain passages of lyric poetry – it is suggested that Medea's father Aeëtes was king of Corinth before leaving for Colchis. This would make Medea Greek, as well as giving her some sort of claim to royal power in Corinth. Euripides ignores this version of the myth, first, because the contrast between Medea as a non-Greek and Jason as a Greek is an essential aspect of the play, and second, because the plot requires that Medea be an outsider in Corinth, with no connection to the royal family.

There are various accounts of the death of Medea's children. In one account, she kills them herself, but accidentally, while trying to make them immortal. In another, the Corinthians kill them in revenge for Medea's murder of their king Creon and his daughter. In a further version, the women of Corinth turn against Medea and murder her children. Euripides rejects all these accounts, and instead has Medea take her children's lives as a means of punishing her faithless husband. He does, however, allude to these alternative versions of the myth. Medea initially voices a desire to murder Jason as well as Creon and his daughter, before deciding to kill the children instead of Jason; the visit by Aegeus of Athens, troubled by his childlessness, perhaps gives her the idea. And before realizing that the children are already dead, Jason expresses concern that the Corinthians may try to kill them to avenge Medea's murder of their king and his daughter. Another significant aspect in which Euripides departs radically from established versions of the myth is in having Medea escape from Corinth in a flying chariot provided by her grandfather Helios, the sun-god. This famous closing scene subsequently became a popular subject of Greek vase-painting.

Euripides' play begins when the heady days of the golden fleece adventure have long passed, although there are frequent references to Medea's actions against her homeland, her own brother, and Pelias, as well as to the assistance she gave Jason in his quest. While in Corinth Medea and Jason have had two sons, but Jason, longing for royal power, has since sought to make an advantageous marriage to the daughter of Creon, the king of Corinth. This intention goes against the oath Jason swore to Medea in Colchis, something to which she draws due attention in the course of the play. As the play starts, Jason's marriage to Creon's daughter – she isn't named in the play but is called Glauce in most versions of the myth – is imminent. Medea, apprised of his betrayal and distraught at the prospect of being forsaken in favour of a younger royal bride, is at a loss as to how to respond to this insult.

Characters

NURSE
TUTOR *to Medea's sons*
MEDEA
CHORUS, *women of Corinth*
CREON, *king of Corinth*
JASON
AEGEUS, *king of Athens*
MESSENGER
CHILDREN *of Medea and Jason*

Scene: Before Jason's house in Corinth.
Enter NURSE.

NURSE

If only they had never gone! If the Argo's hull
Had never winged its way through the grey-blue Clashing
    Rocks
And on towards Colchis! If that pine on Pelion's slopes
Had never felt the axe, and fallen, to put oars
Into those heroes' hands, who went at Pelias' bidding
To fetch the golden fleece! Then neither would my mistress
Medea ever have set sail for the walled city
Of Iolchus, mad with love for Jason, nor would she,
When Pelias' daughters killed their father at her bidding,
Have come with Jason and her children to live here   10
In Corinth. Coming here as an exile, she has earned
The people's welcome, while to Jason she is all
Obedience – in marriage that's the crucial thing,
When a wife dutifully accepts her husband's will.
But now her world is turned to hate, and wounds her
Where her love lies deepest. Jason has betrayed
His own sons – and my mistress – for a royal bed,
And alliance with the king of Corinth. He has married
Creon's daughter. Poor Medea! Scorned and shamed,   20
She raves, invoking every vow and solemn pledge
That Jason made her, and calls the gods to witness
What thanks she has received for her fidelity.
She will not eat; she lies collapsed in misery,

Dissolving the long hours in tears. Since first she heard
Of Jason's wrongdoing she has not raised her eyes,
Or moved her cheek from the floor. Though friends plead
With her she might as well be a rock or wave of the sea
For all she hears – except for when she turns away
30   Her lovely head, speaks to herself alone, and wails
Aloud for her dear father, and for her homeland,
Which she betrayed and left to come here with this man
Who now spurns and insults her. Poor Medea! Now
She learns through pain what blessings they enjoy who are
      not
Uprooted from their native land. She hates her sons:
To see them brings her no pleasure. I am afraid
That some dreadful purpose is forming in her mind. She is
A frightening woman; no one who makes an enemy
Of her will carry off an easy victory.
Here come the boys, back from their running. They know
      nothing
Of this cruel blow that has befallen their mother.
They're young; young heads and painful thoughts don't go
      together.

[*Enter* TUTOR *with* MEDEA'*s* CHILDREN.]

TUTOR

Old nurse and servant of my mistress' house, tell me,
50   What are you doing, standing out here by the door,
All alone, talking to yourself, lamenting troubles?
What does Medea say to being left alone?

NURSE

Old friend, tutor of Jason's sons, an honest slave
Suffers in her own heart the blow that strikes her mistress.
It was too much. I couldn't bear it. I had to come
Out here and tell my mistress' wrongs to heaven and earth.

TUTOR

Poor woman! Has she not stopped crying yet?

NURSE

                                          Stopped crying?
60   I envy you. Her troubles are just born – not yet half-grown.

TUTOR
　　Poor fool – though she's my mistress and I shouldn't say
　　　　so –
　　She had better save her tears. She hasn't heard the worst.
NURSE
　　The worst? What now? Don't keep it from me. What has
　　　　happened?
TUTOR
　　Why, nothing's happened. I'm sorry I said anything.
NURSE
　　Look, we're both slaves together; don't keep me in the dark.
　　Is it so great a secret? I can hold my tongue.
TUTOR
　　All right. I'd gone to the benches where the old men
　　Play dice, next to the holy fountain of Peirene.
　　They thought I wasn't listening, but I heard one say
　　That Creon king of Corinth means to send these boys   70
　　Away from here, to banish them – their mother too.
　　Whether the story's true or not I don't know. I hope not.
NURSE
　　But surely Jason won't stand by and see his sons
　　Banished, despite his quarrel with their mother?
TUTOR
　　Old love is ousted by new; Jason's no friend to this house.
NURSE
　　Then we're lost, if we must add new trouble
　　To the old, before we're rid of what we have already.
TUTOR
　　Listen, it's a bad time to tell Medea this.
　　Keep quiet, don't say a word.   80
NURSE
　　　　　　　　　　　　　Children, do you hear
　　What sort of father Jason is to you? My curse . . .
　　No, not my curse; he is my master. All the same
　　He is guilty: he has betrayed those near and dear to him.
TUTOR
　　What man's not guilty? It's taken you a long time to learn

That everyone loves himself more than his neighbour.
These boys are nothing to their father; he's in love.
NURSE [*to the* CHILDREN]
    Run into the house, boys. Everything will be all right.
      [*to the* TUTOR]
90   You do your best to keep them by themselves. As long
    As she's in this dark mood, don't let them near her.
    I've seen her watching them, her eyes like a wild bull's.
    There's something she means to do. And I know this:
    She'll not relax her rage till it has found its victim.
    God grant she strikes her enemies and not her friends!
      [MEDEA's *voice is heard from inside the house.*]
MEDEA
    Oh! What misery, what unhappiness!
    What shall I do? If only I were dead!
NURSE
    There! Do you hear? It is your mother
    Racking her heart, racking her anger.
100   Quick now, children, hurry indoors,
    And don't go within sight of her,
    Or anywhere near her. Keep a safe distance.
    Her mood is cruel, her nature dangerous,
    Her will fierce and intractable.
    Come, now, in with you both at once.
      [*The* CHILDREN *go into the house followed by the*
      TUTOR.]
    The dark cloud of her lamentation
    Is just beginning. Soon, I know,
    It will ignite as her anger rises.
    Deep in passion and unrelenting,
110   What will she do now, stung by insult?
MEDEA [*still indoors*]
    Do I not suffer? Am I not wronged? Should I not weep?
    Children, your mother is hated, and you are cursed.
    Death take you, and your father! May his whole house
      perish!
NURSE
    Oh dear! Oh god!

Your children – what have they to do
With their father's wrongdoing? Why hate them?
I am sick with worry for you, children; fear
Of what may happen. The mind of a princess
Is a thing to fear – princesses are used
To giving commands, not receiving them –   120
And her rage once roused is hard to appease.
It is better to lead an ordinary
Existence. No grand life for me;
Just peace and quiet as I grow old.
The middle way, neither great nor mean,
Is best by far – in theory and practice.
To be rich and powerful brings no blessings;
Only more utterly are prosperous houses
Destroyed when the gods are angry.   130

[*Enter the* CHORUS OF CORINTHIAN WOMEN.]

CHORUS
I heard her voice, I heard
That unhappy woman from Colchis
Still crying, not yet calm.
Old nurse, tell us about her.
As I stood by the door, I heard her
Crying inside the house.
My own heart suffers too
When Jason's house is suffering,
For that is where my loyalty lies.

NURSE
Jason's house is no more – all that is finished!
Jason is a prisoner in a princess's bed;   140
And Medea is in her room
Melting her life away in tears;
No word from any friend can bring her comfort.

MEDEA [*still indoors*]
Come, lightning bolt,
Pierce through my head!
What do I gain from living any longer?
Oh, how I hate being alive! I want
To end my life, leave it behind, and die.

CHORUS

O Zeus, and Earth, and Light,
Do you hear the woeful prayer
150   Of a wife in her anguish?
      [*addressing* MEDEA]
    What madness is this? The bed you long for
    Is it what others shrink from?
    Is it death that you desire?
    Do not say that prayer, Medea!
    If your husband is won to a new love,
    The thing is common. Why let it upset you?
    Zeus will plead your cause.
    End this desperate grief over your husband
    Which wastes you away.

MEDEA [*still indoors*]

160   Mighty Themis! Dread Artemis!
    Do you see how I am used –
    In spite of those great oaths I swore with him –
    By my accursed husband?
    Oh, may I see Jason and his bride
    Dashed to pieces in their shattered palace
    For the wrong they have dared to do me, unprovoked!
    O my father and my city that I deserted!
    O brother that I shamefully murdered!

NURSE

    Do you hear what my mistress is saying –
    Clamouring to Themis, hearer of prayer,
170   And Zeus, who is guardian of oaths?
    It is no trifling matter
    That can end a rage like hers.

CHORUS

    I wish she would come out here and let us see her
    And talk to her; if she would listen,
    Perhaps she would drop this deep resentment,
    This vehement indignation.
    As a friend I am anxious to do whatever I can.
180   Go, nurse, persuade her to come out to us.
    Tell her we are all on her side.

Hurry, before she does harm to those in there;
This passion of hers is an irresistible flood.

NURSE

I will. I fear I might not persuade her,
Still, I would like to do my best.
But as soon as any of us servants
Gets near her, or tries to speak,
She glares at us like a raging bull
Or a lioness guarding her cubs.

The men of old had little sense;   190
If you called them fools you wouldn't be far wrong.
They invented songs, and all the sweetness of music,
To perform at feasts, banquets and celebrations,
But no one thought of using
Songs and the lyre to banish
The bitterness and pain of life.
Sorrow is the real cause
Of deaths and disasters and ruined families.
If music could cure sorrow it would be precious.   200
But after a dinner why sing songs?
When people are full of food they're happy already.
    [*The* NURSE *goes into the house.*]

CHORUS

I heard her sobbing and wailing,
Shouting shrill, pitiful accusations
Against the husband who has betrayed her.
She invokes Themis, daughter of Zeus,
Who witnessed those promises which drew her
Across from Asia to Greece, setting sail at night,   210
Threading the salty strait that forms
The gateway to the Black Sea.
    [MEDEA *emerges from the house, surprisingly calm and
    self-possessed.*]

MEDEA

Women of Corinth, I would not have you censure me,
So I have come out. Many, I know, are proud at heart,
At home and in public; but others are maligned

As supercilious just because their ways are quiet.
There is no justice in the world's judgemental eyes.
220   People will not wait to learn a person's true character;
Though they have been done no wrong, one look and they
    hate.
Of course a foreigner must conform, but even citizens
Should not annoy their peers by wanton stubbornness.
I accept my place; but this blow that has fallen on me
Was unexpected. It has crushed my heart.
Life has no pleasure left, dear friends. I want to die.
Jason was my whole life; he knows that well. Now he
Has proven himself the most contemptible of men.
230   Surely, of all the creatures that have life and will, we women
Are the most wretched. When, for an exorbitant sum,
We have bought a husband, we must then accept him as
Possessor of our body. This is to aggravate
Wrong with worse wrong. Then the great question: will the
    man
We get be good or bad? For women, divorce is not
Respectable, and to repel the man not possible.
Still more, a foreign woman, coming among new laws
And customs, needs prophetic powers to find out
240   What her home could not teach her: how to treat the man
Whose bed she shares. And if we are successful in
This demanding task, and our husband does not struggle
Under the marriage yolk, our life is enviable;
Otherwise, death is better. If a man grows tired
Of company at home, he can go out and find
A cure for boredom. But we wives are forced to look
To just one man. They say that we at home live free
From danger, while they venture out to battle – fools!
250   I'd rather stand three times in the front line than bear
One child. But the same arguments do not apply
To you and me. You have this city, your father's home,
The enjoyment of your life, and your friends' company.
I am alone; I have no city; now my husband
Insults me. I was taken as booty from a land
At the earth's edge. I have no mother, brother, nor any

Of my own blood to turn to in this predicament.
So I make this one request. If I can find a way   260
To work revenge on Jason for his wrongs to me,
Say nothing. Women are weak and timid in most matters.
The noise of war, the glint of steel, makes her a coward.
But hurt her marriage and there's no bloodier spirit.

CHORUS

I'll do what you ask. To punish Jason would be just.
I hardly wonder that you take such wrongs to heart.
But look, Medea, I see Creon, king of Corinth.
He must be here to tell you of some new decision.   270
    [*Enter* CREON.]

CREON

You there, Medea, venting spleen against your husband!
I banish you from Corinth. Take your sons with you and go
Into exile. Waste no time; I'm here to see this order
Enforced. And I will not go back into my palace
Until I've put you safely beyond my borders.

MEDEA

Oh, this is a cruel end to my ill-fated life!
My enemies have spread full sail. No welcoming shore
Waits to receive and save me. Mistreated as I am,   280
Creon, I ask you for what offence you banish me.

CREON

I fear you. Why wrap up the truth? I fear that you
May do my daughter some irreparable harm.
A number of things contribute to my anxiety.
You are a clever woman, skilled in many evil arts.
And now you're barred from Jason's bed, which angers you.
I learn too from reports that you have uttered threats:
Revenge on Jason, his bride, and her father.
So I'm acting first, in self-defence. I'd rather make you   290
My enemy now than weaken, and pay later with tears.

MEDEA

My reputation, yet again! How often, Creon,
It has been my curse and ruin. A man of shrewdness
Should never have his children taught to use their brains
More than their peers. What do you gain by being clever?

You neglect your own affairs, and all your fellow citizens
Hate you. Those who are fools will call you ignorant
And useless when you offer them unfamiliar knowledge.
300 And as for those deemed wise, if people rank
You above *them*, it is something they will not stand.
I know this from experience: because I am clever,
People are jealous – and the rest dislike me. It would seem
I am not so clever after all. But what are you
Afraid of, Creon? Some harm I might do to you?
Don't let *me* alarm you. I'm in no position – a woman –
To hurt a king. Besides, you have done me no wrong.
You gave your daughter to the man you chose. I hate
310 My husband, true, but you had every right to do
As you have done. So now I bear no grudge against
Your happiness: give your daughter to him and good luck
To you both. But let me live in Corinth. I will bear
My wrongs in silence, yielding to superior strength.

CREON

Your words are gentle, but my blood runs cold to think
What plots you may be nursing deep within your heart.
In fact, I trust you even less now than before.
A woman of hot temper – or, indeed, a man –
320 Is a safer enemy than one who's quiet and clever.
So out you go, and quickly – no more arguments.
I've made up my mind: you're my enemy. No craft
Of yours will find a way of staying in my city.

MEDEA

I kneel before you, and beg you by the young bride, your
        child.

CREON

You're wasting words. You'll never make me change my
        mind.

MEDEA

I beg you! Will you cast off pity and banish me?

CREON

I will. I have more love for my family than for you.

MEDEA

My home, my country! How my thoughts turn to you now!

CREON
I love my country too – next only to my daughter.
MEDEA
Oh, what an evil power love has over people's lives!   330
CREON
That depends on circumstances, I suppose.
MEDEA
Great Zeus, remember who caused all this suffering!
CREON
Go, wretched woman, and take my troubles with you.
MEDEA
I know what trouble is; I have no need of more.
CREON
In a moment you'll be thrown out. Here, men!
MEDEA
No, don't do that! Creon, I have one thing to ask.
CREON
Medea, you're still intent on giving me trouble.
MEDEA
I'll go. It isn't *that* I'm asking for.
CREON
                                    Then why resist?
Why will you not get out?
MEDEA
                                    Let me stay this one day –   340
To fix some plan for my exile, and make provision
For my two sons, since their own father is not concerned
With helping them. Show some pity. You are a father too;
You should feel sympathy for them. For myself, exile
Is nothing. I weep for them; their fate is very hard.
CREON
I'm no tyrant by nature. My soft heart has often
Betrayed me, and I know it's foolish of me now,   350
Nevertheless, Medea, you shall have what you ask.
But mark my words: if tomorrow's light of day
Finds you or them inside my borders, you shall die.
This is my solemn word. Now stay here, if you must,
This one day. You can hardly achieve in one day

What I am afraid of.
    [*Exit* CREON.]

CHORUS

Medea, poor Medea!
Your grief touches our hearts.
A wanderer, where can you turn?
To what welcoming shelter,
360   What protecting land?
How wild with fear and danger
Is the sea where the gods have set your course!

MEDEA

A sore predicament all round – it's true enough.
But don't imagine things will end as they are now.
Trials are yet to come for this newly-wedded pair,
Nor shall those nearest to them get off easily.
Do you think I would have fawned so on this man, except
To gain my purpose and further my plans? I wouldn't
370   Have spoken to him or touched him. But he – oh, what a
        fool!
By banishing me straightaway he could have thwarted me
Entirely; instead, he has let me stay one day.
Today I will strike down three of my enemies:
The father, the daughter, and my husband.
I have in mind so many ways for them to die,
I don't know which to choose. Should I set fire to the
        house,
And burn the bridal chamber? Or creep up to their bed
380   And drive a sharp knife through their guts? There is one
        fear:
If I am caught going into the house, or in the act,
I die, and the last laugh goes to my enemies.
The best way is the simplest, which most suits my bent:
Killing by poison.
So let's say they are dead – what city will receive me then?
What friend will guarantee my safety, offer land
And home as sanctuary? None. I'll wait a little.
390   If some strong tower of help appears, I'll carry out

These murders cunningly and quietly. But if Fate
Banishes me without resource, I will take sword
In hand myself, hardening my heart to the utmost,
And kill them both, even if it means my death.
For, by queen Hecate, whom above all divinities
I worship, my chosen accomplice, to whose presence
My central hearth is dedicated, none of them
Shall hurt me and not suffer for it! Now to work!
In bitterness and pain they shall regret this marriage;
Regret their houses joined; regret my banishment.   400
Come, lay your plan, Medea! Scheme with all your wits.
On to the deadly moment that will test your nerve!
You see now where you stand. Your father was a king;
His father was the Sun-God. You must not invite
Laughter from Jason and his new allies, the tribe
Of Sisyphus. You know what you must do. Besides,
Women were born useless for honest purposes,
But skilled practitioners in every kind of evil.

CHORUS
Streams of the sacred rivers flow uphill;   410
Tradition, order, all things are reversed:
Deceit is men's device now,
Men's oaths are gods' dishonour.
Legend will now reverse our reputation.
A time has come for the female sex to be honoured;
That old discordant slander
Shall no more hold us subject.   420
Male poets of ages past, with their ballads
Of faithless women, shall go out of fashion;
For Apollo, lord of music,
Did not bestow lyric inspiration
Through female understanding –
Or we should have found themes for poems
And countered with our epics against men.
But time is old, and in his store of tales
Men figure no less famous
Or infamous than women.   430

So you, Medea, mad with love,
Set sail from your father's house,
Threading the rocky jaws of the Black Sea;
And here, living in a strange country,
Your marriage lost, your bed lonely,
You are driven beyond the borders –
An exile with no redress.
The grace of sworn oaths is gone.
Honour remains no more

440   In the wide Greek world, but is flown to the sky.
Where can you turn for shelter?
Your father's door is closed against you;
Another is now mistress of your husband's bed;
A new queen rules in your house.

      [*Enter* JASON.]

JASON

I've often noticed – this is not the first time –
What fatal results follow from uncontrolled rage.
You could have stayed in Corinth, still lived in this house,
If you had quietly accepted the decisions

450   Of those in power. Instead, you talked wildly, and now
You're banished. Well, your angry words don't upset me.
Go on as long as you like reciting 'Jason's crimes'.
But after your abuse of the king and the princess
Think yourself lucky to be let off with banishment.
I have tried, all this time, to calm them down; but you
Would not give up your frantic tirades against
The royal family. So you're banished. Even so, I
Will not desert a friend. I've carefully considered

460   Your plight, and have come now, in spite of everything,
To see that you and the children are not sent away
Without money, or unprovided. Exile brings
With it a train of difficulties. You no doubt
Hate me, but I could never bear ill-will to you.

MEDEA

You filthy coward! If I knew any worse name
For such unmanliness I'd use it. So, you've come.
You, my worst enemy, come to me! It isn't courage –

To look friends in the face after betraying them.
It isn't even audacity; it's a disease,   470
The worst a man can have, pure shamelessness. But still,
It's just as well you came; to say what I have to say
Will ease my mind, and to hear it will make you wince.
I'll start at the beginning. When you were sent
To master the fire-breathing bulls, yoke them, and sow
The deadly furrow, I saved your life. That is something
Every Greek who sailed with you in the Argo knows.
The serpent that kept watch over the golden fleece,   480
Coiled round it fold on fold, unsleeping – it was I
Who killed it, and so lit the torch of your success.
I willingly deceived my father, left my home,
And came with you to Iolchus, by Mount Pelion,
Showing much love and little wisdom. There I put
King Pelias to the most horrific of deaths –
By his own daughters' hands – and ruined his whole house.
And in return for this you have the gall
To turn me out and get yourself another wife –
And this after I bore you sons! If you were still   490
Childless, I could have pardoned you for hankering
After this new marriage. But respect for oaths has gone
To the wind. Do you, I wonder, think that the old gods
No longer rule? Or that new laws are now in force?
You must know you are guilty of perjury to me.
My poor right hand, which you so often clasped! My knees
Which then you clung to! How we are besmirched and
     mocked
By this man's broken vows, and all our hopes deceived!
Come, I'll ask your advice as if you were a friend.
Not that I hope for any help from you, but still,   500
I'll ask you and expose your infamy. Where now
Can I turn? Back to my country and my father's house,
Which I betrayed to come with you? Or Iolchus, perhaps,
To Pelias' wretched daughters? What a welcome they
Would give me – I who killed their father! So it stands:
My friends at home now hate me; and in helping you
I have earned the enmity of those I had no right

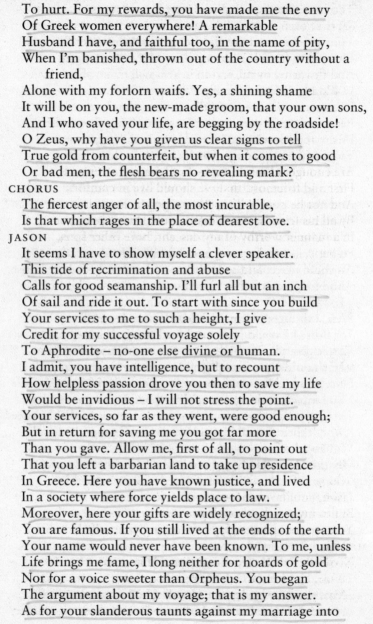

      To hurt. For my rewards, you have made me the envy
510   Of Greek women everywhere! A remarkable
      Husband I have, and faithful too, in the name of pity,
      When I'm banished, thrown out of the country without a
          friend,
      Alone with my forlorn waifs. Yes, a shining shame
      It will be on you, the new-made groom, that your own sons,
      And I who saved your life, are begging by the roadside!
      O Zeus, why have you given us clear signs to tell
      True gold from counterfeit, but when it comes to good
      Or bad men, the flesh bears no revealing mark?

CHORUS
520   The fiercest anger of all, the most incurable,
      Is that which rages in the place of dearest love.

JASON
      It seems I have to show myself a clever speaker.
      This tide of recrimination and abuse
      Calls for good seamanship. I'll furl all but an inch
      Of sail and ride it out. To start with since you build
      Your services to me to such a height, I give
      Credit for my successful voyage solely
      To Aphrodite – no-one else divine or human.
      I admit, you have intelligence, but to recount
530   How helpless passion drove you then to save my life
      Would be invidious – I will not stress the point.
      Your services, so far as they went, were good enough;
      But in return for saving me you got far more
      Than you gave. Allow me, first of all, to point out
      That you left a barbarian land to take up residence
      In Greece. Here you have known justice, and lived
      In a society where force yields place to law.
      Moreover, here your gifts are widely recognized;
540   You are famous. If you still lived at the ends of the earth
      Your name would never have been known. To me, unless
      Life brings me fame, I long neither for hoards of gold
      Nor for a voice sweeter than Orpheus. You began
      The argument about my voyage; that is my answer.
      As for your slanderous taunts against my marriage into

The royal family, I shall show that my actions
Were wise, not swayed by passion, and directed towards
Your interests and my children's. No, keep quiet! When I   550
Came here from Iolchus as a stateless exile, dogged
And thwarted by misfortunes, what better stroke of luck
Could I have had than marriage with the king's daughter?
It was not, as you resentfully assume, that I
Became tired of your attractions and was smitten with
Desire for a new wife. Nor did I especially want
To raise a large family. The sons that we have
Are enough – I'm satisfied – but I wanted to ensure,
First and foremost, that we should live in comfort
And not be poor. I know how a poor man is shunned   560
By all his friends. Next, that I could bring up my sons
In a manner worthy of my descent; have other sons,
Perhaps, as brothers to your children; give them all
An equal place, and so build up a close-knit
And prosperous family. *You* don't want more children, do
        you?
Well, *I* thought it worthwhile to ensure benefits
For those I have, by way of those I mean to have.
Was such a plan so bad? Even you would approve
If you could control your jealousy. But you women
Have reached the stage where, if all's well with your sex-life,   570
You have everything you wish for, but if *that* goes wrong,
Then all that's best and noblest turns at once to dust.
If only children could be got some other way,
Without the female sex! If women didn't exist,
Human life would be rid of all its miseries!

CHORUS
Jason, you have set forth your case plausibly.
But to my mind – though you may be surprised at this –
You are acting wrongly by forsaking your wife like this.

MEDEA
No doubt I differ from many people in many ways.
To me, an evil man who is also eloquent   580
Seems the most guilty of them all. He'll cut your throat
As bold as brass, because he knows he can dress up murder

In fine words. But you're not so clever after all.
You dare outface me now with glib self-righteousness!
One point will undo you: if you were honest, you ought first
To have won me over, not got married behind my back.

JASON

No doubt, if I had mentioned it, you would have proved
Most helpful. Why, even now you cannot bring yourself
590   To calm this raging temper.

MEDEA

                              That wasn't the reason.
You're an ageing man, and an Asiatic wife
No longer seemed respectable.

JASON

                              Understand this:
It's not for the sake of any woman that I have made
This royal marriage but, as I've already said,
To ensure your future, and give my children brothers
Of royal blood, to build security for us all.

MEDEA

I loathe your prosperous future – I'll have none of it.
Nor your security; it galls my very being.

JASON

600   You know, you'll change your mind and be more sensible.
You'll soon stop thinking good is bad, and striking these
Pathetic poses when in fact you're fortunate.

MEDEA

Go on, insult me – you have a roof over your head.
I am alone, an exile.

JASON

                      It was your own choice.
Blame no one but yourself.

MEDEA

                          My choice? What did I do?
Did I make you my wife and then abandon you?

JASON

You called down evil curses on the king and his house.

MEDEA

I did. On your house too Fate sends me as a curse.

JASON
    I won't pursue this further. If there's anything else
    I can provide to meet the children's needs or yours,   610
    Tell me. I'll gladly give whatever you want, or send
    Letters of introduction, if you like, to friends
    Who will help you. Listen, to refuse such help is madness.
    You've everything to gain if you give up this rage.

MEDEA
    Nothing would induce me to have dealings with your
       friends,
    Nor to take any help from you, so offer none.
    A lying traitor's gifts bring no luck.

JASON
                                      Very well.
    I call the gods to witness that I have done my best
    To help you and the children. But you make no response   620
    To kindness. Friendly overtures you stubbornly
    Refuse. So much the worse for you.

MEDEA
                             Go! You have spent
    Too long out here. You are burning with desire for
    Your newly-won bride. Go, enjoy her!
       [*Exit* JASON.]
                             It may
    Turn out – god willing – that this your wedding day
    Will end with your marriage lost, and loathing and horror
       left.

CHORUS
    Visitations of love that come
    Raging and violent on a man
    Bring him neither good repute nor goodness.
    But if Aphrodite descends in gentleness   630
    No other goddess brings such delight.
    Never, queen Aphrodite,
    Fire at me from your golden bow,
    Dipped in sweet desire,
    Your inescapable arrow!

Let innocence, the gods' loveliest gift,
Choose me for her own;
Never may the dread Cyprian
Stir my heart to leave old love for new,
Sending, to assault me,
Angry disputes and unending feuds.

640 But let her judge shrewdly the loves of women
And respect the bed where no war rages.

O my country, my home!
May the gods save me from becoming
A stateless refugee
Dragging out an intolerable existence
In desperate helplessness!
That is the most pitiful of all griefs –
Death is better. Should such a day come to me
I pray for death first.

650 Of all the pains and hardships none is worse
Than to be deprived of your native land.

This is no mere reflection derived from hearsay;
It is something we have seen.
You, Medea, have suffered the most shattering of
        blows,
Yet neither the city of Corinth
Nor any friend has taken pity on you.
May dishonour and ruin fall on the man

660 Who, having unlocked the secrets
Of a friend's open heart, can then disown them!
He shall be no friend of mine.
    [*Enter* AEGEUS.]

AEGEUS

All happiness to you, Medea! Between old friends
There is no better greeting.

MEDEA

                                All happiness to you,
Aegeus, son of Pandion the wise! Where have you come
        from?

AEGEUS
  From Delphi, from the ancient oracle of Apollo.
MEDEA
  The centre of the earth, the home of prophecy.
  Why did you go?
AEGEUS
                        To ask for children; that my seed
  May become fertile.
MEDEA
                              Why? Have you lived all these years   670
  Childless?
AEGEUS
              I am indeed childless; so some fate has ordained.
MEDEA
  You have a wife, or not?
AEGEUS
                        I am married.
MEDEA
                                    And what answer
  Did Phoebus give you about children?
AEGEUS
                                  His answer was
  Too subtle for me or any human interpreter.
MEDEA
  Is it lawful for me to hear it?
AEGEUS
                            Of course. A brain
  Like yours is just what's needed.
MEDEA
                              Tell me, since you may.
AEGEUS
  He commanded me 'not to unstop the wineskin's neck—'
MEDEA
  Yes – until when?   680
AEGEUS
  Until I come home safe again.
MEDEA
  I see. And for what purpose have you sailed to Corinth?

AEGEUS

You know the king of Troezen, Pittheus son of Pelops?

MEDEA

Yes, a most pious man.

AEGEUS

I want to ask his advice

About this oracle.

MEDEA

He is an expert in such matters.

AEGEUS

Yes, and my closest friend. We went to the wars together.

MEDEA

I hope you will get all you wish for, and be happy.

AEGEUS

But you are looking pale and wasted: what's the matter?

MEDEA

690   Aegeus, my husband is the most evil man alive.

AEGEUS

Why, what's this? Tell me why you are unhappy.

MEDEA

Jason has betrayed me, though I never did him wrong.

AEGEUS

What has he done? Tell me in detail.

MEDEA

He has taken

Another wife, and made her mistress of *my* house.

AEGEUS

But such an act is shameful! He can't have dared—

MEDEA

It is so. Once he loved me; now I am disowned.

AEGEUS

Did he tire of you? Or fall in love with someone else?

MEDEA

Head over heels in love. He's not a man his friends can
      trust.

AEGEUS

Well, if – as you say – he's a bad sort, let him go.

MEDEA
  It's royalty and power he's fallen in love with.   700
AEGEUS
                                              What?
  So who's the girl's father?
MEDEA
                              Creon, king of Corinth.
AEGEUS
  I see. Then you have every reason to be upset.
MEDEA
  It is the end of everything! What's more, I'm banished.
AEGEUS
  Worse still – unbelievable! Why, who has banished you?
MEDEA
  Creon has banished me from Corinth.
AEGEUS
                                    And does Jason
  Accept this? How disgraceful!
MEDEA
                              Oh no, he protests.
  But he's resolved to bear it bravely. Aegeus, see,
  I touch your beard as a suppliant, embrace your knees,   710
  And beg you to take pity on my wretchedness.
  Have pity! I'm an exile; let me not be friendless.
  Receive me in Athens. Give me a welcome in your house.
  So may the gods grant you fertility, and bring
  Your life to a happy close. You do not realize
  What good luck fate has brought you. I know certain
      drugs
  Whose power will put an end to your sterility.
  I promise you shall beget children.
AEGEUS
                                    I am eager,
  For many reasons, to help you in some way, Medea.   720
  First, for the gods' sake; then this hope you've given me
  Of children – I've quite despaired of my own powers.
  Look, this is what I'll do: once you arrive in Athens

I'll keep my promise and protect you all I can.
But I must make this clear first: I do not intend
To take you with me away from Corinth. If you make
Your own way to Athens, you shall have sanctuary there –
I will not give you up to anyone. But first
Get clear of Corinth by yourself; the Corinthians too
730   Are friends of mine, and I don't wish to cause offence.

MEDEA

So be it. Now confirm your promise with an oath,
And all is well between us.

AEGEUS

                                Why? Do you not trust me?
What's the problem?

MEDEA

                        I trust you, but I have enemies –
Not only Creon but the house of Pelias.
Once you are bound by oaths you will not give me up
If they should try to take me out of your domain.
But if your promise is verbal, and not sworn to the gods,
Perhaps you will make friends with them, and agree to do
What they demand. I've no power on my side, while they
740   Have wealth and all the resources of a royal house.

AEGEUS

Your foresight is impressive; since you wish it,
I've no objection. In fact, our taking an oath
Safeguards me, as I can confront your enemies
With a clear excuse, while *you* have full security.
So name your gods.

MEDEA

                        Swear by the Earth under your feet,
The Sun, father of my father, and the whole race of gods.

AEGEUS

Tell me what I shall swear to do or not to do.

MEDEA

Never to expel me yourself from your territory;
750   And, if my enemies want to take me away, never
Willingly, while you live, to give me up to them.

AEGEUS

  I swear by Earth, and by the burning light of the Sun,
  And all the gods, to keep the words you have just spoken.

MEDEA

  I am satisfied. And if you break your oath, what then?

AEGEUS

  Then may the gods do to me as to all guilty men.

MEDEA

  Go now, and joy be with you. Everything is well.
  I'll reach your city as quickly as I can, when I
  Have carried out my purpose and achieved my will.
    [*Exit* AEGEUS.]

CHORUS

  May Hermes, protector of travellers, bring you
  Safely to your home, Aegeus. May you   760
  Accomplish all that you so earnestly
  Desire; your noble heart has won our goodwill.

MEDEA

  O Zeus! O Justice, daughter of Zeus! O glorious sun!
  Now I am on the road to victory, now there's hope!
  I shall see my enemies punished as they deserve.
  Just where my plan was weakest, at that very point,
  Help has arrived in this man Aegeus. He is a haven
  Where I shall find safe mooring, once I reach the walls   770
  Of the city of Athens.
    [*Enter* NURSE.]
                  Now I'll tell you all my plans –
  They don't make pleasant hearing. First I'll send a slave
  To Jason, asking him to come to me, and then
  I'll give him soft talk, tell him he has acted well,
  Tell him I think this royal marriage, which he has bought
  With my betrayal, is for the best and wisely planned.
  But I shall beg that the children be allowed to stay;   780
  Not that I would think of leaving sons of mine behind
  On enemy soil for those who hate me to insult,
  But in my plot to kill the princess they must play a part.
  I'll send them to the palace bearing gifts, a dress

Of soft weave and a coronet of beaten gold.
If she takes and puts on this finery, both she
And all who touch her will expire in agony;
With such deadly poison will I anoint my gifts.
790   But enough of that. What makes me cry in pain
Is the next thing I have to do: I must kill my sons.
No one shall take my children from me. When I have left
Jason's whole house in ruins, I will leave Corinth
A murderess, flying from my darling children's blood.
Yes, I can endure guilt, however terrible;
The laughter of enemies I will not stand.
Now let things take their course. What use is life to me?
I have no land, no home, no refuge from despair.
800   My folly was committed long ago, when I
Was ready to desert my father's house, won over
By a Greek's smooth talking, whom with god's help I now
Will punish: he will never see the sons he had
By me alive again. From his new bride he will
Not breed a son. She by my poison, wretched girl,
Will die a hideous death. Let no one think of me
As humble or weak or passive. Let them understand
I am of a different kind: dangerous to my enemies
810   And loyal to my friends. To such a life glory belongs.

CHORUS
Since you have told us everything, and as I want
To be your friend, as well as upholding the laws
Of human life, I tell you, don't do this!

MEDEA
There is no other way. You have good reason
To speak so; you haven't been treated as I have.

CHORUS
But have you the heart to kill your own children?

MEDEA
This is the way to deal Jason the deepest wound.

CHORUS
It will also bring you the deepest misery.

MEDEA
It must be so. There is no point in moderation.

Nurse! You're the one I use for messages of trust.   820
Go, bring Jason to me. As you're a loyal servant,
And a woman, breathe no word about my plans.
　　[*Exit* NURSE.]
CHORUS
The people of Athens, the sons of Erechtheus,
Have enjoyed their prosperity
Since ancient times. Children of the blessed gods,
They grew from holy soil unscorched by invasion.
Among the glories of knowledge their souls are pastured.
They walk always with grace under the sparkling sky.   830
There long ago, they say, was born golden-haired Harmony,
Created by the nine virgin Muses of Pieria.

They say that Aphrodite dips her cup
In the clear stream of the lovely Cephisus;
It is she who blows over the land the breath
Of gentle honey-laden winds; her flowing locks   840
She crowns with a diadem of sweet-scented roses,
And sends the Loves to be enthroned beside Knowledge,
And with her to create excellence in every art.

How, then, will such a city,
Watered by sacred rivers,
A country that gives protection to its friends –
How will Athens welcome
You, the child-killer
Whose presence is pollution?   850
Contemplate the blow struck at a child,
Weigh the blood you take upon you.
Medea, by your knees,
By every pledge and appeal we beseech you,
Do not slaughter your own children!

Where will you find the firmness of purpose?
How will you forge resolution in hand and heart
To face the horror without flinching?
When the moment comes, and you look at them –

The moment for you to assume the role of murderess –
860   How will you do it?
      When your sons kneel to you for pity,
      Will you stain your fingers with their blood?
      Your heart will melt; you will know you cannot do it.
           [*Enter* JASON (*from the palace*) *and maids to attend*
           MEDEA (*from the house*).]
   JASON
      You sent for me; I'm here. Though you hate me I'm ready
      To listen. Do you have some new request? What is it?
   MEDEA
      Jason, I ask you to forgive the things I said.
      You must bear with my violent temper; you and I
870   Share many memories of love. I have been taking
      Myself to task. 'You're a fool!' I told myself,
      'You're mad, when people try to plan things for the best,
      To be resentful, and pick quarrels with the king
      And with your husband. What he has done will help us all.
      His wife is royal; her sons will be my sons' brothers.
      Why not cast off your anger? What is wrong
      If the gods make kind provision? After all
880   I have two children still to take care of, and I know
      We came as exiles and our friends are few enough.'
      When I considered this, I saw my foolishness,
      And saw how pointless anger was. So now I welcome
      What you have done. I think you are wise to gain for us
      This new alliance, and the folly was all mine.
      I should have helped you in your plans, made it a
           pleasure
      To prepare your marriage-bed and attend your bride.
      But we women – I won't say we are bad by nature,
890   But we are what we are. You, Jason, should not copy
      Our poor example, or match yourself with us, trading
      Folly with folly. I give in. I was wrong before,
      I admit. But I have thought more wisely of it since.
      Children, children! Are you inside? Come out here.
           [*The* CHILDREN *come out followed by the* TUTOR.]
      Greet your father, as I do. Put your arms around him.

Forget our quarrel, and love him as your mother does.
We have made friends; we are not angry any more.
There, children, take his hand.
  [MEDEA *breaks into tears.*]
                                            Forgive me. I was recalling
What pain the future hides from us.   900
  [*The* CHILDREN *return from* JASON *to* MEDEA.]
                                        Oh children! Will you
All your lives long stretch out your hands to me like this?
Oh, my tormented heart is full of tears and terror.
After so long, I have ended my quarrel with your father.
And now, see, I have drenched these young faces with tears.

CHORUS
  I too feel fresh tears filling my eyes. May the course of evil
  Be checked at once, and go no further!

JASON
                                        I am pleased, Medea,
That you have changed your mind, though I don't blame
      you for
Your initial anger. It is natural for a woman
To be angry if her husband takes a second wife.   910
You have had wiser thoughts and, though it has taken time,
You have recognized the right decision. This is the act
Of a sensible woman. As for you, my boys, your father
Has taken careful thought and, with the help of the gods,
Ensured a good life for you. Why, in time, I'm sure,
You, with your brothers, will be the leading men in Corinth.
Only grow big and strong. Your father, and those gods
Who support him, have everything else under control.
I hope to see you, when you're strong, full-grown young   920
      men,
Tread down my enemies.
  [MEDEA *breaks into tears again.*]
                                What's this? Why these floods of tears?
Why are you pale? Did you not like what I was saying?
Why do you turn away?

MEDEA
                                It's nothing. I was thinking

About the children.

JASON

                      I'll provide for them. Take heart.

MEDEA

I will. It isn't that I mean to doubt your word.

But women are women; tears come naturally to us.

JASON

Why do you grieve so over the children?

MEDEA

                             I'm their mother.

930   Just now when you prayed for them to live long, I wondered

Whether it would be so; and grief came over me.

But I've said only part of what I had to say.

Here is the other thing: since Creon has resolved

To send me out of Corinth, I fully recognize

That for me too this course is best. If I lived here,

I would become a problem both to you and him.

People believe I bear a grudge against you all.

So I must go. But the boys – I would like *them* to be

940   Brought up in your care. Beg Creon to let them stay.

JASON

I don't know if I can persuade him, but I'll try.

MEDEA

Then get your wife to ask her father to let them stay.

JASON

Why, yes, of course – I'm sure she'll win him over.

MEDEA

She will, if she's like other women. But I too

Can help in this. I'll send gifts to your wife –

The loveliest things that can be found anywhere.

The boys can take them. One of you maids, quickly, bring

950   The dress and golden coronet. These will multiply

Her happiness many times, when she can call her own

A royal, noble husband, and these treasures, which

My father's father the Sun bequeathed to his descendants.

    [*A slave brings in the gifts.*]

Boys, hold these gifts, and take them to the happy bride,

The princess royal. Be sure to put them into her own
    hands.
Go! She will find them all that such a gift should be.

JASON

Foolish woman, why deprive yourself of such things?
Do you think a royal palace is in need of dresses –   960
Or of gold? Keep them, don't give them away.
If my wife values me at all she will yield to me
Rather than costly presents, I am sure of that.

MEDEA

Don't stop me. Gifts, they say, persuade even the gods;
With mortals, gold outweighs a thousand arguments.
The day is hers. From now on her prosperity
Will rise to new heights. She is royal and young. To buy
My sons from exile I would give my life, not just gold.
Come, children, both of you go into that grand palace;
Kneel down and beg your father's new bride – my new   970
    mistress –
That you may not be banished. And above all, see
That she receives the presents into her own hands.
Go quickly, be successful, and bring back good news:
That what your mother longs for has been granted.

    [*Exit* JASON *followed by the* TUTOR *and the*
    CHILDREN.]

CHORUS

Now I have no more hope,
No more hope that the children will live;
They are walking to murder at this very moment.
The bride will receive the golden coronet,
Receive her merciless destroyer;
With her own hands she will carefully fit   980
The trappings of death round her golden hair.

She cannot resist such loveliness, such heavenly lustre;
She will enfold herself
In the dress and the wreath wrought of gold,
Preparing her bridal beauty

To enter a new home – among the dead.
So deadly is the trap she will fall into,
So inevitable the death that awaits her;
From its cruelty there is no escape.

990   And you, unhappy Jason, ill-starred in marriage,
You, son-in-law of kings,
Little do you know that the favour you ask
Will seal your sons' destruction
And fasten on your wife a hideous fate.
O wretched Jason!
So sure of the future and yet so ignorant!

Your sorrow too I weep for, pitiable mother.
You, for the jealousy of your marriage-bed,
Will slaughter your children,
Since, disregarding right and loyalty,
1000   Your husband has abandoned you
To live with another wife.
    [*The* TUTOR *returns from the palace with the*
    CHILDREN.]
TUTOR
Mistress, these two boys are reprieved from banishment.
The princess took your gifts from them with her own hand,
And was delighted. They have no enemies in the palace.
    [MEDEA *remains silent.*]
What's this?
Why do you stand there distressed, when you've heard good
    news?
MEDEA
How cruel, how cruel!
TUTOR
That's not in keeping with the news I brought.
MEDEA
How cruel life is!
TUTOR
                    Have I said something dreadful
1010   Without realizing it? I thought my news was good.

MEDEA

Your news is what it is. I don't blame you.

TUTOR

Then why stand staring at the ground, with streaming
eyes?

MEDEA

Good reason forces me to weep, old friend. The gods,
And my own evil-minded plots, have led to this.

TUTOR

Take heart, mistress. In time your sons will bring you home.

MEDEA

Before then, I have others to send home. Oh, gods!

TUTOR

You're not the only mother to be parted from her sons.
We are all mortal; you must not bear grief so hard.

MEDEA

Yes, friend. I'll follow your advice. Now go indoors
And get things ready for them, as on other days.   1020
    [*Exit* TUTOR.]
O children, children! You have a city and a home,
And when we have parted, there you both will stay
    forever –
You motherless, I miserable. And I must go
To exile in another land, before I can have
My joy of you, before I can see you growing up,
Becoming prosperous. I shall never see your brides,
Adorn your bridal beds, and hold the torches high.
My misery is my own heart, which will not relent.
All was for nothing, then – these years of rearing you,
My care, my aching weariness, and the wild pains   1030
When you were born. Oh, yes, I once built many hopes
Around you; imagined fondly that you would care for me
In my old age, and would yourselves wrap my dead body
For burial. How people would envy me my sons!
That sweet, sad thought has faded now. Parted from you,
My life will be all pain and anguish. You will not
Look at your mother any more with these dear eyes.
You will have moved into a different realm of existence.

1040   Dear sons, why are you staring at me so? You smile
At me – your last smiles. Why? . . .
    [MEDEA *turns to the* CHORUS.]
                           Oh, what am I to do?
Women, my courage is all gone. Their bright young faces –
I can't do it. I'll think no more of it. I'll take them
Away from Corinth. Why should I hurt *them* to make
Their father suffer, when I shall suffer twice as much
Myself? No, I shall bid my plans farewell.

What is the matter with me? Are my enemies
1050   To laugh at me? Am I to let them off unpunished?
I must steel myself to it. What a coward I am,
Even tempting my own resolution with soft talk.
Boys, go indoors!   *is she now compleltly insane.*
    [*The* CHILDREN *go towards the door.*]
                  If there are any here who find it
Unlawful to be present at my sacrifice,
Let them think on it. My hand will not weaken . . .

Oh, my heart, don't do it! Oh, miserable heart,
Let them be! Spare your children! We'll all live together
Safely in Athens . . . and they will make you happy . . . No!
No! No! by all the fiends of hate in hell's depths, no!
1060   And I will not leave sons of mine to be the victims of
My enemies' rage. In any case, there's no escape –
The thing is underway now. Yes, the golden coronet
Is on her head, the royal bride is in her dress,
Dying, I know it. So, since I have a sad road
To travel, and must send these boys on a still sadder road,
I'll speak to them. Come, children. Give me your hand, dear
    son;
1070   Yours too. Now we must say goodbye. Oh, darling hands,
And darling mouths, your noble, childlike faces and bodies!
Dear sons, my blessing on you both – but there, not here.
All blessings here your father has destroyed. How sweet
To hold you! So soft, children's skin, and their breath
    pure . . .

Go! Go away! I can't look at you any longer.
My pain is more than I can bear.
  [*The* CHILDREN *go into the house.*]
                                I know the full
Horror of what I am about to do, but anger,
The spring of all life's horrors, masters my resolve.   1080
CHORUS
I have often engaged in arguments,
And become more subtle, and perhaps more heated,
Than is seen fit for women,
Though in fact women too have intelligence,
Which forms part of our nature and instructs us –
Not all of us, I admit, but a certain few
You might find, in a large number of women,
Are not incapable of reflection.

And this is my opinion: those men and women   1090
Who have never had children of their own
Enjoy the advantage of good fortune
Over those who are parents. Childless people
Have no means of knowing whether children are
A blessing or a burden, but being without them
They live exempt from many troubles.

While those who have growing up in their homes
The sweet gift of children I see always
Burdened and worn with incessant worry.   1100
First, how to rear them in health and safety,
And bequeath them, in time, enough to live on,
And then this further anxiety:
They can never know whether all their toil
Is spent on worthy or worthless children.

And beyond the common ills that attend
All human life there is one still worse.
Suppose at last parents are fairly well off,
Their children have grown up, and, what's more,
They are kind and honest, then what happens?

1110   A throw of chance, and there goes Death
        Bearing off your child into the unknown.

        Why then should mortals thank the gods,
        Who add to their load, already grievous,
        This one more grief, for their children's sake,
        Most grievous of all?
MEDEA
        Friends, I have long been waiting for a message from the
            palace
        About how things have gone. I see a slave of Jason's
1120   Coming, gasping for breath. He must bring grievous news.
            [*Enter* MESSENGER.]
MESSENGER
        Medea! Get away, escape! Oh, what a thing to do!
        What an unholy, horrific thing! Take ship or chariot –
        Any means you can – but escape!
MEDEA
                                          Why should I escape?
MESSENGER
        She's dead – the princess – and her father Creon too.
        They're both dead, by your poison.
MEDEA
                                          Splendid news!
        I count you from now on as friend and benefactor.
MESSENGER
        What? Are you sane, or raving mad? You have committed
1130   This hideous crime against the royal house and you're glad
        At the news? Don't you tremble at such things?
MEDEA
        I could make suitable reply to that, my friend,
        But take your time now; tell me how they died. You'll give
        Me twice the pleasure if their deaths were horrible.
MESSENGER
        When your two little boys came hand in hand, and entered
        The palace with their father, where the wedding was,
        We servants were delighted. We had all felt sorry

To hear how you'd been treated, and now the word went
    round
From one to another, that you and Jason had made up.   1140
So we were glad to see the boys; one kissed their hand,
Another their fair hair. Myself, I was so pleased,
I followed them into the princess's room. Our mistress –
The one we now call mistress in your place – before
She saw your pair of boys coming, had eyes only
For Jason. But seeing them she dropped her eyes, and
    turned
Her lovely cheek away, upset that they should come
Into her room. Your husband then began to soothe
Her sulkiness and girlish temper. 'You must not,'   1150
He said, 'be unfriendly to our friends. Turn your head
    round,
And give up feeling angry. Those your husband loves
You must love too. Now take these gifts,' he said, 'and ask
Your father to revoke their exile for my sake.'
After she saw those lovely things, she was won over,
And agreed to all that Jason asked. At once, before
He and your sons were well clear of the house, she took
The embroidered gown and put it round her. Then she
    placed
The golden coronet over her curls, and began   1160
To arrange her hair in a bright mirror, smiling at
Her lifeless reflection. Then she stood up,
And stepped daintily to and fro about the room
On bare white feet, and many times she would twist back
To see how the dress fell in clear folds to the heel.
Then suddenly we saw a frightening thing. She changed
Colour and staggered sideways, shaking in every limb.
She was just able to collapse on to a chair,
Or she would have fallen flat. Then one of her attendants,   1170
An old woman, thinking that perhaps the anger of Pan
Or some other god had struck her, chanted the cry of
    worship.
But then she saw white froth oozing from the girl's lips;

The pupils of her eyes were twisted out of sight;
The blood was drained from all her skin. The old woman
Knew her mistake and changed the chant to a despairing
    howl.
One maid ran off quickly to fetch the king, another
To look for Jason and tell him what was happening
To his young bride. The whole palace was filled with a
    clatter
1180   Of people running here and there. All this took place
In a few moments, perhaps while a fast runner might run
A hundred yards. And she lay speechless, her eyes closed.
Then she came to, poor girl, and gave a frightful scream,
As two torments made war on her together: first
The golden coronet round her head discharged a stream
Of unnatural devouring fire, then the fine dress
Your children gave her, poor miserable girl, started
1190   To eat her fair flesh. She leapt up from her chair,
On fire, and ran, tossing her head and her long hair
This way and that, trying to shake off the coronet.
But the garland of gold was fitted close and would not
    move –
The more she shook her head the fiercer the flame burned.
At last, overcome by agony, she fell to the ground.
Except to her father, she was unrecognizable.
Her eyes and face were one grotesque disfigurement.
Down from her head dripped blood mingled with flames;
    her flesh,
Meanwhile, attacked by hidden fangs of poison, had melted
1200   From her bare bones like gumdrops from a pine-tree's
    bark –
A ghastly sight! Not one among us dared to touch
Her body. What we saw was lesson enough for us.
But suddenly her father came into the room.
He didn't understand, poor man, what kind of death
Had struck his child. He threw himself down at her side,
Then sobbed aloud, kissed her, and took her in his arms,
Crying, 'Poor darling, what god destroyed your life

So cruelly? Who robs me of my only child,
Old as I am, and near my grave? Oh, let me die   1210
With you, my daughter!' When he stopped his tears and
    cries,
He tried to lift his aged body upright. But then,
As ivy sticks to laurel-branches, so he stuck
Fast to the dress. A ghastly wrestling started next.
He struggled to lift up his knees, but she tugged him down.
If he used force, he tore the old flesh off his bones.
At length the king gave up his pitiful attempts.
Weakened with pain, he yielded, and gasped out his life.
Now, joined in death, daughter and father – such a sight   1220
As tears were made for – both lie there. To you, Medea,
I have no more to say. You yourself will know best
How to evade reprisal. As for human life,
It is a shadow, as I have long believed. And this
I say without any hesitation: those whom most would call
Intelligent, the propounders of wise theories,
Their folly is of all men's the most culpable.
Happiness is a thing no man possesses. Fortune
May come now to one man, now to another, as
Prosperity increases; happiness never.   1230
    [*Exit* MESSENGER.]

CHORUS
Today we see the will of Heaven, blow after blow,
Bring down on Jason justice and calamity.

MEDEA
Friends, now my course is clear: as quickly as possible
To kill the children and then fly from Corinth; I must not
Delay and so consign them to another hand
To murder with a better will. They die
In any case, and since they must, then I who gave   1240
Them birth will kill them. Arm yourself, my heart: the thing
That you must do is awful yet inevitable.
Why wait, then? Come, my accursed hand, take the sword.
Take it, and head towards your frontier of despair.
No cowardice, no tender memories – forget

That once you loved them, that of your body they were
    born.
For one short day forget your children. Afterwards
Weep; though you killed them they were your beloved
    sons.

1250 Life has been cruel to me.
        [MEDEA *goes into the house.*]
CHORUS
Earth, awake! Bright rays of the Sun,
Look! Look down on the accursed woman
Before she lifts up a murderous hand
To pollute it with her children's blood!
They belong to your own golden race;
And for mortals to spill blood that grew
In the veins of gods is a fearful thing.
Heaven-born brightness, hold her, stop her,
Purge the palace of her, this execrable
1260 Bloody-handed fiend of vengeance!

All your care for them lost! Your love
For the babes you bore, all wasted, wasted!
Why did you come from the blue Symplegades
That form the gateway to the barbarous sea?
Why must this rage devour your heart
And spend itself in slaughter of children?
Where kindred blood pollutes the ground
A curse hangs over human lives;
And murder measures the doom that falls
1270 By Heaven's law on the guilty house.
        [A CHILD's *scream is heard from within the house.*]
CHORUS
Do you hear? The children are calling for help.
O cursed, miserable woman!
CHILDREN [*From within*]
Help! Help! Mother, let me go!
Mother, don't hurt us!
CHORUS
Shall we go in?

We have to try to save the children's lives!
CHILDREN [*From within*]
  Help! Help us! Oh god! She's attacking us.
  We can't get away from her sword!
CHORUS
  O miserable mother, to destroy your own issue,
  Murder the babes of your own body!   1280
  Stone or iron you are, as you resolved to be.

  There was but one in times past,
  One woman that I have heard of,
  Who raised her hand against her own children.
  She was Ino, sent out of her mind by a god,
  When Hera, the wife of Zeus,
  Drove her from her home to wander over the world.
  In her misery she plunged into the sea
  Being defiled by the murder of her children.
  From the steep cliff's edge she stretched out her foot,
  And so perished,
  Joined in death with her two sons.

  What can be strange or terrible after this?   1290
  O bed of women, full of passion and pain,
  What wrongdoing, what sorrow you have caused!
    [*Enter* JASON, *running and breathless, with
    attendants.*]
JASON
  You women standing round the door there! Is Medea
  Still in the house – sick murderess! Or has she gone
  And escaped? I swear she must hide in the deep earth
  Or soar on wings into the sky's abyss to escape
  My vengeance for the royal house. She has killed the
        king
  And the princess! Does she expect to go unpunished?   1300

  Still, I am less concerned with her than for the children.
  Those who have suffered at her hands will make her suffer;
  I've come to save my sons, before Creon's family

Murder them in revenge for this unspeakable
Crime of their mother's.

CHORUS

                       Jason, you have yet to learn
How great your troubles are; or you would not have
   spoken so.

JASON

What now? Is Medea trying to kill me too?

CHORUS

Your sons are dead. Their mother has killed them both.

JASON

1310   What? Killed my sons? Your words destroy me!

CHORUS

                                     Both dead.

JASON

Where are they? Did she kill them out here, or indoors?

CHORUS

Open that door, and see them lying in their blood.

JASON

You slaves! Unbar the doors! Open up, let me see
Two horrors: my dead sons, and the woman I shall kill.

   [JASON *batters at the doors.* MEDEA *appears above the*
   roof in a chariot drawn by winged serpents, with the
   bodies of the two CHILDREN *beside her.*]

MEDEA

Jason, why are you battering at these doors? Seeking
The dead children and me who killed them? Stop! Be quiet.
1320   If you have any business with me, say what you wish.
Touch us you cannot, in this chariot which the Sun
Has sent to save us from the hands of enemies.

JASON

You anathema! Of all women most detested
By every god, by me, by the whole human race!
How could you bring yourself – a mother – to take a sword
To your own children, leaving me childless, my life wrecked.
And after such a murder you dare outface both Sun and
   Earth,
Guilty of gross pollution? May the gods strike you down!

I am sane now, but I was mad before, when I
Brought you from your palace in a land of savages   1330
Into a Greek home – you, a living curse, already
A traitor both to your father and your native land.
The vengeance due for your crimes the gods have cast on
        me.
You had already murdered your brother at his own hearth
When first you stepped on board my lovely Argo's hull.
That was how you began. Then you became my wife, and
        bore
My children. Now, out of mere sexual jealousy,
You've murdered them! In all of Greece there is not one
        woman
Who could have done such a thing, yet in preference to them   1340
I married you, chose hatred and murder for my wife:
No woman but a tigress – Tuscan Scylla, only fiercer.
But what's the use? If I cursed you all day, no remorse
Would touch you – your heart is proof against feeling. Go!
Out of my sight, polluted fiend, child-murderer!
Leave me to mourn over my destiny: I have lost
My young bride; I have lost the two sons I fathered
And brought up; I shall never see them alive again.   1350

MEDEA
I would if necessary answer at full length
Every charge you have made; but Zeus the father of all
Knows well what service I once rendered you, and how
You repaid me. You were mistaken if you thought
You could dishonour my bed, live a pleasant life,
And laugh at me. The princess was wrong too, and so
Was Creon, when he took you for his son-in-law
And thought he could exile me with impunity.
So now I am a tigress, Scylla? Hurl at me what names
You will! I've touched your heart, and that is only fair.   1360

JASON
You suffer too; my loss is yours no less.

MEDEA
                                    That's true,
But my pain is a fair price to wipe away your smile.

JASON

O children, what an evil mother Fate gave you!

MEDEA

O sons, your father's treachery cost you your lives.

JASON

It was not my hand that killed my sons.

MEDEA

No, not your hand,

But your insult to me, and your new-wedded wife.

JASON

You thought *that* reason enough to murder them, that I

No longer slept with you?

MEDEA

And is that injury

A slight one, do you suppose, to a woman?

JASON

A decent one – yes! But to you – the whole world lost.

MEDEA

1370   I can wound too: your sons are dead!

JASON

Dead? No! They live –

To haunt your life with vengeance.

MEDEA

Who began this feud?

The gods know.

JASON

Yes, they know the evil of your heart.

MEDEA

Rage on! Your bitter voice – how I abhor the sound!

JASON

As I loathe yours. Let us make terms and part at once.

MEDEA

Gladly. What terms? What do you bid me do?

JASON

Give me my sons for burial and mourning rites.

MEDEA

Oh no! I will take them myself to the temple

Of Hera Acraea. There in the holy precinct I

Will bury them with my own hand, to ensure that none
Of their enemies can violate or insult their graves.   1380
And I will ordain an annual feast and sacrifice
To be observed forever by the people of Corinth,
To expiate this unholy murder. I myself
Will go to Athens, city of Erechtheus, to make my home
With Aegeus son of Pandion. You, as you deserve,
Shall die an unheroic death, your skull shattered
By a falling relic from the Argo. So, wretchedly,
Your fate shall end the story of your love for me.

JASON
Of their enemies can violate or insult their graves.

The curse of children's blood be on you!
Avenging Justice strike you down!   1390

MEDEA
What god will hear your imprecation,
Oath-breaker, guest-deceiver, liar?

JASON
Unclean, abhorrent child-destroyer!

MEDEA
Go home: your wife waits to be buried.

JASON
I'll go – a father once, now childless.

MEDEA
You grieve too soon. Old age is nearing.

JASON
Children, how dear you were!

MEDEA
Yes, to their mother, not to you.

JASON
Dear – and you murdered them!

MEDEA
I did, Jason, to break your heart.

JASON
I long to fold them in my arms;
To kiss their faces would give comfort.   1400

MEDEA
Now you have loving words, and kisses;
Then you disowned them, exiled them.

JASON
    For God's sake, let me touch their gentle flesh.
MEDEA
    You can't. Don't waste your breath by asking.
JASON
    Zeus, do you hear how I am treated,
    Spurned by this savage beast
    Polluted with her children's blood?

    But now, as time and strength permit,
    I will lament this grievous day,
    And call the gods to witness, how
1410   You killed my sons, and then refused
    To let me touch or bury them.
    Would that I had not fathered them,
    Or ever lived to see
    Them dead, you their destroyer!
        [*During this speech* MEDEA *and the dead* CHILDREN
        depart in the chariot.]
CHORUS
    Many the fates which Zeus in Olympus dispenses;
    Many matters the gods bring to surprising ends.
    The things we thought would happen do not happen;
    The unforeseen the gods make possible,
    And such is the conclusion of this story.

EXTRACTS FROM
FROGS
BY
ARISTOPHANES

Preface to *Frogs*

Aristophanes was a younger contemporary of Sophocles and Euripides. His career as a comic playwright began in 427 and lasted into the second decade of the fourth century, a total of about forty years. The main reason for including selections from the *Frogs* in this volume is that the play presents us with a comic version of the tragic competition. Not only does the play tell us a great deal about the reception of tragedy by its original Athenian audience, but it also offers an invaluable critical assessment, admittedly filtered through a comic lens, of the three tragedians included in this volume. The *Frogs* is also one of Aristophanes' finest plays, and one that attests the key role played by tragedy in the artistic, political and cultural life of Athens.

The recognized starting date for the performance of comedy in Athens is 486 BC, half a century after the start of the tragic competition. Athenian (or Attic) Comedy may be divided into two main periods, Old and New Comedy, which differ radically.[1] Old Comedy directly confronts topical socio-political and cultural issues; it includes vitriolic abuse of well-known individuals as well as uninhibited obscenity and slapstick; it shows a marked propensity to the fantastic and the absurd; and it regularly makes reference to itself both as comedy and as a theatrical performance, frequently collapsing the notional boundary between stage and audience.

New Comedy is considerably more regulated and inhibited. It tends to be based around a generic household with stock comic characters (the witty slave, the earnest young master, the irascible old master, the socially aspirant mother, the braggart soldier, and so on); it combines social observation

with sentimental situation comedy; it also conforms closely to
Aristotle's realist principles as set out in *Poetics*.[2]

While most of Aristophanes' output belongs to Old Comedy,
his career also extends into what is usually seen as a transitional
period between Old Comedy and New Comedy. His extant
plays up to and including the *Frogs* belong unequivocally to Old
Comedy, but in his last two surviving works, *Assembly Women*
(*c*.392) and *Wealth* (388), we see a decisive shift in the direction
of New Comedy. In both these plays, especially *Wealth*, the
vigorous examination of the cultural and ideological preoccu-
pations of the Athenian polis evident in Aristophanes' earlier
plays, including the *Frogs*, and in the tragedies of Aeschylus,
Sophocles and Euripides, is significantly less apparent.[3]

Old Comedy was performed at two annual festivals. In the
Dionysia, five comedies were performed when the festival was
a full four days, but only three in those years where, because of
war, the festival was curtailed to three days. In the Lenaea
festival, which took place in midwinter (probably also in the
theatre of Dionysus), comedy was given much greater promin-
ence: there seem to have been five comedies but no tragedies.
The festival also involved an exclusively Athenian audience in
contrast to the broader audience of the Dionysia (see General
Introduction p. xiii).

The *Frogs* was written for performance at the Lenaea of 405.
The play presents Dionysus, the god of theatre, as its comic
hero. The basic plot is as follows. Dionysus laments the lack of
good tragedians left alive (both Sophocles and Euripides died
shortly before the play was written) and hankers after
Euripidean tragedy in particular. He therefore resolves to venture down to the underworld with his slave Xanthias and bring
Euripides back to the world of the living. On his way he visits
his half-brother Heracles, who has experience in such matters
having brought Cerberus up from the gates of Hades and rescued
Alcestis for her grieving husband Admetus.[4] After a comic
exchange about the state of tragedy, Heracles advises Dionysus
how to get to Hades. While crossing the river Styx, Dionysus
encounters a chorus of Frogs, after which he sees a second
chorus of Initiates for the Mysteries (a major religious cult

involving Demeter, Persephone and Dionysus under the name Iacchus). Comic scenes with Aeacus, who polices Hades, and other minor characters follow. These largely involve the cowardly, dim-witted Dionysus and the braver, wittier Xanthias exchanging places and clothes. Once they arrive in Hades proper, we learn that there is a contest for the throne of tragedy about to take place: Euripides, who has recently arrived, is challenging the long-time incumbent Aeschylus. Dionysus is asked, as the patron of drama, to judge the contest.

What follows is a substantial piece of literary criticism. Euripides and Aeschylus examine and criticize one another's style of tragedy, while Dionysus looks on as judge. All the play's literary criticism is mediated both through the characters on stage and through the comic interests of the dramatist behind the scenes (namely, Aristophanes). Still, there is much that we may infer about the critical issues that were raised about tragedy in the late fifth century.

The result of the contest is victory for Aeschylus. We should, however, be wary of interpreting this outcome as a verdict in favour of Aeschylean over Euripidean tragedy (as some scholars have done). Aeschylus' victory involves indecision on Dionysus' part followed by a spontaneous choice. Although Dionysus decides against taking Euripides back with him, he nevertheless remains first and foremost a lover of Euripidean tragedy; throughout the play, he quotes far more from Euripides than he does from Aeschylus. Moreover, it is common in Aristophanic comedy to find unexpected changes to the comic plan as originally envisaged. What we may confidently infer, however, is that the participation of Aeschylus and Euripides in the contest for supreme tragedian serves to confirm their respective standings as tragedians. The same may be said of Sophocles, who is presented as capable of entering the contest in his own right.[5] It is out of respect for Aeschylus that he offers only to contend (on Aeschylus' behalf) if Euripides is victorious.

Sophocles' reluctance to compete directly against Aeschylus may allude to the fact that the two did indeed compete against each other in 468; it was the first year Sophocles entered the tragic competition, and he was victorious. This indirectly supports the view that Sophocles is presented as being more than capable of contending for the throne of tragedy in his own right. Euripides never competed against Aeschylus; he first entered the tragic competition in 455 BC, the year after Aeschylus died.[6] By having Euripides compete against Aeschylus face to face in a fictional Hades, Aristophanes offers us the one confrontation among these three tragedians that never actually took place.

The *Frogs* has the distinction of being the only play of Aristophanes, and seemingly the only play of Old Comedy, that was granted a second performance. The reason for this privilege is generally taken to be the advice given in the parabasis of the play.[7] A number of Athenian captains, whose ships were lost in a naval battle in 406 with the Spartans at Arginusae – Athens won what proved to be a Pyrrhic victory – had been sentenced, both hastily and on dubious grounds, to be executed. Aristophanes advised strongly that they be spared. While the *Frogs* raises numerous topical and political issues and links them to its literary interests – after the analysis of their respective work, Aeschylus and Euripides are tested on political questions (e.g., whether to recall from exile the brilliant but temperamental general Alcibiades) – the literary dimension of the play may be treated independently of its political concerns.

The characterization of Aeschylus and Euripides in the *Frogs* is largely based on a caricature of Aeschylean and Euripidean characters and the general features of their respective plays. Aeschylus is moody and silent (like his eponymous heroine Niobe, and like Achilles from his trilogy based on events of the *Iliad*). He is also irascible, and dislikes glib speakers and those who break with or debase traditional values. Euripides is verbose, inventive and argumentative (like his eponymous heroes Telephus and Palamedes) and generally avant-garde. Aeschylus is presented as a composer of martial, heroic tragedy while Euripides is shown as a playwright who focuses on beggarly or injured heroes and immoral heroines. Such a portrayal is partly based on comic distortion, but it is also partly informed by a dramatic requirement, namely, to establish an antagonism between Aeschylus and Euripides as participants in a contest.

Their presentation is also influenced by a general thematic interest throughout the play in the polarity between the Old and the New.

Aristophanes' presentation of the two tragedians perhaps encourages a view of Aeschylus as the grand old man of the theatre and of Euripides as an upstart and iconoclast; it also encourages a view of Sophocles, who remains an implicit presence in the *Frogs*, as poised between these two poles. Such a picture, however, is potentially misleading. The real Aeschylus was very much an innovator, even if his work had become largely canonical by Aristophanes' day (Aeschylus was the only playwright whose plays were regularly performed posthumously). As Aristotle notes, he added a third actor and went some way towards reducing the choral part of tragedy, even though Aristophanes makes Euripides complain about the length of Aeschylean choral odes compared with those of his own plays. While Euripides may have courted greater controversy with his subject matter, treatment and presentation, Sophocles was a highly innovative playwright too. Sophocles presented shockingly transgressive female heroines, such as Procne in his lost play *Tereus*, who murders her own children to punish her husband for his wrongdoings (not unlike the Euripidean Medea).[8] He managed, however, to handle controversial material without being perceived as a radical in the same way as Euripides. This is partly because Euripides had a reputation for being reclusive and misanthropic, and because he cultivated close connections with a number of controversial intellectual figures (e.g., Socrates and Protagoras). Sophocles, by contrast, was renowned for his geniality and good nature; moreover, he played a more active part in Athenian public life, serving in high office in various capacities throughout his life and distinguishing himself as a general.

In terms of the specific criticism of Aeschylean tragedy, Euripides convincingly suggests that Aeschylean drama, as perceived by the time the *Frogs* was written, involves certain shortcomings or outdated tendencies. These include a reliance on prolonged silences; a relative lack of dialogue; very long choral passages; and obscure poetic language and imagery. Dionysus, however, while partly agreeing with Euripides, nonetheless expresses a nostalgic fondness for a number of these characteristics. Aeschylus, in response, criticizes Euripidean tragedy for a number of its innovations. These include presenting beggarly or injured heroes (e.g., Telephus and Bellerophon); presenting immoral heroines (e.g., Phaedra and Stheneboea); having over-talkative characters, especially low characters such as nurses and slaves; and using language that is insufficiently elevated and belongs more to the law courts. Euripides defends himself on the grounds that he is making tragedy more realistic and relevant to a modern, democratic audience, but Aeschylus construes this as a debasement of the art. There is also criticism on more technical artistic and stylistic grounds. Aeschylus criticizes Euripides' style of prologue as formulaic and metrically predictable: he makes his point by interrupting to add the same ridiculous phrase – 'and lost his little flask of oil' – each time Euripides tries to complete opening lines from various plays. Euripides then parodies Aeschylus' odes as a way of demonstrating their archaic obscurity and repetitiveness. Aeschylus responds with a parody of Euripidean odes that exposes their melodramatic character and fondness for certain kinds of imagery, specifically images of sleep, night and dreams.

The play ends with Aeschylus departing with Dionysus for the world of the living. As he goes he is lavished with praise by the chorus. Euripides, by contrast, is roundly berated by the chorus for being an idle, chattering intellectual who spends his time huddling with Socrates. This nostalgic hankering for the good old days, as embodied in Aeschylus, and harsh criticism of all that is novel, as represented by Euripides, is a common posture for Old Comedy, and is not to be seen as a personal stance of Aristophanes. The presentation of Euripides here is less favourable than in other plays largely because the role he plays is one of a losing antagonist in a two-way contest. In *Thesmophoriazusae*, where he is the hero of the play, Euripides is presented far more sympathetically.

Aristophanes' preoccupation with tragedy is evident throughout his plays. His predominant interest elsewhere is Euripides and aspects of Euripidean tragedy. The *Frogs* is the one extant play where Aristophanes' primary interest is the evolution of the genre as a whole. By pitting two tragedians from different generations who never actually competed against one another, one regarded as the greatest tragedian from the first half of the fifth century and the other considered the most radically innovative of the second half, Aristophanes is able to offer a disinterested, humorous critique of tragedy over the century or so from the establishment of democracy (509 BC) to the deaths of Sophocles and Euripides (*c*.407–5). In making Dionysus incapable of deciding between Aeschylus and Euripides on artistic grounds alone, Aristophanes avoids revealing a readily extricable personal viewpoint.

Given that Aristophanes only considers Aeschylus, Sophocles and Euripides as potential candidates for the throne of tragedy, we may conclude that the *Frogs* actively seeks to canonize them. The same process of canonization is continued later by Aristotle, who makes use of these three tragedians above all others in his *Poetics*.

NOTES

1. Some scholars also suggest a transitional period known as Middle Comedy.
2. The only writer of New Comedy for whom whole works, or substantial parts thereof, survive is Menander.
3. While we have very few fragments of fourth-century tragedy, the premise of the plot of the *Frogs* and Aristotle's tendency in *Poetics* to use fifth-century plays as exemplars of good tragedy give us reason to suppose that the tragic genre as a whole went into decline after the deaths of Sophocles and Euripides.
4. The latter of these feats is treated in Euripides' earliest surviving play, *Alcestis*, written in 438.
5. Heracles expresses surprise that Dionysus does not want to fetch Sophocles instead of Euripides; later, Dionysus expresses surprise that Sophocles is not competing for the throne of tragedy.
6. While Euripides never competed against Aeschylus in person, he may nonetheless have competed against his plays, some of which were re-performed posthumously (see note on line 868, p. 283).

7. The parabasis is a section of the play where the chorus members temporarily step out of their fictional roles (this involves the removal of their masks and part of their costume) and address the audience directly. In doing so they seemingly speak on the poet's behalf, but this 'voice' is itself a fictional construct and, as such, should not necessarily be taken at face value.

8. In some ways Sophocles' *Tereus* is more shocking than *Medea*. It presents a worse atrocity: Procne not only killed her son but also diced him, cooked him, and served him up to her husband Tereus. Moreover, while Euripides showed a foreign Medea killing her children, Sophocles showed a heinous infanticide committed by a *Greek* woman.

Frogs 52ff.

DIONYSUS
So anyway, I was on a ship reading
Andromeda to myself when a sudden urge
Came upon me – I can't tell you how strong.

HERACLES
An urge? How big?   55

DIONYSUS
About Molon's size.

HERACLES
For what? A woman?

DIONYSUS
No.

HERACLES
A boy then?

DIONYSUS
Certainly not!

HERACLES
Surely not a man?

DIONYSUS
Give me a break!

. . .

HERACLES
What kind of urge was it, little bro?

DIONYSUS
I can't put it into words. Still, perhaps I   60
can explain it to you through an analogy.

Have you ever had a sudden craving for pea soup?

HERACLES
Pea soup? You're kidding, at least a thousand times!

DIONYSUS
Am I making myself clear, or should I use another way?

HERACLES
65   Not at all – I'm with you all the way on the soup.

DIONYSUS
Well, that's the kind of consuming urge I've got
For Euripides.

HERACLES
What? Even though he's dead?

DIONYSUS
Absolutely. And no one can talk me out of
Going to find him.

HERACLES
Even if it means going down to Hades?

DIONYSUS
70   I'd go down further still, if I had to.

HERACLES
What is it you're after?

DIONYSUS
I need a gifted poet.
Unfortunately, they're all dead – and those alive are rank.

HERACLES
What? Isn't Iophon still going?

DIONYSUS
Well, he's the only good one left – if, that is,
75   He's really any good. I'm still not totally convinced.

HERACLES
But if you are planning to bring a tragedian back,
Shouldn't you take Sophocles over Euripides?

DIONYSUS
Not before I've had a chance to see what Iophon
Can do on his own, without Sophocles' help.
80   Besides, Euripides is such a shifty customer
He might well try to run away with me, but Sophocles
Lived life contented and is probably content in death.

HERACLES
  What about Agathon?
DIONYSUS
  He's gone and forsaken me – a fine playwright,
  And one who's sorely missed by his friends.
HERACLES
  Where's he gone to?
DIONYSUS
  The banquets of the Blest.   85

  . . .

HERACLES
  But haven't you got other fledgling tragedians
  Up there in their thousands, churning out   90
  Plays that out-talk Euripides by miles?
DIONYSUS
  They're all imitators, mere second-raters, 'Choirs
  Of swallows', defilers of the art. If they're ever
  Granted a chorus – their one chance to piss all over
  Tragedy – their efforts are soon forgotten.   95
  Try as you will, you won't find a poet among them
  That's bona fide, one who can coin a decent phrase.
HERACLES
  What do you mean, bona fide?
DIONYSUS
  I mean someone who can
  Produce something that's truly innovative, like
  'Ether, boudoir of Zeus' or 'The tread of Time'   100
  Or that 'Heart averse' to vowing by 'what is sacred',
  Or that bit with the 'tongue' swearing 'but not the
      mind'.
HERACLES
  You don't go in for that stuff, do you?
DIONYSUS
  I'm mad for it!
HERACLES
  It's absolute twaddle – you must see that!

DIONYSUS
105   'Seek not to rule my mind' – you have your own.
HERACLES
      But surely you accept that it's complete filth.
DIONYSUS
      Stick to teaching me about eating, but . . .
XANTHIAS
      . . . Never a word about me!

Frogs 757ff.

XANTHIAS
      But what's this kerfuffle inside, all this
      Shouting and squabbling?
AEACUS
      That'll be Aeschylus and Euripides.
XANTHIAS
      Eh?
AEACUS
      Big, big trouble's afoot among the dead.
760   It more or less amounts to open civil war.
XANTHIAS
      Over what?
AEACUS
      There's a tradition in existence here,
      Applying to all the high and prestigious arts,
      That the man who's the best in his own field
      Is granted dining rights in the town hall
      And given a seat beside Pluto himself.
XANTHIAS
765   I see.
AEACUS
      Until, that is, a greater exponent arrives,
      In which case the incumbent must give way.
XANTHIAS
      So why is this a problem for Aeschylus?
AEACUS
      He's the man who, as the best in his field,
      Was the holder of the throne of tragedy.

XANTHIAS
  And now?   770
AEACUS
  Well, when Euripides got here he started
  Showing off to all the cut-throats, thieves,
  Parricides and looters – they seem to form
  The majority in Hades. After hearing
  His speeches against, his contentions, and his
  Twists of reasoning, they went berserk and hailed   775
  Him as the wisest. Then, all excited, he laid
  Claim to the throne that Aeschylus was sitting in.
XANTHIAS
  Wasn't he given a whipping?
AEACUS
  Good god, no! The public cried out for a trial
  To see who was the greatest in the art.   780
XANTHIAS
  You mean criminal types?
AEACUS
  A mob as high as heaven.
XANTHIAS
  But surely Aeschylus had his supporters?
AEACUS
  Good men are hard to find – just like the world up there.
XANTHIAS
  So what does Pluto intend to do?
AEACUS
  To hold a contest straightaway, and make   785
  A test of their respective skills.
XANTHIAS
  In that case, how come
  Sophocles isn't laying claim to the throne as well?
AEACUS
  He wouldn't dream of it. When he arrived here
  He kissed Aeschylus, shook him by the hand,
  And renounced any claims to the throne.   790
  Now, according to Cleidemides, he'll sit
  On the sidelines. If Aeschylus wins

He'll do nothing; otherwise, he says he'll fight
Against Euripides in defence of his art.

XANTHIAS

Is this really going to happen?

AEACUS

795   Yes, in just a few moments.
Then there's going to be a real commotion,
With poetry being measured on the scales!

XANTHIAS

What? They're going to weigh tragedy like sides of meat?

AEACUS

And they'll bring out rulers and measures
(800)   And sliding scales . . .
. . . Euripides says he'll test
Individual tragedies phrase by phrase.

XANTHIAS

I imagine Aeschylus didn't take too kindly to that.

AEACUS

No, he looked down and glowered like a bull.

XANTHIAS

805   So who's going to judge this contest?

AEACUS

That was tricky.
They both thought there was a shortage of qualified
        people.
810   . . . In the end they turned to your master,
On account of his familiarity with the art.

. . .

[*Enter* EURIPIDES, AESCHYLUS *and* PLUTO. PLUTO
*sits while the other two stand at opposite sides of the
stage.* DIONYSUS, *who has remained on stage
throughout, stands between the two antagonists.*]

EURIPIDES

830   Don't lecture me! I'm not letting go of this chair!
I say I'm better at our art than he is.

DIONYSUS

Aeschylus, why so quiet? You heard what he said.

EURIPIDES

First, he'll be all aloof, the same way he used
To try and con us in his tragedies.

DIONYSUS

Careful, old friend, don't get carried away!   835

EURIPIDES

I know the man. I got his number long ago:
A crude composer, and stubborn-tongued, with
An unbridled, unruly, and unstoppable mouth;
A stranger to discursive talk, just full of bluster.

AESCHYLUS

Is that so, you child of the allotment queen?   840
You dare say that of *me*, you gleaner of garbage,
You creator of beggars, you rag-stitcher!
You're going to rue what you said!

DIONYSUS

Stop it, Aeschylus!
'Warm not your inward parts with baleful rage!'

AESCHYLUS

I won't stop till I've shown this cripple-maker up   845
For what he is, despite his gall.

DIONYSUS

A lamb, boys, bring out a black lamb! I think
There's a hurricane blowing our way.

AESCHYLUS

You collector of Cretan arias,
Debasing our art with perverted unions!   850

DIONYSUS

Steady on, my exalted Aeschylus!
And you, poor Euripides, if you know what's good
For you, get out of the way of this hailstorm,
Or else in anger he may hit you on the head
With a pronouncement, and make you shed your
    Telephus.   855
And, Aeschylus, less anger please. Exchange

Arguments calmly. It's unseemly for poets
To brawl like breadwomen, yet you start roaring
Like a blazing oak right from the word go.

EURIPIDES

860   I'm ready – I won't back out – to peck or be pecked
First, if it suits him; over words, songs, and the very
Fibres of tragedy, including my *Peleus*, by god,
And *Aeolus* and *Meleager* – why, even *Telephus*!

DIONYSUS

865   Tell me, Aeschylus, what do you intend to do?

AESCHYLUS

I would have preferred not to compete here;
The contest cannot be on equal terms.

DIONYSUS

Why not?

AESCHYLUS

Because my poetry hasn't died with me.
His is as dead is he is – he'll have it here to recite.

870   Still, if this is what you want, it's what we must do.

DIONYSUS

Right, someone fetch me some fire and incense
So that, before the intellectualities
Begin, I can pray to judge this contest
With the utmost artistic sensibility.

          . . .

DIONYSUS

885   Now each of you say a prayer before you say your
          piece.

AESCHYLUS

Demeter, goddess who nurtures my mind,
May I be worthy of your Mysteries!

DIONYSUS [*to* EURIPIDES]

You take some incense too and put it on the fire.

EURIPIDES

890   Thank you,
But the gods I pray to are of a different kind.

DIONYSUS
Some ones of your own, eh? Newly created?
EURIPIDES
Exactly.
DIONYSUS
Go on then, pray to these personal gods.
EURIPIDES
Sky, my sustainer, and Axle of Tongue,
Perception, and Sensitive Nostrils, may I
Successfully refute all arguments I seize on.

. . .

EURIPIDES
As for myself, what kind of poet I am, I shall leave
Till last. First, I'll expose my rival, showing how he was
A charlatan and fraud, and how he duped the audiences,
Which he inherited from Phrynichus, already trained
As idiots. He would always start with a lone figure,   910
Maybe Achilles or Niobe, sitting there all wrapped up,
Not showing us their faces – a lame pretence at drama –
And not making so much as a peep.
DIONYSUS
That's true, they didn't!
EURIPIDES
The chorus, in the meantime, would rattle off four rounds
Of lyrics in a row, while the main characters sat in silence.   915
DIONYSUS
I used to like those silences – no less than the motor-mouths
We get these days.
EURIPIDES
And I can tell you why: because
You were stupid.
DIONYSUS
I think so too. So what was he playing at?
EURIPIDES
It was a total scam. The audience sat waiting for the
        moment

920   When Niobe made a sound; meanwhile the play went on.
DIONYSUS
       What a swindler! Now I see how he took me in!
          [*to* AESCHYLUS]
       Why are you wriggling and fretting?
EURIPIDES
       Because I've exposed him.
       After he'd done all that nonsense and the play was already
       Half over, he'd come out with a dozen bulldozing words,
925   All beetling brows and crests, terrifying bogey-faced things
       Which the audience knew nothing of.
AESCHYLUS
       God damn you!
DIONYSUS
       Be quiet!
EURIPIDES
       And what he said didn't make any sense—
DIONYSUS [*to* AESCHYLUS]
       And don't gnash your teeth!
EURIPIDES
       —nothing but Scamanders, and moats, and shields
       Blazoned with bronze griffin-eagles, and sheer verbiage
       That was impossible to figure out.
DIONYSUS
930   You're right, by god,
       Before now I've 'lain awake through swathes of night, trying
       To fathom' what kind of bird a tawny Hippocock is.
AESCHYLUS
       An emblem carved on the ships, you imbecile!

          . . .

EURIPIDES
935   But is it right to put poultry in a tragedy?
AESCHYLUS
       And you, you god-detested scum? What did you write
          about?
EURIPIDES
       Not horsecocks and goatstags, that's for sure – not

The sort of thing you find on Persian tapestries.
No, as soon as I took over the art from you,
Bloated with pomp and lardy verbiage, straightaway   940
I put it on a diet to take off excess weight with a course
Of wordlets, exercises and small white beets, while giving it
A dose of babble-juice freshly squeezed from books.
Then I fed it on arias, fortified with Cephisophon.
And I didn't spout any old rubbish that came to mind,   945
Rather the first character on stage would at once explain
The play's background.

AESCHYLUS
That's because it was better than your own!

EURIPIDES
What's more, right from the start, I'd leave no character
    idle.
The wife would speak, and the slave no less; the same goes
    for
The master, the unwed daughter, the old woman.

AESCHYLUS
And didn't you   950
Deserve to die for such shamelessness?

EURIPIDES
Not at all, by Apollo –
I did it in the name of democracy.

DIONYSUS
I'd steer clear of that subject, old boy,
You're not best qualified to speak on it!

EURIPIDES [pointing to the audience]
Next I taught these people here how to talk—

AESCHYLUS
Indeed you did!
I only wish you'd been split in two beforehand!   955

EURIPIDES
And how to apply subtle rules and test the spin of their
    words,
To perceive, discern, apprehend, change perspective,
    scheme,
Suspect others, consider every angle—

AESCHYLUS
Indeed you did!

EURIPIDES
By putting everyday events on stage, things we were used to
960   And lived with, which spectators knew about and so could
            have
Exposed any faults in my art.

. . .

EURIPIDES
That's how I got these
People to think, by putting
Reason and scrutiny into
My art. Now they grasp
975   And discern everything.
Above all, they run their households
Better than they used to, always
Checking – 'How's this going?
Where did that go? Who's taken this?'

DIONYSUS
980   My god, yes! These days
Every Athenian comes home
And bellows at his slaves,
'Where did the pot go?
Who bit the head off this
985   Sprat? That bowl I bought
Last year has had it! Where's
Yesterday's garlic bulb? Who's
Been nibbling those olives?'
Before now they used to
990   Sit there like idiots, yawning
Fools, simpletons, dunces.

CHORUS
'You witness these things, glorious Achilles!'
But what will you say in reply to them?

. . .

AESCHYLUS
  I'm furious at this turn of events, and it sickens my bones
  That I am required to compete with this man.
  But so that he cannot claim that I was at a loss, let him
  Answer me this: for what qualities should a poet be
        admired?
EURIPIDES
  For expertise and sound advice, and for making people
  Better members of the community.
AESCHYLUS
  And if you haven't done this,   1010
  But instead have made first-rate citizens patently worse,
  What punishment, would you say, you deserve?
DIONYSUS
  Death! No need to ask.
AESCHYLUS
  Then merely consider what they were like when he took
  Them over from me – noble six-footers, not the shirking
  Citizens, boorish louts and criminals they are today   1015
  But men with an air about them of spears, lances,
        white-crested
  Helmets, berets, greaves, and the spirit of sevenfold ox-hide.

      . . .

EURIPIDES
  And how exactly did you teach them to become so noble?
DIONYSUS
  Speak up, Aeschylus, don't be so proud and difficult.   1020
AESCHYLUS
  By writing a play suffused with martial spirit.
DIONYSUS
  Which was?
AESCHYLUS
  Seven Against Thebes.
  Every man who watched it burned with belligerence.

      . . .

AESCHYLUS

. . . my imagination created many paradigms of heroism –
Patroclus and lionhearted Teucer – in the hope of inspiring
Every citizen to measure up to their standards whenever
He heard the call of the bugle. But I never created whores
Like Phaedra and Stheneboea. No one can ever say that I
Created a woman who was driven by lust.

EURIPIDES

Of course not; Aphrodite never had anything to do with
    you.

AESCHYLUS

I pray she never does. She did, however, sit heavily on you
And yours. In fact, she flattened you completely.

DIONYSUS

1047   That's true enough!
What you wrote about others' wives, you were hit by
    yourself.

EURIPIDES [*to* AESCHYLUS]

What harm, you scumbag, did my *Stheneboea* do the
    public?

AESCHYLUS

You induced respectable women married to respectable men
1050   To take hemlock, seized by shame at your Bellerophons.

EURIPIDES

But didn't the story I told about Phaedra exist already?

AESCHYLUS

Of course. But it is the duty of the poet, most of all, to
    conceal
What is evil and not to stage or teach it. Children have
Teachers to guide them; adults have poets. It is vital that we
Tell them things that are good.

EURIPIDES

1056   So if you give us things the size
Of Lycabettus or great Parnassus, that's good teaching, is it?
Shouldn't you use the language of men?

AESCHYLUS

Look, you wretch, it's vital to
Create language equal to great thoughts and ideas. Besides,

It's natural for demigods to use greater words than ours,   1060
Just as they wear more impressive clothes than we do.
Here I set a good example that you totally perverted.

EURIPIDES
How?

AESCHYLUS
First, you made men of royal birth wear rags so that they
    would
Appear to people as objects of pity.

EURIPIDES
What harm did I do by that?   1064

AESCHYLUS
For one thing, there are no rich men prepared to take charge
Of warships. Instead, they wrap up in rags and plead
    poverty.

    . . .

AESCHYLUS
But what evils is he not to blame for?
Didn't he show women playing bawds,
Giving birth in holy sanctuaries,   1080
Having sexual congress with their brothers,
Claiming such things as life is not life?
Because of all this our city has
Become filled with undersecretaries
And inane monkeys as politicians   1085
Who are always hoodwinking the public.
And physical fitness is so neglected that
There's no one left to run the torch!

    . . .

EURIPIDES
Now then, let's have a look at his prologues.
I'll begin by putting the openings   1120
Of this great man's tragic drama to the test.
I think he was obscure in his exposition of plot.

DIONYSUS
And which of his prologues do you plan to examine?

EURIPIDES
A good many.
[*to* AESCHYLUS]
But first give me one from the *Oresteia*.
DIONYSUS
1125   Now then, everyone, be quiet! Go on, Aeschylus.
AESCHYLUS
'Netherworld Hermes, who guard the paternal realm,
Be my ally now and my saviour too, I pray,
For I am come back to this land and have returned.'
DIONYSUS
Any complaints as yet?
EURIPIDES
More than a dozen.
DIONYSUS
1130   But the whole passage is only three lines long!
EURIPIDES
And each of those lines has maybe twenty faults.

. . .

AESCHYLUS
What faults?
EURIPIDES
Say it again.
AESCHYLUS
'Netherworld Hermes, who guard the paternal realm,'
EURIPIDES
Doesn't Orestes say this at his father's tomb?
AESCHYLUS
1140   Yes he does.
EURIPIDES
Is he saying, then, that Hermes was 'guarding'
His father as he perished violently
At his own wife's hands in a secret ambush?
AESCHYLUS
Of course not! He calls on Hermes *Eriounios*
1145   As 'netherworld Hermes', and says that he possesses
This function as an inheritance from his father.

EURIPIDES

That is an even worse mistake than I'd imagined.
If he has the underworld as a paternal inheritance—

DIONYSUS

That makes him a hereditary grave robber!

. . .

DIONYSUS

Recite him another bit.
    [*to* EURIPIDES]
And you watch out for faults.

AESCHYLUS

'Be my ally now and my saviour too, I pray,
For I am come back to this land and have returned.'

EURIPIDES

The great Aeschylus has told us the same thing twice.

AESCHYLUS

What do you mean, twice?

EURIPIDES

Look at the words and I'll show you.   1155
'For I am come back', he says, 'and have returned'.
But coming back is the same thing as returning.

DIONYSUS

You're right! It's like someone saying to a neighbour,
'Lend me a kneading trough or else a bowl for kneading'.

AESCHYLUS

It's not the same thing at all, you drivelling idiot!   1160
It's an excellent piece of phraseology.

DIONYSUS

How so? Explain yourself.

AESCHYLUS

'Coming back' is something anyone belonging to a place
Can do; he arrives home without any other circumstance.
But an exile both 'comes back' and 'returns'.   1165

DIONYSUS

Very good, by Apollo! What do you say, Euripides?

EURIPIDES

I say Orestes didn't *return* home; he came in secret

Without informing the proper authorities.

DIONYSUS
Very good, by Hermes! Though I'm not sure what you
mean.

EURIPIDES [*to* AESCHYLUS]
Give us the next bit.

DIONYSUS
1170   Yes, Aeschylus, hurry up
And give us the next bit.
        [*to* EURIPIDES]
And you look out for faults.

AESCHYLUS
'And by this burial mound I call on my father
To hear and hearken'.

EURIPIDES
That's another thing he's said twice.
'To hear and hearken' are patently the same.

DIONYSUS
1175   Ah, but he was calling on the dead, you fool,
And we can't reach them even if we call three times!
Anyway, how did you compose your prologues?

EURIPIDES
I'll show you.
And if anywhere I say the same thing twice, or you
See anything extrinsic to the plot you can spit on me.

DIONYSUS
1180   Come on then, recite one. I simply have to listen to
The lexical precision of your openings.

EURIPIDES
'Oedipus was a fortunate man at first—'

AESCHYLUS
No he wasn't! He was born ill-fated.
Even before his birth Apollo said that he
1185   Would kill his father – before he was even conceived!
How can such a man be 'fortunate at first'?

EURIPIDES
'But then became the most wretched of mortals'.

AESCHYLUS
  He hardly 'became' wretched – he never stopped!
  How could he? As soon as he was born his parents
  Put him in a pot and exposed him in winter so that   1190
  He wouldn't live to become his father's killer.
  Then he came to Polybus with two swollen feet.
  When he was young he married an old woman
  And, to top it all, she turned out to be his mother!

  . . .

AESCHYLUS
  Now look, I don't want to nitpick over every word
  And phrase of yours. Instead, with heaven's help,
  I'll wipe out your prologues with a little flask of oil.   1200
EURIPIDES
  My prologues, with a flask of oil!
AESCHYLUS
  Just one.
  You see, the way you write I can tack any little thing
  On to your iambics – a 'tuft of wool', a 'flask of oil',
  A 'tiny pouch' – and I'll prove it right now.
EURIPIDES
  You will, will you?
AESCHYLUS
  I will.
EURIPIDES
  All right then, I'd better recite one: 1205
  'Aegyptus, as the story is told far and wide,
  Together with his fifty sons, by sailor's oar,
  On reaching Argos—'
AESCHYLUS
                            '—lost his little flask of oil'.
DIONYSUS
  What is this flask of oil? Away with it!
  Give him another opening, so we can see again.   1210
EURIPIDES
  'Dionysus, bedecked with fennel wands and fawnskins,

Amid the pine trees on the ridge of Mount Parnassus,
Leaped to the dance and—'

AESCHYLUS

'—lost his little flask of oil'.

DIONYSUS

Yikes, we've been undone by that flask of oil again!

EURIPIDES

1215   It doesn't bother me. Here's a prologue on which
He won't be able to stick his flask of oil:
'There lives no man possessed of complete happiness.
He may have been noble and short of wealth; he may
Have been lowborn and—'

AESCHYLUS

'—lost his little flask of oil'.

DIONYSUS

Euripides!

EURIPIDES

What?

DIONYSUS

1220   I'd trim your sails;
This flask of oil is blowing up a storm.

EURIPIDES

Not at all! I'm not in the least bit worried.
This time I'm going to knock it right out of his hand!

DIONYSUS

Go on then, say another one, but watch out for the flask.

EURIPIDES

1225   'Long ago Cadmus, son of Agenor, departed
Sidon's city and—'

AESCHYLUS

'—lost his little flask of oil'.

DIONYSUS

Look here, old boy, let's buy the oil-flask off him.
If not, he'll chew all our prologues to pieces.

EURIPIDES

Me buy from him!

DIONYSUS

If you want my advice.

EURIPIDES

Well, I don't! I've got plenty of prologues where   1230
He won't be able to attach his flask of oil:
'Pelops, the son of Tantalus, arrived in Pisa
On pacy steeds and—'

AESCHYLUS

'—lost his little flask of oil'.

DIONYSUS

You see? He fixed that little flask of oil again.
Old chap, there's still time – you must put in a bid.   1235
You'll get it for an obol, and it's a neat little piece.

EURIPIDES

No way – not yet! I've still got plenty left.
'On his lands Oeneus—'

AESCHYLUS

'—lost his little flask of oil'.

EURIPIDES

At least let me finish the line!
'On his lands Oeneus one year reaped an ample harvest   1240
And while giving thanks—'

AESCHYLUS

'—lost his little flask of oil'.

DIONYSUS

During a sacrifice? Who can have taken it?

. . .

DIONYSUS

That oil-flask grows on your prologues like a stye on an eye.
For goodness' sake, let's turn to choral lyrics now.

EURIPIDES

All right. I have evidence to show that he is
A poor lyricist, and that he writes repetitively.   1250

CHORUS

What will happen now?
I cannot imagine
What faults he will find
With the man who has written
More – and better – lyrics

1260   Than anyone else to this day.
       EURIPIDES
       Marvellous lyrics indeed! We'll soon see.
       I'll cut all his lyrics down to a single size.
       DIONYSUS
       All right, I'll get some pebbles to keep count.
       EURIPIDES
       'Phthian Achilles, when you hear the sound of slaughter –
1265   *Ai, ai,* a strike! – why do you not come to the rescue?
       We, the people of the marsh, honour Hermes our forbear –
       Ai, ai, a strike! – why do you not come to the rescue?'
       DIONYSUS
       That's two strikes against you, Aeschylus.
       EURIPIDES
1270   'Noblest of the Achaeans, sovereign son of Atreus, hear me.
       Ai, ai, a strike! – why do you not come to the rescue?'
       DIONYSUS
       That's your third strike, Aeschylus.
       EURIPIDES
       'Keep Silence! The Bee-Priestesses are near to open
       The temple of Artemis –
1275   *Ai, ai,* a strike! – why do you not come to the rescue?
       I have the power to declare the lucky sign for travellers –
       Ai, ai, a strike! – why do you not come to the rescue?'
       DIONYSUS
       Lord Zeus, what a barrage of strikes! I think
       I need to get to a bathhouse. These strikes
1280   Have left me with swellings in my kidneys.
       EURIPIDES
       No, not before you've heard another set
       Of lyrics composed from tunes for the lyre.
       DIONYSUS
       Go on, then, only don't put in any more strikes.
       EURIPIDES
       'How the twin-throned Greek leaders, the pick of Hellas—
1286   *Phlattothrattophlattothrat—*
       Sent the Sphinx, bitch who presided over evil days—
       Phlattothrattophlattothrat—

With spear and avenging arm, a bird of warlike omen—
Phlattothrattophlattothrat—   1290
Gave them as prey to cruel sky-wandering hounds—
Phlattothrattophlattothrat—
The contingent that clung to Ajax—
Phlattothrattophlattothrat.'   1295

DIONYSUS

What's this '*Phlattothratt*' business? Is that picked up
From the rope-winders' songs at Marathon or somewhere?

AESCHYLUS

The point is that I took them from a reputable source –
So that I wouldn't be caught stealing from the same
'Sacred mead of the Muses' as Phrynichus did.   1300
   [*pointing to* EURIPIDES]
He, on the other hand, plunders from any old place –
Tarts' songs, drinking songs by Meletus, and pipe songs,
   dirges
And dances from Caria. He'll soon be shown up. Someone
Bring me my lyre. On second thoughts, who needs a lyre
For this job? Where's the girl who plays percussion   1305
On pot shards? Come here, Muse of Euripides,
You're the ideal accompaniment for these songs.
   [*Enter Muse of* EURIPIDES.]

DIONYSUS

She used to be – well, she never played the Lesbian way!

AESCHYLUS

'You halcyons, who twitter by
The everflowing waves of the sea,   1310
Spraying and moistening the coat
Of your wings with liquid droplets;
And you spiders in the rooftop nooks,
Who with your digits spi-i-i-i-i-n
The loom-tightened thread,   1315
The art of the tuneful shuttle;
Where the pipe-fond dolphin leapt
At the prows with their azure rams
For oracles and the racetrack.
Gleam of the wine-laden vine blossom,   1320

The grape's pain-dispersing tendril.
Flings your arms about me, child!'

...

So much, then, for your choral lyrics. Now I'd like
1330   To look in detail at your monodies.

'O dark-lit gloom of night,
What dread dreams do you send me
Emanating from opaque Hades,
Possessed of lifeless life,
A child of black Night,
1335   A chilling, fearful sight,
Cloaked in cadaverous black,
With murderous, murderous stare,
And extended talons?

But you, my attendants, light a lamp!
Fetch some river dew in pails, warm some water,
1340   That I may purge the heaven-sent dream.
O god of the deep!
It is done! O my housemates,
Witness these portents! My cockerel –
Snatched by Glyce. It is vanished!
You Nymphs of the mountains,
1345   And you, Mania, save me!
I, poor me, happened
To be busy with my chores,
Spi-i-i-i-i-nning with my hands
A spindleful of flax,
1350   Making a piece of cloth
To take down to the Agora
Before dawn to sell –
But he flew up, flew up to the sky
On the feathery tips of his wings,
Leaving me only grief, grief,
1355   And tears, tears in my eyes,
That I shed, shed in my misery.

But you Cretans, children of Ida,
Take up your bows and help me!
Strain your limbs and surround her house!
And with you may fair Artemis,
With her pack of bitch-pups,
Run riot through her halls!   1360
And you, Hecate, daughter of Zeus,
Wielding in your hands the scorching
Flame of your twin torches,
Guide me to Glyce's house,
That I may enter and search.'

DIONYSUS
Now both of you stop these songs.

AESCHYLUS
I've had enough as well.
I want to take him over to the scales;   1365
That's the only thing that will truly test our poetry.
The weight of our words will be the final proof.

DIONYSUS
Come here, then, if that's what has to be done –
To weigh the art of poets like a cheese-seller.

. . .

Right then, you two, stand next to the two scale-pans.
    [AESCHYLUS and EURIPIDES *take up their positions.*]

BOTH
We're ready.

DIONYSUS
Now each of you take hold of your pan and say a line
Into it, and don't let go until I say, 'cuckoo'.   1380

BOTH
We're in position.

DIONYSUS
Now recite your lines into the scales.

EURIPIDES
'Would that the Argo had never winged its way'

AESCHYLUS
'River Spercheius, and your haunts where cattle graze'

DIONYSUS
 Cuckoo!
BOTH
 We've let go.
DIONYSUS [*moving to* AESCHYLUS' *scale-pan*]
 Look, this side is going down
 A lot lower.
EURIPIDES
1385 Why is that?
DIONYSUS
 Why? He put a river in, which made
 His line wet, like a wool-seller pre-soaking his wool,
 While you put in a line that soared like a bird.
EURIPIDES
 Well, let him say another.
DIONYSUS
 All right. Take the scales.
BOTH
 Ready!
DIONYSUS
1390 And speak.
EURIPIDES
 'Persuasion has no temple save the spoken word'
AESCHYLUS
 'For Death alone, of all the gods, yearns for no gift'
DIONYSUS
 Let go!
BOTH
 We have.
DIONYSUS
 His has gone down further again;
 He put in death, the heaviest blow of all.
EURIPIDES
1395 But I put in Persuasion, which is always apt.
DIONYSUS
 Persuasion is a flimsy thing, with no mind of its own.
 Try to come up with something really heavy this time.
 Something mammoth and hulking to weigh down your pan.

EURIPIDES
  Where can I find something like that?
DIONYSUS
  I suggest,
  'Achilles threw' two singles and a four.   1400
  Both your lines please – this is your final weigh-in.
EURIPIDES
  'He took up in his hand the cast-iron handle'
AESCHYLUS
  'For chariot on chariot, and corpse on corpse'
DIONYSUS
  He's outdone you again.
EURIPIDES
  How come?
DIONYSUS
  He put in two chariots and two corpses;   1405
  Too much to lift even for a hundred Egyptians.
AESCHYLUS
  Let's have no more of this line-by-line stuff! Let him
  Get into the scales with his children and his wife,
  And Cephisophon – why, his books as well!
  I'd only have to recite two lines of my verse.   1410
    [PLUTO *rises from his seat and approaches* DIONYSUS.]
DIONYSUS [*to* PLUTO]
  These two men are my friends, and I don't wish to judge
  Between them – I don't want to be in either's bad books.
  The one I regard as a master and the other I enjoy.
PLUTO
  Then you'll have failed to achieve what you came here for.
DIONYSUS
  And if I do reach a decision?
PLUTO
  You can take the one you choose   1415
  Back up with you; that way you won't have come for
      nothing.
DIONYSUS
  Bless you!
  Now listen to me both of you.

I came down here for a poet. What for? So that
Our city might survive and still have choral festivals.
1420   So whoever is going to offer the city good advice
Is the one I've decided to take back with me.
First of all, what is each of your opinion
About Alcibiades? The city's in a quandary.

. . .

EURIPIDES
I despise the citizen who proves slow to help
His country but is quick to do her harm, who is
Alert to his own good but useless for the city's.
DIONYSUS
Well said, by Poseidon.
    [*to* AESCHYLUS]
1430   And what do you think?
AESCHYLUS
It isn't good to rear a lion cub within
The city walls, but if you do, and it has grown
To maturity, you must pander to its moods.
DIONYSUS
By Zeus our saviour, I can't make up my mind!
One spoke with insight, the other with clarity.
1435   Just tell me, each of you, one more suggestion
About a way the city might be saved.

. . .

EURIPIDES
I've got an idea I'd like to share with you.
DIONYSUS
Go on.
EURIPIDES
When we put our trust in what is now untrusted,
And untrust what now we trust—
DIONYSUS
How? I don't understand.
1445   Try to speak less unintelligibly and more clearly.

EURIPIDES
> If we stop trusting the politicians that we do, and start
> Making use of those we don't use at present—

DIONYSUS
> Then we come to safety?

EURIPIDES
> Yes – if we're faring badly with one we elected,
> We'll surely find salvation by doing the opposite.   1450

. . .

DIONYSUS [*to* AESCHYLUS]
> What about you? What do you say?

AESCHYLUS
> First tell me this: What kind
> Of people does the city uphold? Honest men?

DIONYSUS
> Of course not!   1455
> She hates them with a vengeance.

AESCHYLUS
> So she delights in worthless men?

DIONYSUS
> Not exactly, but she's forced to make do with them.

AESCHYLUS
> How can anyone save such a city, if
> She won't accept the woollen cloak or goatskin mantle?

DIONYSUS
> You'd better think of something if you want to head back
>   up.

AESCHYLUS
> I'll tell you up on earth; I don't want to down here.   1461

DIONYSUS
> Oh no you don't. Send your blessings from here.

AESCHYLUS
> The city will be safe when they regard the enemy's
> Land as their own and their own as the enemy's;
> The fleet as their wealth and their wealth as poverty.   1465

. . .

PLUTO
Please give your verdict.
DIONYSUS
This will be my decision between you:
'I'll choose whomsoever my soul desires'.
EURIPIDES
Now don't forget the gods by whom you swore
1470   That you would take me back home; choose your friends.
DIONYSUS
'It was my tongue that swore' – but I choose Aeschylus.
EURIPIDES
What have you done, you utter scum!
DIONYSUS
Me?
I just deemed Aeschylus the winner, and why not?
EURIPIDES
How can you look me in the eye after stooping so low?
DIONYSUS
1475   'What is low, if it seems not so' to the audience?
EURIPIDES
You bastard! Will you stand by and watch me die?
DIONYSUS
'Who knows if living is in fact dying', and breathing
Is eating, and sleep just a woolly blanket?
        [*Exit* EURIPIDES.]
CHORUS
Happy the man who has
Accurate perception.
Examples are plenty.
1485   This man, for his evident good sense,
Will be returning home again,
A blessing to his people,
A blessing also to his
Family and friends;
1490   All because of his intelligence.

So it is not becoming to sit
Next to Socrates and jabber,

Discarding artistic merit
And passing up what is best
Of the tragedian's craft.   1495
To squander time idly
On pretentious discussions
And pedantic twaddle
Is the mark of a mindless man.

EXTRACTS FROM
POETICS
BY
ARISTOTLE

Preface to *Poetics*

Aristotle was born at Stagira, in Macedonia, in 384 BC. He studied in Athens for twenty years under Plato at his Academy before returning home to become the tutor of Philip II of Macedon's youngest son, later Alexander the Great. When Alexander became king, Aristotle went back to Athens to establish his own academic institution, the Lyceum. After Alexander's death, Aristotle fled Athens, where there was hostility towards Macedonians, to Chalcis in Euboea. He died there a year later in 322.

The date of the *Poetics* is uncertain, although the fact that it seems to presume a knowledge of other works by Aristotle (mainly *Ethics* and *Rhetoric*) suggests that it may have been a relatively late work. The surviving text resembles lecture notes, and was probably intended for Aristotle's students at the Lyceum rather than being a completed version for publication. The unpolished form of the *Poetics* as we have it has both advantages and disadvantages. It means that Aristotle does not make compromises for a wider readership, but it also means that ideas are often elliptically expressed and contain ambiguities. Still, the *Poetics* is arguably the more intriguing for coming down to us in the form that it is.

There are many reasons for including selections from *Poetics* in a volume such as this. The vast influence of *Poetics* upon subsequent criticism – both later European criticism (despite its sometimes questionable interpretation of Aristotle's views) and our own literary-critical perspectives – and the quality of Aristotle's thought are justification enough. There are, however, two specific reasons for its inclusion here. The first is that

Poetics is the earliest extant work of literary criticism to offer a systematic and self-contained theoretical investigation of poetry in general and tragedy in particular. Before Aristotle, the only substantial examinations of poetry occur in Old Comedy and Plato;[1] and the only detailed considerations of tragedy are in Aristophanes.[2] What literary criticism exists elsewhere, in poetry or philosophy, tends to involve passing reflections on the nature of poetry or poets. Homer and Hesiod, for example, both see poetry as divinely inspired, the former regarding its main function as providing pleasure, while the latter sees it as primarily instructive. Philosophers before Socrates (known as the Pre-Socratics) criticize Homeric passages on a variety of grounds. Xenophanes, for example, disapproved of Homer's presentation of the gods as having scant regard for morality. But the most significant consideration of poetry in philosophy prior to the *Poetics* is in Plato's *Republic* (books 3 and 10), where Socrates adopts a famously hostile attitude towards it.[3] He criticizes poetry on moral grounds: much of it, he argues, misrepresents gods and heroes by showing them in an unfavourable light; and poetry in which people behave in immoral ways may also have a negative effect on the young.

Plato also denounces poetry on metaphysical grounds. A major idea developed in the *Republic* is that everything which exists in the world is an imperfect copy of a perfect version – or 'form' – in another, ideal metaphysical realm (this is usually referred to as the Theory of Forms). For Plato poetic imitation (*mimêsis*) is an imitative representation of what is already imperfect, and is therefore at an even greater remove from the truth.[4] Aristotle's positive account of poetry in the *Poetics* may be seen, in part, as an implicit response to Plato's attack on it.

A second reason for including the *Poetics* in this volume is that it provides a radically different ancient perspective on tragedy from that of Aristophanes' *Frogs*. The *Frogs* was written by an Athenian contemporary of Euripides and Sophocles, at the end of the period in which Athens was the dominant imperial power among the Greeks; *Poetics* was written some time in the mid-fourth century by a non-Athenian, after the period in which tragedy (and Old Comedy) flourished, and at a time when

Athens' hegemony within the Greek world was long past. In Aristophanes' day, Euripides was seen as a controversial, avant-garde figure. By the time Aristotle was writing, his plays were arguably more popular and more widely known than those of Aeschylus and Sophocles.[5] A further difference lies in the nature of the two works. As an exuberant work of comic drama the *Frogs* could not be more different in spirit or temperament from the *Poetics*, a philosophically grounded theory of art in the form of lecture notes. *Poetics* also reflects certain general changes from fifth- to fourth-century perceptions of tragedy. Very little importance is attached to the role of the chorus and it is suggested that the role of gods in the action of the play should be kept to a minimum. In the fifth century both gods and the chorus were still major aspects of tragedy, although the direction of change is made evident in Aristophanes' *Frogs* by Euripides, who criticizes Aeschylus' long choral odes and the relative lack of complexity in the action of his plays.

As a complementary perspective on tragedy to that of the *Frogs* from a time when tragedy was still being written and performed, and as the work of an extraordinary philosopher and polymath, Aristotle's *Poetics* is an invaluable text for our understanding both of Greek tragedy in general and of its reception in the ancient world in particular. There is no room here for a detailed explanation of the ideas running through *Poetics*, either in isolation or in the context of Aristotle's broader philosophical thought; nor is there scope for discussing the place of the *Poetics* within ancient literary criticism as a whole.[6] What follows is a simple outline of the main ideas developed in *Poetics* that are of particular interest to the student of Greek tragedy. Attention will also be drawn to key areas of contention in the interpretation of *Poetics*, and to Aristotle's positive response to some of Plato's seemingly negative pronouncements on poetry.

In the opening paragraph of the *Poetics* Aristotle announces a dual interest in the interpretation of existing poetry and in setting out prescriptions for poetic composition. While this is couched in general terms, it soon becomes clear that his

principal interest, in the surviving book of *Poetics* at any rate,
is tragedy.[7]

1. Mimesis

Aristotle begins his theoretical examination of poetry by con-
struing it as a species of imitation (*mimêsis*). It is notoriously
difficult to capture the full sense of the Greek word *mimêsis* in
English. It is sometimes translated as 'representation' or simply
left as 'mimesis'.[8] No single term is wholly satisfactory. While
'imitation' captures the sense in which *mimêsis* is a copy or
version of its object, 'representation' reflects the potentially
altered or oblique relationship between *mimêsis* and its object.
For Plato *mimêsis* is straightforwardly imitative representation
(he therefore sees poets as guilty of misrepresentation when they
show gods, who should be perfect, acting immorally). Aristotle
sees *mimêsis* as a potentially more variable form of imitation.
He suggests, for example, that dancers can show character,
emotion and action through *mimêsis* (47a). Significantly, he
does not conceive of *mimêsis* as negative in itself, as Plato does
(see above, p. 228). Mimetic art is not considered false or
removed from the truth on metaphysical grounds, rather it is
seen simply as *fictional*. This is further suggested by Aristotle's
observation that while both Homer and Empedocles write in
dactylic hexameter verse, the former is a poet and the latter a
natural scientist (47b).[9] Aristotle's later point that poetry, while
fictional, is interested in universal truths (51a–b) further serves
to exempt mimetic art from Plato's charge of being counterfeit
and unreal.

Mimetic art is categorized according to its having different
media, objects or modes. Different media include literature (for
which, Aristotle notes, there was no name in his day), painting,
dance and music. With certain genres, two or more media
may be combined (tragedy and comedy, for example, involve
literature or poetry, music and dance). By different objects,
Aristotle means that poetry presents people who are either better
than us, worse than us, or the same as us. Tragedy presents
characters who are better than us, while comedy presents

characters who are worse. The way in which Aristotle couches
this distinction (i.e., as 'different objects') is somewhat unhelpful. Tragedy does not present better people so much as render
the people it presents as more admirable or elevated. Comedy,
likewise, does not necessarily show worse people – comedies
involving mythological burlesque may include the same figures
who also appear in epic and tragedy (e.g., Dionysus, Heracles,
Odysseus) – so much as portray its characters as more ridiculous.
What Aristotle regards as a case of different 'objects' seems
closer to being a different overall treatment of characters and
their actions. By different modes Aristotle means forms such as
dramatic, narrative and lyric poetry.

2. The Origins and Evolution of Poetry

In chapter four Aristotle considers the origins and evolution
of poetry. He counters Plato's assessment of poetry in strict
metaphysical and moral terms by offering a more psychologi-
cally and aesthetically grounded view of poetry as a mimetic
art. As creators of art, he says, we take pleasure in the act of
mimêsis. As consumers of art, we take pleasure in understanding
things for what they are meant to be. He further suggests,
with reference to painting, that whether or not we recognize
something for what it is, we still appreciate aesthetic criteria
such as colour and execution (48b).

Aristotle divides poetry into serious and trivial genres. In
doing so he makes a highly questionable set of alignments
between a genre, its content and its author. He sees writers of
serious genres, who concern themselves with fine actions (i.e.,
those of fine persons), as serious-minded themselves; conversely,
he sees writers of trivial genres, who concern themselves with
inferior people, as trivial themselves. This position is somewhat
undermined by the subsequent postulation that Homer is the
pivotal figure in the evolution both of serious and trivial genres.
Homer is seen as reaching perfection within epic by making it
as dramatic as possible (i.e., having as much dialogue and as
little narration as the narrative form allows), thereby pointing
the way towards tragedy. He is also seen as anticipating the

form of comedy: his humorous work *Margites* is regarded by Aristotle as standing in the same relation to comedy as the *Iliad* and *Odyssey* to tragedy. Though Aristotle does not make it clear at this point, the evolution from epic to tragedy is seen as an indication of tragedy's superiority. The point is taken up in the closing section of *Poetics* (61b–62a; not included in this selection), where Aristotle argues that the dramatic mode is better than the narrative mode inasmuch as it is a more economical means of organizing action or plot. Here it is merely stated that epic and comedy – the former a serious but less evolved mode than drama, the latter dramatic but trivial – will be treated later, and that tragedy, the most evolved of all forms of poetry, will be examined forthwith.

3. A Definition of Tragedy

In chapter six Aristotle offers a formal definition of tragedy as the imitation of an action that is admirable (i.e., serious/not trivial), complete and of sufficient magnitude. Other conditions are also specified: tragedy has certain distinct formal units or sections; it is performed by actors; it is dramatic. There is also a final specification, one of the most widely known and commonly debated remarks in the *Poetics*, namely that tragedy brings about 'through pity and fear the purification of such emotions'. The original Greek is ambiguous and, largely as a result of this, Aristotle's precise meaning is unclear. The word for 'purification', *catharsis*, may alternatively be translated as 'purgation'. If *catharsis* means purgation then Aristotle seems to be saying that tragedy rids us of pity and fear; if, on the other hand, it does mean purification then Aristotle's meaning seems to be that tragedy renders harmless, or neutralizes, the harmful emotions of pity and fear. There is at least one further possibility. The Greek may be construed as meaning that tragedy brings about, through events involving pity and fear, the purification of such events (rather than the emotions themselves).[10] Aristotle only uses the term *catharsis* once in *Poetics*. It appears in the *Politics* but the meaning there is unclear since Aristotle refers the reader to his discussion of *catharsis* in the *Poetics*; this discussion is missing from our text and must therefore come from the lost, published version of *Poetics*. While the issue of interpretation remains an open one, what does emerge more clearly is that for Aristotle pity and fear are emotions that have a special connection with tragedy.

4. The Component Parts of Tragedy

Aristotle offers six component parts of tragedy. These are listed on more than one occasion with slight variations in the order, but the order of importance is clearly indicated. The terms are usually given as plot, character (or characterization), reasoning, diction, song and spectacle.[11] It is clear throughout chapters four to nine that, as far as Aristotle is concerned, plot is of paramount importance. We are told that the plot must have a clear beginning, middle and end; also, that it must be of a certain length, one that can be kept in the memory at a single reading or viewing. Other significant aspects of Aristotle's principles for representing action are that the plot must be unified; that it must have a determinate structure; that it must have nothing unnecessary or extraneous; and that it should be such that the removal or alteration of any one part would (adversely) affect the whole. An important part of Aristotle's attempt to raise the status of poetry as a whole, and tragedy in particular, is his insistence that the poet does not deal in particulars, as the historian does, but in universal truths. Tragedy presents hypothetical, or fictional, situations and follows them through to their conclusion in accordance with necessity and probability. Thus, Aristotle contends, poetry is more philosophical and serious than history.[12]

Aristotle expresses a preference for plots which involve a change of fortune through reversals (actions with outcomes contrary to expectation) or recognition (a change from ignorance to knowledge). Such plots are termed complex rather than simple. He also regards a double plot involving a change from bad fortune to good for good characters and from good fortune to bad for bad characters as improper for tragedy (and more in keeping with comedy). Instead he suggests that tragedy should involve a single change from good fortune to bad. Aristotle's description of the sort of character who should suffer such a change of fortune is another well-known and contentious passage. The sufferer in a tragedy should not, he suggests, be conspicuously good or bad, but should be from a noble family (from mythology). His or her bad fortune should come about not through any inherent immorality but through what Aristotle simply calls an 'error' (*hamartia*). This idea of *hamartia* is vital to Aristotle's understanding of tragedy. He says that tragedy should not provide moral satisfaction (in the way that tragedies with a double plot do; see above), because moral satisfaction is incompatible with the effect of pity and fear. As an example Aristotle suggests that a man rightfully injuring his enemies does not evoke pity or fear, whereas a person harming his own family or friends does. To create pity and fear tragedy must present characters acting against the interests of those near to them, or their own interests, through some sort of error of judgement. *Hamartia* may have a moral component but it does not imply that the character committing the error is immoral by nature. In later European criticism the notion of *hamartia* was reinterpreted as an ingrained 'tragic flaw'. While *hamartia* may be symptomatic of a deep-seated characteristic, there is nothing in Aristotle to suggest that he sees a tragic figure as requiring a clearly identifiable character flaw.

As far as character is concerned, Aristotle says that characters should be good, appropriately characterized (men, women and slaves should be characterized as befits their station), lifelike and consistent. He adds that characterization, like plot, should be in accordance with necessity and probability. On diction or poetic style, while valuing clarity, Aristotle nonetheless suggests that tragedy must balance clarity with dignity (the clearest or most simple style being too plain or conversational).

The final third of the *Poetics* is largely concerned with detailed points about style and the classification of literary and linguistic terms. It concludes with a comparison of epic and tragedy, in which tragedy emerges as superior. There are, however, two interesting remarks made in passing about the imaginative faculties of the poet. The first concerns the poet's ability to visualize the action, something which is seen as essential to the composition of a good plot. Aristotle suggests that gesture is a useful means of imagining the emotions of a play's characters. He concludes that, to create action authentically and empathize successfully with his characters, the poet must be naturally gifted or mad. The second remark is made in connection with diction. Aristotle says that the most important aspect of style is metaphor. He warns that this cannot be learnt but that it is 'a sign of natural talent'.

5. Conclusion

One of the most impressive qualities of the *Poetics* is the way in which Aristotle successfully balances competing interests. He integrates his theory of poetry both with his views of human nature and habits and with his general method of starting from first principles and considering the ultimate end or aim (*telos*) of his object of inquiry. At the same time his approach is in many ways a pragmatic one. There is a carefully sustained ambivalence throughout the *Poetics* as to the extent to which poetry is a discipline (the Greek word is *techne*, which can mean any or all of art, craft, skill or expertise) and the extent to which it is dependent upon instinct and natural ability. As far as interpretation of poetry (and, more specifically, tragedy) is concerned, Aristotle largely draws on works he admires, and makes his prescriptions for composition accordingly. So despite being theoretically integrated with Aristotle's wider philosophical thought, *Poetics* is a strongly aesthetic theory. This is a vital aspect of his response to Plato. Plato's approach to poetry is very much a moral one, in which he considers whether poetry is harmful or beneficial; arguing the case on metaphysical as well as moral grounds, he concludes that poetry is harmful in the ideal community. Aristotle plays down moral or political considerations about the effect of poetry. He primarily considers what makes for good or bad poetry in accordance with its stated artistic objectives.

Aristotle's view of tragedy is nonetheless a reductive one. Tragedy is seen as having a specific end or *telos* (i.e., the definition given in chapter six; see above), and assessed solely in terms of its successful pursuit of that end. This is consistent with Aristotle's manifest preference for Sophocles above all other tragedians. What partly distinguishes Sophoclean tragedy from Aeschylean and Euripidean tragedy is its tighter control of action and its greater economy and sense of cumulative effect. Aeschylus' plays are perhaps too simple in their plot structure for Aristotle's tastes, and they place too much emphasis on the role of the chorus and the gods. Euripidean tragedy, while consistent with a number of Aristotelian principles, makes a point of debunking tragic grandeur and heroism. This is something that is inimical to Aristotle's outlook: for him tragedy should show people as admirable or dignified. In addition, Euripides does not adhere as strictly as Sophocles to Aristotelian prescriptions for action and characterization.[13]

Aristotle makes it clear that he regards tragedy and epic as the two highest genres of poetry. One of his main reasons for considering tragedy to be superior to epic is that it is a more concentrated form of poetry, which achieves its end more economically. It is hardly surprising, then, that for Aristotle Sophocles is the greatest exponent of tragedy. The most important part of tragedy, according to Aristotle – what he calls 'the source and (as it were) the soul of tragedy' – is the organization of action. Such a perspective tallies closely with features of Sophoclean tragedy. The respective merits of Aeschylean and Euripidean tragedy – and there are many – are less closely connected with the organization of action itself. As such their styles of tragedy are more open to objections on the grounds of taste, as is evident from passing remarks in the *Poetics* and from Aristophanes' *Frogs*. Sophocles' intense concentration on the development of action to its logical conclusion means that there is very little that is non-essential in his plays. It is telling in this regard that while Aristotle in the *Poetics* and Aristophanes in the *Frogs* differ significantly in their overall outlook on tragedy, they concur in having little or nothing to find fault with in the plays of Sophocles.

NOTES

1. There are a number of plays by writers of Old Comedy centred on particular poets (e.g., Hesiod and Archilochus) and their poetry, but there is no evidence of a play based specifically on tragedy, or on one or more tragedians, by any comic playwright other than Aristophanes; on Plato see below.

2. Aristophanes shows a preoccupation with tragedy throughout his extant works. The *Frogs* is the only extant play to assess the evolution of the genre as a whole. Elsewhere Aristophanes tends to focus primarily on Euripides and particular aspects of Euripidean tragedy. In *Acharnians*, Euripides appears in one scene and the play itself is largely based on a comic reworking of one of his plays (*Telephus*). In *Thesmophoriazusae*, Euripides is the hero of the play and there is a detailed examination of various aspects of Euripidean tragedy from his earlier works to his most recent. Euripides is also known to have appeared as a character in at least one other lost play of Aristophanes.

3. The views of Socrates are filtered through Plato's representation of them in his dialogues. Issues concerning the extent to which Plato's dialogues are a reflection of Socrates' views or Plato's own are extraordinarily complex and cannot be addressed here.

4. It should be borne in mind that Plato's aim in the *Republic* is to outline a model for the ideal city-state, and that the view of poetry expressed there is subordinate to this interest; elsewhere, Plato expresses his admiration for poets (he also wrote poetry himself).

5. Aristotle discusses or cites Euripides and Sophocles on a comparable number of occasions; Aeschylus is mentioned a number of times, but less frequently than the other two.

6. There is a vast amount of critical literature – ancient, early modern and modern – on both these areas.

7. The content of Aristotle's lost second book of *Poetics*, which deals with comedy, has been the subject of much speculation and debate.

8. Other possible translations include 'enactment' or 'version'. *Mimêsis* has even been translated differently at different points within the same translation. In this translation 'imitation' is used throughout.

9. See note 7 to the text of *Poetics*.

10. This suggestion first appears in G. Else, *Aristotle's Poetics* (Cambridge, Mass.: Harvard University Press, 1957).

11. It has been suggested that the ordering of the parts of tragedy may also refer to a chronological order for the composition of tragedy.

12. Aristotle suggests in his *Ethics* that the highest calling of man is to be engaged in philosophical contemplation (*theoria*). The poet is therefore not in danger of achieving the same status as the philosopher. The dictum about universals is also applied to comedy. This strongly suggests that Aristotle sees Old Comedy, which frequently includes real-life characters (such as Aeschylus and Euripides in the *Frogs*) and therefore deals in particulars, as inferior to New Comedy, which is peopled by generic (i.e., universalized) characters.

13. Aristotle cites what he considers the improbable and unnecessary escape in a flying chariot at the end of *Medea* as an example of an unsatisfactory departure from his prescriptions for action.

1. Introduction

Let us discuss the art of poetry in general and its species – the effect which each species of poetry has and the correct way to construct plots if the composition is to be of high quality, as well as the number and nature of its component parts, and any other questions that arise within the same field of enquiry.[1] We should begin, as is natural, by taking first principles first.

2. Poetry as a Species of Imitation

Epic poetry and the composition of tragedy, as well as comedy and the arts of dithyrambic poetry and (for the most part) of music for pipe or lyre, are all (taken together) *imitations*.[2] They can be differentiated from each other in three respects: in respect of their different *media* of imitation, or different *objects*, or a different *mode* (i.e. a different manner).[3]

2.1 Medium

Some people use the medium of colour and shape to produce imitations of various objects by making visual images (some through art, some through practice); others do this by means of the voice.[4] Similarly in the case of the arts I have mentioned: in all of them the medium of imitation is rhythm, language and melody, but these may be employed either separately or in combination. For example, music for pipe or lyre (and any other arts which have a similar effect, e.g. music for pan-pipes) uses melody and rhythm only, while dance uses rhythm by itself and without melody (since dancers too imitate character, emotion and action by means of rhythm expressed in movement).

The art which uses language unaccompanied, either in prose 47b or in verse (either combining verse-forms with each other or using a single kind of verse), remains without a name to the present day.[5] We have no general term referring to the mimes of Sophron and Xenarchus and Socratic dialogues,[6] nor to any imitation that one might produce using iambic trimeters, elegiac couplets or any other such verse-form. Admittedly people attach 'poetry' to the name of the verse-form, and thus refer to 'elegiac poets' and 'hexameter poets'; i.e. they do not call people 'poets' because they produce imitations, but indiscriminately on the basis of their use of verse. In fact, even if someone publishes a medical or scientific text in verse, people are in the habit of applying the same term. But Homer and Empedocles have nothing in common except the form of verse they use; so it would be fair to call the former a poet, but the latter a natural scientist rather than a poet.[7] . . .

There are also some arts which use all the media mentioned above (i.e. rhythm, melody and verse), e.g. dithyrambic and nomic poetry,[8] tragedy and comedy; these differ in that the former use them all simultaneously, the latter in distinct parts.

These, then, are what I mean by differences between the arts in the medium of imitation.

2.2 *Object*

Those who imitate, imitate agents; and these must be either 48a admirable or inferior. (Character almost always corresponds to just these two categories, since everyone is differentiated in character by defect or excellence.) Alternatively they must be better people than we are, or worse, or of the same sort.[9] . . . These dissimilarities are possible in dance and in music for pipe or lyre, and also in connection with language and unaccompanied verse (for example, Homer imitates better people; Cleophon people similar to us; Hegemon of Thasos, who invented parodies, or Nicochares, the author of the *Deiliad*, worse people).[10] . . . The very same difference distinguishes tra-

gedy and comedy from each other; the latter aims to imitate
people worse than our contemporaries, the former better.

2.3 Mode

A third difference between them is the mode in which one may
imitate each of these objects. It is possible to imitate the same
objects in the same medium sometimes by narrating (either using
a different *persona*, as in Homer's poetry, or as the same person
without variation), or else with all the imitators as agents and
engaged in activity.[11]

So imitation can be differentiated in these three respects, as
we said at the outset: medium, object and mode. So in one
respect Sophocles would be the same kind of imitator as Homer,
since both imitate admirable people, but in another the same as
Aristophanes, since both imitate agents and people doing things.
This is the reason – some say – for the term 'drama': i.e. that the
poets imitate people doing things.[12] . . .

3. The Anthropology and History of Poetry

3.1 Origins

In general, two causes seem likely to have given rise to the art
of poetry, both of them natural.[13]

Imitation comes naturally to human beings from childhood
(and in this they differ from other animals, i.e. in having a strong
propensity to imitation and in learning their earliest lessons
through imitation); so does the universal pleasure in imitations.
What happens in practice is evidence of this: we take delight in
viewing the most accurate possible images of objects which
in themselves cause distress when we see them (e.g. the shapes
of the lowest species of animal, and corpses). The reason for
this is that understanding is extremely pleasant, not just for
philosophers but for others too in the same way, despite their
limited capacity for it.[14] This is the reason why people take
delight in seeing images; what happens is that as they view them
they come to understand and work out what each thing is (e.g.
'This is so-and-so'). If one happens not to have seen the thing

before, it will not give pleasure as an imitation, but because of its execution or colour, or for some other reason.[15]

Given, then, that imitation is natural to us, and also melody and rhythm (it being obvious that verse-forms are segments of rhythm),[16] from the beginning those who had the strongest natural inclination towards these things generated poetry out of improvised activities by a process of gradual innovation.

3.2 Early history

Poetry bifurcated in accordance with the corresponding kinds of character: more serious-minded people imitated fine actions, i.e. those of fine persons; more trivial people imitated those of inferior persons (the latter at first composing invectives, while the others composed hymns and encomia).[17] . . . Just as Homer was the outstanding poet of the serious kind, since he did not just compose well but also made his imitations dramatic,[18] so too he was the first to adumbrate the form of comedy; what he composed was not an invective, but a dramatization of the laughable. His *Margites* stands in the same relation to comedy as the *Iliad* and *Odyssey* do to tragedy.[19] When tragedy and comedy made their appearance those who inclined towards either kind of poetry became, in accordance with their nature, poets of comedy (instead of lampoons) or of tragedy (instead of epic), because these forms were greater and more highly esteemed than the others.[20]

49a

3.3 Tragedy

. . . Originally it developed from improvisations. (This is true of tragedy, and also of comedy: the former arose from the leaders of the dithyramb, the latter from the leaders of the phallic songs which are still customary even now in many cities.[21]) Then tragedy was gradually enhanced as people developed each new aspect of it that came to light. After undergoing many transformations tragedy came to rest, because it had attained its natural state.

The number of actors was increased from one to two by Aeschylus, who also reduced the choral parts and made the spoken word play the leading role;[22] the third actor and scene-painting were introduced by Sophocles.[23] In addition, the magnitude increased from short plots; and in place of comic diction, as a consequence of a change from the satyric style, tragedy acquired dignity at a late stage, and the iambic verse-form was adopted instead of the trochaic tetrameter.[24] (They used tetrameters at first because the composition was satyric in manner, and more akin to dance. But when speech was introduced nature itself found the appropriate form of verse, iambic being the verse-form closest to speech. There is evidence of this: we speak iambics in conversation with each other very often, but rarely dactylic hexameters – and only when we depart from the normal conversational tone.) . . .

3.4 Comedy

Comedy is (as we have said) an imitation of inferior people – not, however, with respect to every kind of defect: the laughable is a species of what is disgraceful. The laughable is an error or disgrace that does not involve pain or destruction; for example, a comic mask is ugly and distorted, but does not involve pain.[25]

. . . Comedy already had some of its features before there is any mention of those identified as comic poets, and it is not known who introduced masks, prologues, the number of actors and so forth. But plot-construction came originally from Sicily; among Athenian poets it was Crates who first abandoned the form of a lampoon and began to construct universalized stories and plots.[26]

3.5 Epic

Epic poetry corresponds to tragedy in so far as it is an imitation in verse of admirable people. But they differ in that epic uses one verse-form alone, and is narrative. They also differ in length, since tragedy tries so far as possible to keep within a single day, or not to exceed it by much, whereas epic is unrestricted in time, and differs in this respect.[27] (At first, however, people used to make no distinction between tragedy and epic in this respect.)

Some of the component parts are common to both, others are peculiar to tragedy. Consequently anyone who understands what is good and bad in tragedy also understands about epic, since anything that epic poetry has is also present in tragedy, but what is present in tragedy is not all in epic poetry.

4. Tragedy: Definition and Analysis

4.1 Definition

... Tragedy is an imitation of an action that is admirable, complete and possesses magnitude; in language made pleasurable, each of its species separated in different parts; performed by actors, not through narration; effecting through pity and fear the purification of such emotions.[28]

(By 'language made pleasurable' I mean that which possesses rhythm and melody, i.e. song. By the separation of its species I mean that some parts are composed in verse alone; others by contrast make use of song.)

4.2 Component parts

Since the imitation is performed by actors, it follows first of all that the management of the *spectacle* must be a component part of tragedy. Then there is *lyric poetry* and *diction*, since these are the medium in which the actors perform the imitation. (By 'diction' I mean the actual composition of the verse; what is meant by 'lyric poetry' is self-evident.)

Now, tragedy is an imitation of an action, and the action is performed by certain agents. These must be people of a certain kind with respect to their character and reasoning. (It is on the basis of people's character and reasoning that we say that their 50a actions are of a certain kind, and in respect of their actions that people enjoy success or failure.) So *plot* is the imitation of the action (by 'plot' here I mean the organization of events); *character* is that in respect of which we say that the agent is of a certain kind; and *reasoning* is the speech which the agents use to argue a case or put forward an opinion.

So tragedy as a whole necessarily has six component parts, which determine the tragedy's quality: i.e. plot, character, diction, reasoning, spectacle and lyric poetry. The medium of imitation comprises two parts, the mode one, and the object three; and there is nothing apart from these.

4.3 The primacy of plot

Virtually all tragedians, one might say, use these formal elements; for in fact every drama alike has spectacle, character, plot, diction, song and reasoning. But the most important of them is the structure of the events:

(i)   Tragedy is not an imitation of persons, but of actions and of life. Well-being and ill-being reside in action, and the goal of life is an activity, not a quality; people possess certain qualities in accordance with their character, but they achieve well-being or its opposite on the basis of how they fare. So the imitation of character is not the purpose of what the agents do; character is included along with and on account of the actions. So the events, i.e. the plot, are what tragedy is there for, and that is the most important thing of all.[29]

(ii) Furthermore, there could not be a tragedy without action, but there could be one without character. The tragedies of most modern poets lack character, and in general there are many such poets. Compare, among painters, the relation between Zeuxis and Polygnotus: the latter is good at depicting character, but Zeuxis' painting has no character.

(iii) Also, if one were to compose a series of speeches expressive of character, however successful they are in terms of diction and reasoning, it will not achieve the stated function of tragedy; a tragedy which, though it uses these elements less adequately, has a plot and a structure of events will do so much more effectively.

(iv) Additionally, the most important devices by which tragedy sways emotion are parts of the plot, i.e. reversals and recognitions.

(v)   A further indication is that those who are trying to write poetry are capable of accuracy in diction and character before they can construct the events; compare too almost all the early poets.

4.4 *The ranking completed*

So the plot is the source and (as it were) the soul of tragedy;
character is second. (It is much the same in the case of painting:
if someone were to apply exquisitely beautiful colours at random
he would give less pleasure than if he had outlined an image in
black and white.) Tragedy is an imitation of an action, and on
account above all of the action it is an imitation of agents.

Third is reasoning. This is the ability to say what is implicit
in a situation and appropriate to it, which in prose is the function
of the arts of statesmanship and of rhetoric. Older poets used
to make people speak like statesmen; contemporary poets make
them speak rhetorically.[30] Character is the kind of thing which
discloses the nature of a choice; for this reason speeches in which
there is nothing at all which the speaker chooses or avoids do
not possess character. Reasoning refers to the means by which
people argue that something is or is not the case, or put forward
some universal proposition.

Fourth is diction. By 'diction' I mean, as was said before,
verbal expression; this has the same effect both in verse and in
prose speeches.

Of the remaining parts, song is the most important of the
sources of pleasure. Spectacle is attractive, but is very inartistic
and is least germane to the art of poetry. For the effect of tragedy
is not dependent on performance and actors; also, the art of
the property-manager has more relevance to the production of
visual effects than does that of the poets.[31]

5. Plot: Basic Concepts

5.1 *Completeness*

We have laid down that tragedy is an imitation of a complete,
i.e. whole, action, possessing a certain magnitude. (There is such
a thing as a whole which possesses no magnitude.) A *whole* is
that which has a beginning, a middle and an end. A *beginning*
is that which itself does not follow necessarily from anything
else, but some second thing naturally exists or occurs after it.
Conversely, an *end* is that which does itself naturally follow

from something else, either necessarily or in general, but there is nothing else after it. A *middle* is that which itself comes after something else, and some other thing comes after it. Well-constructed plots should therefore not begin or end at any arbitrary point, but should employ the stated forms.[32]

5.2 Magnitude

Any beautiful object, whether a living organism or any other entity composed of parts, must not only possess those parts in proper order, but its *magnitude* also should not be arbitrary; beauty consists in magnitude as well as order. For this reason no organism could be beautiful if it is excessively small (since observation becomes confused as it comes close to having no perceptible duration in time) or excessively large (since the observation is then not simultaneous, and the observers find that the sense of unity and wholeness is lost from their observation, e.g. if there were an animal a thousand miles long). So just as in the case of physical objects and living organisms, they should possess a certain magnitude, and this should be such as can readily be taken in at one view, so in the case of plots: they should have a certain length, and this should be such as can readily be held in memory.[33] . . .

51a

5.3 Unity

A plot is not (as some think) unified because it is concerned with a single person. An indeterminately large number of things happen to any one person, not all of which constitute a unity; likewise a single individual performs many actions, and they do not make up a single action. So it is clear that a mistake has been made by all those poets who have composed a *Heracleid* or *Theseid*, or poems of that kind, on the assumption that, just because Heracles was one person, the plot too is bound to be unified. Just as Homer excels in other respects, he seems to have seen this point clearly as well, whether through art or instinct.[34] When he composed the *Odyssey* he did not include everything which happened to Odysseus (e.g. the wounding on Parnassus and the pretence of madness during the mobilization: the occurrence of either of these events did not make the occurrence of

the other necessary or probable); instead, he constructed the
Odyssey about a single action of the kind we are discussing.
The same is true of the *Iliad*.[35]

5.4 *Determinate structure*

Just as in other imitative arts the imitation is unified if it imitates
a single object, so too the plot, as the imitation of an action,
should imitate a single, unified action – and one that is also a
whole. So the structure of the various sections of the events must
be such that the transposition or removal of any one section
dislocates and changes the whole. If the presence or absence of
something has no discernible effect, it is not a part of the whole.[36]

5.5 *Universality*

It is also clear from what has been said that the function of the
poet is not to say what *has* happened, but to say the kind of
thing that *would* happen, i.e. what is possible in accordance
with probability or necessity. The historian and the poet are not
distinguished by their use of verse or prose; it would be possible
to turn the works of Herodotus into verse, and it would be a
history in verse just as much as in prose. The distinction is this:
the one says what has happened, the other the kind of thing that
would happen.

For this reason poetry is more philosophical and more serious
than history. Poetry tends to express universals, and history
particulars. The *universal* is the kind of speech or action which
is consonant with a person of a given kind in accordance with
probability or necessity;[37] this is what poetry aims at, even
though it applies individual names. The particular is the actions
or experiences of (e.g.) Alcibiades.

In the case of comedy this is in fact clear. The poets construct
the plot on the basis of probabilities, and then supply names
of their own choosing; they do not write about a particular
individual, as the lampoonists do.[38] In the case of tragedy they
do keep to actual names. The reason for this is that what is
possible is plausible; we are disinclined to believe that what
has not happened is possible, but it is obvious that what has

51b

happened is possible – because it would not have happened if it were not . . .

6. Plot: Species and Components

6.1 Astonishment

The imitation is not just of a complete action, but also of events that evoke fear and pity. These effects occur above all when things come about contrary to expectation but because of one another. This will be more astonishing than if they come about spontaneously or by chance, since even chance events are found most astonishing when they appear to have happened as if for a purpose – as, for example, the statue of Mitys in Argos killed the man who was responsible for Mitys' death by falling on top of him as he was looking at it . . .

6.2 Simple and complex plots

Some plots are simple, others complex, since the actions of which the plots are imitations are themselves also of these two kinds. By a *simple* action I mean one which is, in the sense defined, continuous and unified, and in which the change of fortune comes about without reversal or recognition. By *complex*, I mean one in which the change of fortune involves reversal or recognition or both. These must arise from the actual structure of the plot, so that they come about as a result of what has happened before, out of necessity or in accordance with probability . . .

6.3 Reversal

A *reversal* is a change to the opposite in the actions being performed, as stated – and this, as we have been saying, in accordance with probability or necessity. For example, in the *Oedipus* someone came to give Oedipus good news and free him from his fear with regard to his mother, but by disclosing Oedipus' identity he brought about the opposite result.[39] . . .

6.4 Recognition

Recognition, as in fact the term indicates, is a change from ignorance to knowledge, disclosing either a close relationship or enmity, on the part of people marked out for good or bad fortune. Recognition is best when it occurs simultaneously with a reversal, like the one in the *Oedipus*.[40] . . .

6.6 Quantitative parts of tragedy

We have already mentioned the component parts of tragedy which should be regarded as its formal elements. In quantitative terms, the separate parts into which it is divided are as follows: prologue; episode; finale; choral parts, comprising entry-song and ode – these are common to all tragedies, while songs from the stage and dirges are found only in some.

The *prologue* is the whole part of a tragedy before the entry-song of the chorus; an *episode* is a whole part of a tragedy between whole choral songs; the *finale* is the whole part of a tragedy after which there is no choral song. Of the choral part, the *entry-song* is the first whole utterance of a chorus; an *ode* is a choral song without anapaests or trochaics; a *dirge* is a lament shared by the chorus and from the stage . . .

7. The Best Kinds of Tragic Plot

7.1 First introduction

What, then, should one aim at and what should one avoid in constructing plots? What is the source of the effect at which tragedy aims? . . .

7.2 First deduction

The construction of the best tragedy should be complex rather than simple; and it should also be an imitation of events that evoke fear and pity, since that is the distinctive feature of this kind of imitation. So it is clear first of all that decent men should not be seen undergoing a change from good fortune to bad fortune – this does not evoke fear or pity, but disgust. Nor should depraved people be seen undergoing a change from bad fortune to good fortune – this is the least tragic of all: it has none of the right effects, since it is neither agreeable, nor does it evoke pity or fear. Nor again should a very wicked person fall 53a from good fortune to bad fortune – that kind of structure would be agreeable, but would not excite pity or fear, since the one has to do with someone who is suffering undeservedly, the other with someone who is like ourselves (I mean, pity has to do with the undeserving sufferer, fear with the person like us); so what happens will evoke neither pity nor fear.

We are left, therefore, with the person intermediate between these. This is the sort of person who is not outstanding in moral excellence or justice; on the other hand, the change to bad fortune which he undergoes is not due to any moral defect or depravity, but to an error of some kind.[41] . . .

It follows that a well-formed plot will be simple[42] rather than (as some people say) double, and that it must involve a change not *to* good fortune *from* bad fortune, but (on the contrary) *from* good fortune *to* bad fortune – and this must be due not to depravity but to a serious error on the part of someone of the kind specified (or better than that, rather than worse) . . .

So the best tragedy, in artistic terms, is based on this structure. This is why those who criticize Euripides for doing this in his tragedies, most of which end in bad fortune, are making the same mistake . . . On stage and in performance people recognize that plays of this kind (provided that they are successfully executed) are the most tragic, and Euripides, even if his technique is faulty in other respects, is regarded as the most tragic of poets.

Second-best is the structure which some say comes first – that which has a double structure like the *Odyssey*, and which ends with the opposite outcome for better and worse people.[43] It is thought to come first because of the weakness of audiences; the poets follow the audiences' lead and compose whatever is to their taste. But this is not the pleasure which comes from tragedy; it is more characteristic of comedy . . .

7.3 Second introduction

It is possible for the evocation of fear and pity to result from the
53b spectacle, and also from the structure of the events itself. The
latter is preferable and is the mark of a better poet. The plot
should be constructed in such a way that, even without seeing
it, anyone who hears the events which occur shudders and feels
pity at what happens; this is how someone would react on
hearing the plot of the *Oedipus*.[44] ...

7.4 Second deduction

Let us therefore take up the question of what classes of events
appear terrible or pitiable ... What one should look for are
situations in which sufferings arise within close relationships,
e.g. brother kills brother, son father, mother son, or son mother
– or is on the verge of killing them, or does something else of
the same kind.

Now, one cannot undo traditional stories ... but one has to
discover for oneself how to use even the traditional stories well
... It is possible for the action to come about in the way that
the old poets used to do it, with people acting in full knowledge
and awareness; this is in fact how Euripides portrayed Medea
killing her children. It is also possible for the action to be
performed, but for the agents to do the terrible deed in ignorance
and only then to recognize the close connection, as in Sophocles'
Oedipus ... A third possibility besides these is for someone to
be on the verge of performing some irreparable deed through
ignorance, and for the recognition to pre-empt the act ...

Of these, being on the verge of acting wittingly and not doing
so is worst; this is disgusting, and is not tragic since there is no
54a suffering. So no one composes in this way, or only rarely (e.g.
Haemon and Creon in the *Antigone*).[45] Performing the action is
second; but it is better if the action is performed in ignorance
and followed by a recognition – there is nothing disgusting in
this, and the recognition has great emotional impact. But the
last case is best.[46] ...

8. Other Aspects of Tragedy

8.1 *Character*

... As for character, there are four things to aim at:

(i)   First and foremost, *goodness*. As was said earlier, speech
      or action will possess character if it discloses the nature of
      a deliberate choice; the character is good if the choice is
      good. This is possible in each class of person: there is such
      a thing as a good woman and a good slave, even though
      one of these is perhaps deficient and the other generally
      speaking inferior.[47]

(ii) Secondly, *appropriateness*: it is possible for the character
      to be courageous, but for this to be an inappropriate way
      for a woman to display courage or cleverness.

(iii) Thirdly, *likeness*: this is not the same as making character
      good and appropriate, as has already been stated.[48]

(iv) Fourthly, *consistency*: even if the subject of the imitation
      is inconsistent, and that is the kind of character that is
      presupposed, it should nevertheless be consistently incon-
      sistent.[49]

An example of unnecessary badness of character is Menelaus
in the *Orestes*; of impropriety and inappropriateness, Odysseus'
lament in the *Scylla* and Melanippe's speech. An example of
inconsistency is the *Iphigeneia in Aulis*: when she pleads for her
life to be spared she is not at all like her later self – but in
characterization, just as much as in the structure of events, one
ought always to look for what is necessary or probable ...

The resolutions of plots should also come about from the plot   54b
itself, and not by means of a theatrical device, as in the *Medea*.[50]
... A theatrical device may be used for things outside the play
– whether prior events which are beyond human knowledge, or
subsequent events which need prediction and narration – since
we grant that the gods can see everything. But there should be
nothing irrational in the events themselves; or, failing that,
it should be outside the play, as for example in Sophocles'
Oedipus ...

8.3 Visualizing the action

When constructing plots and working them out complete with their linguistic expression, one should so far as possible visualize what is happening. By envisaging things very vividly in this way, as if one were actually present at the events themselves, one can find out what is appropriate, and inconsistencies are least likely to be overlooked.[51] . . . .

One should also, as far as possible, work plots out using gestures. Given the same natural talent, those who are actually experiencing the emotions are the most convincing; someone who is distressed or angry acts out distress and irritation most authentically. (This is why the art of poetry belongs to people who are naturally gifted or mad; of these, the former are adaptable, and the latter are not in their right mind.) . . .

8.5 Complication and resolution

Every tragedy consists of a complication and a resolution. What is outside the play, and often some of what is inside, comprises the complication; the resolution is the rest. By *complication* I mean everything from the beginning up to and including the section which immediately precedes the change to good fortune or bad fortune; by *resolution* I mean everything from the beginning of the change of fortune to the end . . .

8.8 Astonishment

In reversals and in simple actions poets use astonishment to achieve their chosen aims; this is tragic and agreeable. This happens when someone who is clever but bad (like Sisyphus) is deceived, or someone who is courageous but unjust is defeated. There is no violation of probability in this; as Agathon said, it is probable for many improbable things to happen.[52]

8.9 The chorus

One should handle the chorus as one of the actors; it should be part of the whole and should contribute to the performance – not as in Euripides, but as in Sophocles.[53] . . .

9. Diction

... The most important quality in diction is clarity, provided there is no loss of dignity. The clearest diction is that based on current words; but that lacks dignity ... diction is distinguished and out of the ordinary when it makes use of exotic expressions – by which I mean non-standard words, metaphor, lengthening, and anything contrary to current usage. However, if one used nothing else the result would be a riddle or gibberish ...

A major contribution to a style that is both clear and out of the ordinary is made by lengthenings, abbreviations and alterations. The variation from current usage makes the diction out of the ordinary, because we are not used to it; but it has something in common with what we are used to, so it will be clear ... Admittedly, obtrusive use of this style is absurd; but moderation is equally necessary in all aspects of diction; using metaphors, non-standard words and the other categories in an inappropriate and deliberately absurd way would produce the same effect ...

It is important to use all the things I have mentioned appropriately ... but the most important thing is to be good at using metaphor. This is the one thing that cannot be learnt from someone else, and is a sign of natural talent; for the successful use of metaphor is a matter of perceiving similarities.

Notes

AGAMEMNON

0   PALACE AT ARGOS: Just in front of the palace are altars of Zeus, Apollo and Hermes. 'Argos' may be used to mean the city of Argos in particular or, in a more general sense, to mean the region or state of the north-eastern Peloponnese known as the Argolid. The two principal cities of the Argolid were Mycenae and Argos (see map, p. 306). Homer gives Mycenae as Agamemnon's capital, but at the time Aeschylus was writing, Argos had recently destroyed its rival Mycenae and had become an Athenian ally. This may inform the ambiguous use of the name 'Argos' throughout the play.

0   THE PALACE ROOF: In the ancient theatre the watchman would probably have been on the roof of the stage-building (*skene*), known as the *theologeion* – so-called because it is where divine characters usually appeared. On whether he is there as the play opens or he 'enters' on the stage-building see O. Taplin, *The Stagecraft of Aeschylus* (Oxford: Oxford University Press, 1977), pp. 276–7.

11 *A man-like will*: One of several descriptions of Clytemnestra's disposition and behaviour as man-like. Like Euripides' heroine Medea, she is presented as dangerous because she thinks like a man and can act decisively in conventionally male spheres of activity.

16 *Music is the one cure*: Such reflections by minor or lowly characters, or the chorus, are not uncommon in tragedy, especially in Euripides. The nurse in the prologue of *Medea* also reflects, somewhat cynically, on the healing power of music (see p. 143).

35 *My tongue is held*: Literally 'an ox sits on my tongue'. The ox was proverbial for an immovable weight.

37 *those / Who understand me*: The watchman presumably means

those who are aware of machinations in Argos during Agamemnon's absence.

00 CLYTEMNESTRA ENTERS: During the chorus' entrance-song (*parodos*) Clytemnestra performs sacrificial rituals at the altar of Zeus and possibly those of Apollo and Hermes. The precise moment of her entry has been much debated. It has been argued that she enters at the same time as the chorus, but most scholars suggest that she enters shortly before the chorus address her directly ('daughter of Tyndareus . . .', 84). For a discussion see Taplin, *The Stagecraft of Aeschylus*, pp. 40ff. and Frankel's commentary on the relevant lines in *Agamemnon* (Oxford: Oxford University Press, 1950).

The situation here, in which a major character is present on stage for some time without speaking while the chorus deliver a string of odes, is one for which Euripides criticizes Aeschylus in Aristophanes' *Frogs* (see p. 201).

44 *Hellas*: Hellas, throughout this translation, is synonymous with Greece.

49 *As eagles cry*: This simile involving Agamemnon and Menelaus being likened to birds of prey is adapted from two Homeric similes. In *Iliad* 16.428–30, the heroes Sarpedon (a son of Zeus, fighting on the Trojan side) and Patroclus, facing each other in a duel, are compared to screaming vultures; in *Odyssey* 16.216–18, in a very different context, Telemachus and Odysseus are likened to crying vultures when they embrace, after the disguised Odysseus has revealed his true identity.

58 *a swift Fury*: The Furies were three female deities (Allecto, Tisphone and Megaera) who avenged those who have been wronged. They appear as the chorus in the *Eumenides* (the third play of the *Oresteia* trilogy), where they persecute – and prosecute – Orestes for the murder of his mother Clytemnestra, until finally being appeased by Apollo and Athena. Here, the term is used metaphorically to mean a spirit of vengeance.

61 *Zeus, protector*: Protecting the guest-host relationship was one of Zeus' important functions; he was known, in this capacity, as Zeus *Xenios*.

82 *Three-footed*: The idea is that an old man's walking stick, mentioned a few lines earlier, is a third foot or leg (as in the riddle of the Sphinx).

00 CHORUS . . . ADDRESSES CLYTEMNESTRA: In choral passages that are addressed directly to the audience (i.e., not to other characters in the play) the Chorus still largely retain their dramatic

identity. Even so such passages may be seen as somehow removed from the dramatic action; they variously comment on, preface, anticipate, speculate about, and reflect on both onstage and background events (Aeschylus makes greater use of the chorus in most of these ways than Sophocles or Euripides). Here the Chorus Leader turns directly to Clytemnestra to ask about an immediate concern.

84   *Tyndareus*: Tyndareus was the father, by Leda, of the sisters Clytemnestra and Helen and the twin brothers Castor and Polydeuces (Pollux in Latin). In some versions of the myth Helen and Polydeuces were said to have been fathered by Zeus, who seduced Leda in the guise of a swan (see genealogical table, p. 303).

101   *These altars*: i.e., the altars of Zeus, Apollo and Hermes that stood outside the palace.

104   *the evil that has been*: This is probably the sacrifice of Iphigenia, which the Chorus later condemn in the presence of Agamemnon.

112   *four wings' furious beat*: A reference to the omen of the two birds that encouraged Agamemnon and Menelaus as they set out.

114   *spear-side of the road*: The right-hand side.

122   *learned seer*: The seer of the Greek army was Calchas, who was blind but never wrong.

134   *hounds of Zeus*: Aeschylus' use of the term 'hounds of Zeus' to mean the two eagles (eagles were associated with Zeus) is characteristic of his fondness for complex imagery. Aristophanes pokes fun at this tendency in the *Frogs* (see p. 202).

137   *Artemis*: Artemis was associated not only with hunting but also caring for wildlife; she is the 'lovely child of Zeus' invoked by Calchas a few lines on (140).

148   *Apollo's healing power*: Apollo, besides being the god of prophecy, the arts and hunting, was the god of healing (and disease). His sister was Artemis.

150   *a different sacrifice ... murdered child*: The 'different sacrifice' refers to the killing of Agamemnon's daughter Iphigenia. The 'house' in question is the house of Atreus (see genealogical table, p. 303), in which the spilling of 'kindred blood' dates back to the murder by Atreus' grandfather Tantalus of his son Pelops and Atreus' own murder of his nephews, and looks forward to the murder of Agamemnon by Clytemnestra and Aegisthus and the subsequent murder of Clytemnestra and Aegisthus by Clytemnestra's son Orestes (see *Preface* to the play, p. 3).

167   *first of the gods*: Uranus (Heaven) and Gaia (Earth) were the two
      primordial deities that form the first generation of ruling gods.

171   *Cronos ... stronger power*: Cronos was the youngest child of
      Uranus (the children of Uranus and Gaia were known as the
      Titans). He overthrew his father but was, in turn, overthrown by
      Zeus, his youngest child.

190   *Chalcis ... Aulis bay*: Chalcis was the chief city of Euboea. Aulis
      was a port in northern Boeotia and had a famous temple of
      Artemis.

192   *Strymon*: Strymon was a river in north-east Greece. It ran along
      the ancient border between Macedonia and Thrace.

202   *Her remedy*: Artemis' 'remedy' was that Agamemnon sacrifice
      his daughter Iphigenia in return for a favourable wind to sail to
      Troy.

205   *The elder king*: i.e., Agamemnon (he was older than his brother
      Menelaus).

218   *harness of Necessity*: Necessity (*Ananke*) was seen by the ancient
      Greeks as an abstract divine force.

224   *wheels of doom*: Agamemnon's decision itself is seen as an act of
      will, but one that conforms, nevertheless, to a predetermined
      wider pattern of kindred slaughter within the royal house.

249   *Calchas prophesied*: A suggestion, in keeping with Homer (*Iliad*
      1.68–72), of Calchas' infallibility.

250   *The killer will be killed*: The first clear intimation of Agamem-
      non's death.

258   *Argive land*: 'Argive' is used here to mean belonging to Argos or
      the Argolid. Occasionally Aeschylus uses the term, usually in
      connection with the Greeks at Troy, simply to mean 'Greek'.

275   *A dream*: Ancient Greeks believed that some dreams were sent
      by the gods. Agamemnon, for example, in book 2 of the *Iliad*, is
      deceived by a false dream sent by Zeus. Aeschylus is fond of using
      dreams and other kinds of visions in his plays.

280   *The god of fire*: Clytemnestra means this metaphorically. What
      follows is a description of how fire signals were sent from Troy
      to Argos. A few of the places mentioned by Clytemnestra cannot
      be identified with certainty.

281   *Ida first launched*: Ida was the mountain close to Troy where
      Paris, while tending sheep, was asked to judge a beauty contest
      between the three goddesses Hera, Aphrodite and Athene. All
      three goddesses made promises of gifts, but he adjudicated in
      favour of Aphrodite, who offered him Helen, the most beautiful

of mortals, as a reward. Zeus watched the Trojan War from the summit of Ida.

282 *Lemnos*: Lemnos is an island in the northern Aegean, halfway between Asia Minor and the north-eastern Greek coast.

283 *Athos*: Athos is a huge pyramid-shaped peak on the eastern-most of the set of three large promontories on the Chalcidean coast. It was associated, possibly on account of its sheer size, with Zeus.

289 *Makistos*: The location of Makistos is uncertain but it must be on the east coast of Euboea, if Athos is meant to be visible from it.

292 *Euripus' channel . . . Messapian guards*: The Straits of Euripus separate the island of Euboea from Boeotia on the mainland. Mount Messapium is in Boeotia, overlooking the Straits.

297 *Asopus . . . Cithaeron's crags*: Asopus is a plain in eastern Boeotia not far from Mount Cithaeron. Cithaeron is not far from Thebes, and was where the infant Oedipus was exposed (see p. 111).

300 *Lake Gorgopis*: The identity and precise location of Lake Gorgopis is not known. It is likely to be in Southern Boeotia or the Megarid.

301 *Aegiplanctus*: According to the scholiasts, Aegiplanctus is a mountain in the environs of Megara.

308 *high Arachneus*: The Saronic Gulf lies between Attica (to the east) and the Peloponnese (to the west) with the Megarid to its north. Mount Arachneus is in the Argolid and must, from what Clytemnestra says ('which neighbours our streets'), be fairly close to Argos or Mycenae (see opening note, p. 256, on the ambiguous use of 'Argos' throughout the play).

329 *slaves' cries*: It was common practice in the archaic Greek world for the women of a conquered people to be led into slavery. Euripides' *Andromache*, *Hecuba* and *Trojan Women* all involve Trojan women who are either facing or living out a life of servitude.

346 *the forgotten dead*: Ostensibly these are the fallen Trojans, but Clytemnestra primarily has in mind her daughter Iphigenia.

351 *like a man's*: See note on line 11.

355 *Kindly night*: The significance of night is that the Greeks succeeded in capturing Troy when the soldiers hidden in the wooden horse (dragged within the walls by the Trojans) emerged at night, killed the guards and unlocked the city gates for the rest of the Greek army.

378 *A middle course*: The Chorus in tragedy often affirm a credo of

moderation. Lowly characters sometimes do the same (e.g., the nurse in Euripides' *Medea*; see p. 141).

416 *statues' sweet proportions*: The image, like Pygmalion in reverse, is one of Menelaus taking cold comfort for the loss of Helen from looking at beautiful statues.

441 *His scales*: This image may look to Homer. In the *Iliad* Zeus weighs the fates of opposing fighters (most poignantly Hector and Achilles) in scales to see whose fate is heavier, thereby signifying their appointed death.

455 *soil . . . Covers its conquerors*: The Chorus' point here is that the very soil which the Greeks have conquered has been used to bury Greek soldiers.

473 *lose / Freedom and life*: Here, before the return of Agamemnon, the Chorus express marked anti-war sentiments; afterwards, when greeting Agamemnon, they seem to change their tune.

000 THE FOLLOWING REMARKS: In what follows the Chorus seem to be responding to some discernible excitement or news (probably rendered in performance by offstage cries). Speculation of this sort, in which lines would usually be distributed among different chorus members, are not uncommon in tragic choruses (see 1346ff., when the Chorus speculate about the fate of Agamemnon).

000 GAP IN THE ACTION: Usually the action of tragedy is fixed in terms of time and place to a single day and single location. Aeschylus is less strict in the application of this notional rule than Sophocles and Euripides. In the *Eumenides*, for example, there is a shift of location from Delphi to Athens for the trial of Orestes.

493 *crown of olive-leaves*: A crown or garland may be indicative of victory or celebration. Olive-leaves, an emblem of the goddess Athena, were associated with peace and prosperity.

510 *his immortal bow*: Apollo is the god who sends disease. In the first book of the *Iliad*, he is memorably described as descending to earth from Olympus, crouching by the Greek ships and firing arrows at men to strike them down with the plague (a punishment for Agamemnon's mistreatment of a priest of Apollo).

Apollo was called the Pythian (the name may be connected with a giant mythical snake Pytho, which lived near Delphi and was killed by Apollo). The Pythian temple of Apollo was where the Delphic Sybil (or Pythia) proclaimed her oracles, inspired by the god.

511 *Phoebus*: The name Phoebus is synonymous with Apollo. Sometimes the two names are used together (Phoebus Apollo; cf. Pallas

Athena). Apollo was regarded, like Hermes, as an averter of evil.

515   *Hermes . . . herald's god*: Hermes was one of the divine heralds or messengers; the other was Iris.

519   *deities . . . rising sun*: These are the images of Zeus, Apollo and Hermes, which presumably 'watch the rising sun' because they face eastwards.

575   *Argive army*: Here 'Argive' seems to mean the Greek army as a whole (especially in view of the later mention of the 'Hellene Race').

618   *beloved Menelaus*: Menelaus was king of Sparta, but as Agamemnon's brother and a fellow Greek he elicits the Chorus's concern and affection.

648   *angry gods*: The angry god in question is Athena, who is described by Nestor, in *Odyssey* 3, as the author of the storm that wrecked the returning Greek fleet.

687   *Helen, the Wrecker*: Aeschylus here makes a wordplay on Helen's name and the Greek verb *helein*, which can mean 'to wreck' or 'ruin'. This kind of explanation of names and their meanings, or linking of names to events, is not uncommon in Greek tragedy (see, for example, the allusion to Oedipus' name in Sophocles' *Oedipus Rex*, p. 112).

691   *Zephyr*: The West Wind.

694   *Simois' shingly bank*: The Simois was one of the two main rivers of Troy; the other was the Scamander (see note on line 1157).

734   *The whelp . . . now grown a beast*: It is not entirely clear what the lion cub is meant to represent. Aeschylean imagery is often deliberately enigmatic. There seems to be an allusion to Helen, who only revealed her true potential for destruction when fully grown to womanhood. The fact that she is clearly the subject of what follows supports such a view. At the same time, the 'feast unbidden' seems to point to Tantalus and Atreus, both of whom served up meals prepared from murdered relatives.

747   *god of host and guest*: Zeus *Xenios* (see note on line 61).

000   ENTER AGAMEMNON: Agamemnon and Cassandra enter by chariot. It is unclear whether they are in one vehicle or separate vehicles, though one seems likelier and would arguably be more pointed. For a discussion see Taplin, *The Stagecraft of Aeschylus*, pp. 304–6.

804   *offering sacrifice*: The first clear indication, in a dramatic rather than purely choral section of the play, that the Chorus strongly opposed the death of Iphigenia.

816 *urn for acquittal*: The method of voting in the Athenian legal system was for jury members to place a pebble (*psephos*) in one of two jars, marked guilty and not guilty respectively.

825 *womb of the horse*: Agamemnon is describing the Greek soldiers emerging from the wooden horse (see note on line 355).

841 *Odysseus . . . unwillingly*: Odysseus tried to avoid going to Troy by feigning madness. Palamedes, a man famed for his wiliness, outwitted Odysseus, who was driving his oxen when the Greek delegation arrived, by throwing Odysseus' son Telemachus before him. When Odysseus stopped the plough so as not to run over his son, he was proved to be feigning madness. Odysseus later murdered Palamedes at Troy.

870 *a second Geryon*: Geryon was a three-headed, three-bodied monster who tended a magnificent herd of cattle on an island far to the west. One of Heracles' labours was to capture the cattle; he killed Geryon in the process.

880 *Phocis*: Phocis was a region in central Greece, whose main city was Delphi. Strophius was king of Phocis. It is from here that Orestes arrives with Strophius' son Pylades in the *Libation Bearers*, the second play of the *Oresteia* trilogy, to avenge his father's death.

930 *harboured in tranquillity*: Vellacott's translation follows the highly unusual order of the text of A.Y. Campbell. Here the order followed by almost all other translations and editions of the Greek text has been restored.

950 *this girl*: i.e., Cassandra.

956 *There is a sea*: Much of this speech has double meanings. The sea and the colours purple and crimson all carry a secondary meaning of blood. The staining of clothes, accordingly, also means the spilling of blood.

968 *Dog Star's heat*: The Dog Star is visible during the hottest part of the year.

970 *the unripe grape*: The 'unripe grape' here probably carries a reference to the unmarried Iphigenia; the departure of heat and onset of coolness, in this context, seems to refer to her death.

973 *Eleleleleu*: This is a cry of victory. Here it is ostensibly a cry for Agamemnon's victory against Troy but it also celebrates Clytemnestra's victory over her husband: by getting Agamemnon to walk on the lavish tapestries Clytemnestra has made him commit an act of hubris, which (to her mind at any rate) gives added justification to his impending death.

974 *Zeus, Fulfiller*: One of Zeus' many roles is that of bringing about

divine justice; in this capacity he is known as Zeus *Teleios* or Zeus the Fulfiller.

1022 *That sage's skill*: The sage in question is Aesculapius (son of Apollo and Coronis), who was killed by Zeus' thunderbolt for bringing Hippolytus (and others) back to life. He was, nevertheless, worshipped as a divinity of healing.

1040 *Heracles . . . was sold*: Heracles was a slave of king Eurystheus of Tiryns (on the eastern coast of the Peloponnese) when he performed his twelve labours.

1051 *Some weird . . . language*: Clytemnestra suggests, somewhat witheringly, that the Trojan Cassandra may not speak Greek. By and large, in tragedy, as in Homer, Trojan characters not only share the same gods and religious beliefs as Greeks but are able to speak Greek perfectly well. Cassandra even alludes to the fact later (1254).

1062 *interpreter*: The Chorus, like Clytemnestra, mistake her apprehension for a failure to understand what is being said to her.

1066 *frothed her rage*: This suggests that Cassandra is already in a state of severe agitation.

1074 *O Apollo*: It is likely that Cassandra's sudden alarm springs from seeing the altar of Apollo. A little later she calls him 'Leader of Journeys' (Greek: *Aguiatos*), a title used in connection with the symbol of Apollo – a stone that is either cone-shaped or with a rounded top – placed by the entrance or gates to a house.

1079 *may not stand . . . grief*: Songs of mourning or grief were inappropriate for Apollo. At the time the play was written, on Delos, the island where Apollo was born and which was sacred to the god, no death was permitted. The unwell were removed from the island as a precaution.

1080 *my destroyer*: In the Greek there is a play on words; the name 'Apollo' sounds very similar to the word for 'destroyer' or 'one who destroys' (*apolôn*).

1082 *even in slavery*: The Chorus's remark implies that they think it perfectly possible that someone with prophetic powers might forego them, passing into slavery; this is consistent with a world view in which gods too put store by human social standing (prophecy was generally considered a gift – in Cassandra's case, a curse – from the gods).

1098 *their father fed*: The event Cassandra refers to here is Atreus' murder of his nephews, the children of Thyestes.

1109 *This cleansing ritual*: Clytemnestra herself has used the language of cleansing in an ambivalent way. Here Cassandra alludes to the fact that Clytemnestra sees the murder of Agamemnon as an act of cleansing and atonement for the death of her daughter Iphigenia.

1123 *her utterance chokes*: This line is an amplification of Cassandra's condition; it is not present in the original Greek.

1143 *the shrill nightingale*: According to myth, the nightingale was originally a woman called Philomela, the daughter of Pandion, a legendary king of Athens. Her elder sister Procne married Tereus, a Thracian king. Tereus, however, fell in love with Philomela when he came to Athens in order to take her to Thrace at Procne's request. On returning to Thrace he raped her, cut out her tongue, and locked her away in a remote dwelling so that she would not be able to proclaim his crime. But Philomela managed to send news to Procne via a tapestry, delivered by a servant, in which she depicted her sufferings.

Procne took revenge on Philomela's behalf. First, she smuggled Philomela out of her hideaway in disguise, then she murdered Itys, her son by Tereus, and fed him to his father in a meal. After the meal, Procne and Philomela confronted Tereus with the child's (uncooked) head. He immediately attempted to kill them both, but all three were transformed into birds: Tereus the hoopoe; Procne the swallow; and Philomela the nightingale. The song 'Itys, Itys' is Philomela's lament for her sister's innocent child.

1156 *His family and city*: Cassandra, as Paris' sister, is part of his family as well as his city.

1157 *river Scamander*: The Scamander (also known as Xanthus) is mentioned often in the *Iliad* as the principal river of Troy. Scamander was also the river-god, who fought against Achilles in *Iliad* 21.

1160 *Cocytus / And Acheron*: Cocytus and Acheron are two of the rivers of the underworld. Others include Lethe, Phlegethon and the Styx, over which the dead had to pass, usually with the help of the ferryman Charon. (In some accounts the river patrolled by Charon is given as Acheron.)

1193 *defiler of his brother's bed*: i.e., Thyestes, who had committed adultery with Atreus' wife Aerope.

1208 *God of Words*: The title used for Apollo in the original is *Loxias*, which may have some connection with the Greek word for 'word' (*logos*). Cassandra seems to be saying that she agreed to sleep with Apollo and then changed her mind.

1224 *cowardly lion*: The cowardly lion is Aegisthus. Though the whole grim history of the house of Atreus is present throughout in the background events and imagery of the play, this is the first specific indication that Aegisthus, as well as Clytemnestra, is involved in the plot to kill Agamemnon.

1233 *basilisk*: It is not uncommon to find women who take drastic action in tragedy being compared to wild creatures of myth. The basilisk was a mythical serpent that could kill with a single glance or breath. The Greek word here is not basilisk but *amphisbaina*, which means a snake that can move in both directions. Scylla was a sea monster that lived on one side of the straits of Messina (between Sicily and Italy), the other side being the home of Charybdis, a giant whirlpool. Scylla used to devour sailors as they passed through if they strayed towards her in attempting to avoid Charybdis, and wore the heads of her victims on a necklace. In Euripides' *Medea*, Jason likens Medea to Scylla after she has murdered their children (see p. 179).

1255 *oracles . . . understand*: The oracles from Delphi were in hexameter verse (the same metre as Homeric epic) and famously difficult to decipher.

1267 *an end of you*: Presumably she throws the emblems of prophecy to the ground, possibly trampling them.

1280 *A third shall come*: Cassandra here utters a new prophecy that looks forward to the action of the next play, in which Orestes will take revenge upon his mother Clytemnestra for her murder of his father.

1307 *I have lived enough . . .*: There is some uncertainty over line order here. While most texts place these two lines later, in Campbell's text (followed here by Vellacott) they are brought forward. Cassandra may make to leave at this point but suddenly check herself, prompting the Chorus' startled response immediately afterwards.

1343 *Here, inside*: Violence in Greek tragedy was not, as a rule, shown onstage (the only exception, in an extant play, is Ajax's suicide in Sophocles' *Ajax*). Consequently, the shouts of characters being injured or killed, while aimed at creating suspense or excitement, also tend to give clear indications of what is happening to them. They may, therefore, come across as somewhat stilted and unrealistic (compare the deaths of the children in Euripides' *Medea*, pp. 176–7).

0000 CHORUS: 1: In scenes of extreme commotion or activity, the Chorus's part may be split among individual chorus members (see 474ff.).

1363 *disgracers . . . royal house*: They disgrace the royal house not

only because of their actions against it but because they belong
to it; Clytemnestra by marriage and Aegisthus by blood.

0000 THE PALACE DOORS OPEN: Clytemnestra appears with the
bodies of Agamemnon and Cassandra in a macabre tableau. How
this was originally staged is unclear. Possibilities include the use
of a central platform that could be wheeled out to show interior
scenes (the *ekkuklêma*), the use of silent stage hands to bring out
the bodies along with various accoutrements (bath, net, axe, etc.),
or the revealing of the bodies inside the stage-building through
the stage doors. These are all discussed in Taplin, *The Stagecraft
of Aeschylus*, pp. 325–7 and in Frankel's commentary on the
relevant lines in *Agamemnon*.

1438 *Chryseis*: Chryseis was a captured girl given to Agamemnon in
the division of spoils after a Greek raid on a settlement near Troy.
Her father Chryses, a priest of Apollo, tried unsuccessfully to
ransom her – Agamemnon rudely dismissed him – and then
prayed to Apollo to punish the Greeks. This the god did by
sending a plague. Agamemnon was forced to return the girl when
Calchas revealed the cause of Apollo's anger. As a replacement,
he took Achilles' girl Briseis; this is what caused Achilles to
withdraw from the fighting until the death of Patroclus. Clytemnestra seems to be suggesting that Agamemnon had a weakness
for captive women.

1469 *curse weighs / Hard*: Tantalus was the founder of Agamemnon's
family. He also started the hideous chain of murder within the
family by murdering his son Pelops and feeding him to the
gods.

1475 *fed three times*: In describing the Fury as having 'fed three times'
Clytemnestra is referring to three separate instances of kindred
slaughter: the butchering of Thyestes' children, the sacrifice of
Iphigenia and the murder of Agamemnon.

1501 *Atreus ... abhorrent deed*: Clytemnestra's suggestion that
Agamemnon's death atones for the deaths of Thyestes' children
– she has already made the point that his death was payment for
Iphigenia's life – anticipates the arrival of Aegisthus.

1507 *the black-robed king*: The 'black-robed king' here is either Ares
or another similar war deity.

1556 *the porchway ... perish young*: Clytemnestra suggests that there
is a special place reserved in the underworld for those who die
young. Such compartmentalization of the dead in Hades is also
hinted at in Odysseus' voyage to the underworld in *Odyssey* 11.

1559 *gagged and silent tongue*: The Chorus in their opening lyrics

(p. 19; line 236) describe Agamemnon asking for Iphigenia to be gagged in case she should utter a curse against his house.

1629 *voice of Orpheus*: Orpheus, the child of one of the Muses, was a celebrated musician and singer, with a voice sweet enough to charm wild beasts and trees, and halt rivers.

1651 *Our swords are ready*: The Chorus, as a rule, do not intervene physically in the action of the play, though in scenes of drastic action or extreme emotion they sometimes seem on the point of doing so (see the earlier scene in which they debate intervening during the murder of Agamemnon). Here, Aeschylus has them on the brink of fighting with Aegisthus and his men before Clytemnestra restores the peace.

1667 *I know*: Aegisthus spent his childhood and early adulthood in exile.

OEDIPUS REX

0   BY THE ALTARS: The main altar (at which Jocasta later offers incense) is that of Apollo.

3   *branches and garlands*: Suppliants often carried branches (usually of olive or laurel) with tufts of wool tied round them. These would be laid at the altar of the god to whom supplication was being made and left there until their prayers were granted.

21   *river Ismenus*: The Ismenus was one of the two rivers of Thebes; the other is the Dirce.

36   *that cruel enchantress*: i.e., the Sphinx.

71   *Pythian shrine*: The Pythian shrine of Apollo (who was known as the Pythian) was the home of the Delphic Sybil or oracle (also known as the Pythia or Pythian priestess). The oracles, uttered by the Sybil in a trance-like state of possession, were seen as coming from Apollo himself.

78   *they are making signs*: In the ancient theatre, because it took some time for characters to reach the stage, their appearance is often prefaced by remarks from other characters on stage. Here, Oedipus and the priest anticipate Creon's arrival.

83   *crowned with bay*: Bay (or laurel) was associated with Apollo.

109 *that distant crime*: The timescale between the death of Laius and the action of the play is not made clear. There are indications within the play that the accession of Oedipus, which was shortly after he solved the riddle of the Sphinx, was not long after Laius' death. Still, the passage of time from Oedipus' accession to the

action of the play must be a substantial period, probably something in the region of ten to fifteen years; Oedipus' daughters are still young children, and his sons, while they do not yet seem to have grown to adulthood, are described as capable of fending for themselves (1460).

122 *not one but many*: The survivor's suggestion that 'not one but many' attacked Laius' party seems to be a lie rather than a mistake. This is supported by his later request to leave royal service upon finding Oedipus the new king (760) and his evasive behaviour during the scene in which he is questioned (1120ff.).

133 *Phoebus*: Phoebus is an alternative name for Apollo; the two names were often used together (Phoebus Apollo).

136 *the god's cause*: i.e., Apollo's.

151 *Pythian House of Gold*: The 'Pythian House of Gold' is the temple of Apollo. Though prophecy comes from Apollo, here he is seen as the spokesperson of Zeus, the supreme deity.

154 *Healer of Delos*: Apollo was seen as a god of healing. The tiny island of Delos, one of the Cyclades, was the birthplace of Apollo and his sister Artemis; it was a major centre for their worship. Apollo was often called the god of Delos or Delian.

163 *Lord of the Bow*: Another title of Apollo. He and Artemis were both patron divinities of hunting.

166 *Save us . . . clean*: Apollo was seen both as the sender and averter of plague.

205 *Lycean . . . Lycian*: 'Lycean' was a cult title of Apollo. The Lycian hills are in south-west Asia Minor. The similarity of the two names seems to hint at the fact that Apollo and Artemis are siblings.

210 *Bacchus . . . Euoe*: Bacchus was another name of Dionysus. Dionysus, the god of wine and the theatre, was of Theban origin. He was the son of Zeus and Semele, one of Cadmus' daughters (see genealogical table, p. 304). Thebes was traditionally seen as the first place in Greece to have celebrated his rites, which were established first in the Near East. The female worshippers of Dionysus were called maenads. 'Euoe!' was the cry of ecstatic delight uttered in honour of Dionysus.

284 *Tiresias*: Tiresias is a prophet who received the gift of prophecy as compensation for being blinded (by Athena according to one tradition, Hera according to another). He is intimately connected with a number of Theban myths and plays that deal with those myths (of other extant plays he appears in Sophocles' *Antigone* and Euripides' *Phoenician Women* and *Bacchae*).

367 *In shameful union with the ones you love*: The wording of Tiresias' claim is deliberately imprecise; moreover, Oedipus by this stage is not really listening carefully to what is being said to him, partly because he is furious and partly because he is under the impression that the prophet is simply making wild accusations. It is therefore reasonable to suppose that he does not register the fact that Tiresias is questioning his relationship with Jocasta and his children.

378 *Was this trick his*: Oedipus mistakenly senses a possible connection with Creon's embassy to Apollo's oracle at Delphi.

391 *Riddling Bitch*: i.e., the Sphinx.

402 *as old / As you appear to be*: Tiresias had lived through many generations before the events of this play.

410 *Loxias*: Loxias is another name of Apollo; it tends to be used in connection with his role as the god of prophecy (see Jocasta's speech, 854; and Cassandra, in *Agamemnon*, p. 52).

420 *Cithaeron*: Cithaeron is the mountain just outside Thebes where the infant Oedipus was nailed down and left to die (before being saved).

449 *I add this*: It has been suggested (by Bernard Knox in 'Sophocles, *Oedipus Tyrannos* 446: Exit Oedipus?' in *Greek, Roman and Byzantine Studies* 21(4), 1980, pp. 321–32) that the prophetic utterance by Tiresias that follows is not actually heard by Oedipus, who exits, or at least turns his back on Tiresias and starts to walk away, after saying, 'We can well do without you', line 446. This suggestion is strongly supported by the fact that if Oedipus had heard this shocking claim, he could hardly have ignored it, especially as it tallies with the one half of the prophecy he obtained about himself from Delphi (see p. 103); he would also have been able to piece together the riddle of his birth far more quickly than he does.

463 *the Delphian rock*: i.e., the oracle at Delphi.

470 *son of Zeus*: i.e., Apollo.

474 *high Parnassus*: Parnassus is a large mountain overlooking Delphi, which lay to its south.

482 *the earth's core*: this has a double meaning, as Delphi was also known as the navel or centre of the earth (*omphalos gês*).

492 *the son of Polybus*: i.e., Oedipus. Polybus, the ostensible father of Oedipus, was king of Corinth.

507 *Winged Enchantress*: i.e., the Sphinx.

543 *men and moneybags*: Oedipus seems to overlook the fact that he won his throne neither through 'men' nor 'moneybags'.

612 *Cast out ... dearest treasure*: this line, which adds little to the text, may be a later interpolation during the text's history.

625 *Still clinging*: The text here is uncertain and a line may be missing, possibly between the end of this line and the beginning of the next.

641 *death or banishment*: There seems to be a slight discrepancy. Earlier Oedipus said that he would sooner see Creon killed than banished, whereas here both Creon and Oedipus talk as though Creon has a choice between death and banishment. The simplest solution is that Oedipus' remark about wanting Creon dead was made in the heat of the moment and was not meant to be taken at face value.

649 *Consent, my lord*: The following section (marked in the translation by shorter rhyming lines of varying length) is energetic lyrics in the original. Such passages, which were reserved for scenes of high tension and emotion, would have been performed with musical accompaniment and may have been sung or, at least, delivered with some kind of vocal modulation. The first lyric section (two strophes) is from 'Consent, my lord, consent' to 'To our old misery' (668); the second (two antistrophes) is from 'Madam, persuade the king' to 'This storm into tranquillity' (678–97). The lines between, spoken by Oedipus and Creon, are in the usual metre of dialogue (iambic trimeters).

688 *see what you have done*: Oedipus chastises the Chorus for their well-meaning but, in his eyes, unhelpful efforts to stay his anger in order to resolve his dispute with Creon. Oedipus does not want an amicable resolution; he wants Creon to be put to death or, at least, banished.

711 *Not from Phoebus, but from his ministers*: Jocasta seems here to be questioning not Apollo himself but the reliability of those who claim to interpret his will; she later says, 'the god will show his will in his own good time', line 725. Even so, her attitude may have seemed controversial to Sophocles' original audience; the Delphic oracle was still consulted and treated with utmost seriousness by the Greeks of Sophocles' day.

734 *Daulia*: Daulia is on the other side of Mount Parnassus from Delphi (see map, p. 306).

775 *a Dorian*: Doris is a small area in central Greece to the northwest of Phocis. Oedipus does not make it clear here that Polybus was, in fact, king of Corinth.

787 *I went to Delphi*: By 'went to Delphi' Oedipus means that he consulted the oracle there.

794 *kill my father*: It does not occur to Jocasta or Oedipus that this prophecy is the same as the one Jocasta has just mentioned (the one which led her and Laius to seek to kill their child), since both Jocasta and Oedipus believe that Oedipus is from Corinth, and that Jocasta's cursed child died long ago, there is no apparent reason for them to be alarmed by the coincidence.

797 *brought me to the region*: Oedipus was heading from Delphi towards Thebes and Laius was going the other way.

853 *Loxias*: See note on line 410.

873 *Pride breeds the tyrant*: The condemnation of pride or excess is not uncommon for a tragic chorus; the Chorus of Elders in Aeschylus' *Agamemnon* do likewise (see p. 24).

898 *Abaean and Olympian altars*: There was a hilltop sanctuary of Apollo at Abae in the northwest of Phocis. There was a sanctuary of Zeus at Olympia in Elis in the northwest Peloponnese.

000 ENTER JOCASTA: She enters carrying paraphernalia for performing rites at the altars on the stage.

940 *the Isthmus*: i.e., the Isthmus of Corinth.

981 *Many a man has dreamt*: This is a remark of which Freud made much in his idea of the Oedipus complex.

1035 *from the cradle*: Oedipus seems not to have known until now that the weakness in his ankles was received rather than a defect from birth. Otherwise he would, one imagines, have had some kind of reaction to Jocasta's earlier mention of the fact that her child had had its ankles riveted (718), although at the time he was, admittedly, preoccupied with her saying that Laius had been killed at a place where three roads meet.

1036 *your present name*: The name 'Oedipus' means 'swollen foot'.

1042 *one of Laius' men*: The mention of the name 'Laius' must come as a profound shock to Jocasta, who is now faced with the full horror of the truth before the others. Her fears were probably raised initially at the moment that the messenger said that he found Oedipus on Cithaeron. The mention of riveted ankles would have pointed very strongly in the direction of the truth, but it is the mention of Laius that provides incontrovertible proof.

1063 *your honour*: Oedipus misconstrues Jocasta's motive. She does not fear that he may be of low birth; she knows that he is in fact of the very highest birth.

1097 *Was this offspring born*: In this stanza the Chorus speculate on Oedipus' birth. Such choral speculation, in which guesses tend to be plausible but never correct, occurs elsewhere in Sophoclean tragedy (the Chorus of Ajax, for example, speculate on the source of Ajax's divine possession).

1105 *Cyllene's Lord*: 'Cyllene's Lord' is Hermes (he was born there). Cyllene is a high mountain (*c.*7300ft) in the northeast of Arcadia, visible from Cithaeron.

1107 *Helicon*: Mount Helicon was in southwest Boeotia, not far from Cithaeron. It was traditionally seen as the home of the nine Muses.

0000 AN ELDERLY SHEPHERD: This shepherd is not only the man present when Oedipus killed Laius, whom Oedipus wishes to question to confirm whether or not he is the killer of Laius, but also the man who gave the infant Oedipus to the Corinthian messenger/shepherd. Jocasta earlier explained that he sought to leave when he saw that Oedipus – the killer of Laius – had become king (760). It is not entirely clear whether he already believes that the killer of Laius (whom he knows to be Oedipus) and the infant he saved are one and the same person (in which case he would already know all that Jocasta has just found out).

1199 *she-devil ... Taloned Lady*: i.e., the Sphinx.

1227 *Ister and Phasis*: The river Ister is the Danube; the river Phasis is either a river that divides Colchis from Asia Minor and flows into the Black Sea or one that flows into the Caspian Sea (possibly the Araxes). The Attendant's point is that even the waters of such mighty, distant rivers are not enough to cleanse the house of Labdacus.

The Attendant prefaces what he is about to describe as 'wilfully chosen', to contrast these actions with Oedipus' past crimes, which were unwitting.

1348 *this riddle*: i.e., the riddle of his birth (as opposed to the riddle of the Sphinx).

1414 *Don't be afraid*: His words suggest that at this point Oedipus approaches the Chorus who shrink away in fear and disgust.

1481 *your brother's hands*: Oedipus attributes his self-blinding not to his being the children's father and their mother's husband, but to his being their brother and their mother's son – it is in this latter role that he cannot face seeing himself, or them.

MEDEA

o   JASON'S HOUSE: While in most plays that are based in a city,
      such as Aeschylus' *Agamemnon* and Sophocles' *Oedipus Rex*, the
      scene for the action is before the royal palace, here the scene
      is before a private house, with the royal palace being located
      offstage.

o   ENTER NURSE: All entrances and exits by the Nurse and Medea
      are from and to the house.

2   *Clashing Rocks*: The Clashing Rocks (or Symplegades) were on
      the Bosporus at the entrance to the Black Sea (see map, p. 307).
      According to legend, they used to close together whenever an
      attempt was made to pass through them, until Jason succeeded,
      with Hera's help, in negotiating them in the Argo (see *Odyssey*
      12.59–72).

3   *Pelion's slopes*: Pelion is a mountain in Thessaly with steep
      wooded slopes.

20   *Creon's daughter*: Creon is the king of Corinth. He is not to be
      confused with the Creon at Thebes, who was the brother of
      Jocasta (the mother/wife of Oedipus).

28   *a rock*: It is not uncommon for intransigent tragic figures to be
      compared to natural phenomena such as rocks or the sea, or to
      stubborn animals, such as bulls (Medea is later likened to a bull;
      see 188).

36   *forming in her mind*: lines 37–43 of the Greek are omitted here
      as they are commonly regarded as spurious.

oo   MEDEA'S VOICE: The device of having a character cry out
      offstage prior to appearing on stage is sometimes used for belea-
      guered heroes or heroines who are in the midst of a crisis at the
      start of the play (e.g., Sophocles' *Ajax*).

118   *The mind of a princess*: Though a foreigner here in Greece, Medea
      is a princess by birth.

125   *The middle way . . . is best*: The praising of moderation is not
      uncommon among low characters (especially in Euripidean tra-
      gedy; see, for example, the nurse in *Hippolytus*), and choruses
      (for example, the Chorus in *Agamemnon*, p. 24).

147   *and die*: Beleaguered tragic heroes and, in particular, heroines
      often pray for death in this way.

157   *Zeus will plead your cause*: Zeus was the guardian of oaths (the
      Nurse mentions this below, 170).

160   *Themis . . . Artemis*: Themis was a primordial goddess, the daugh-

ter of Uranus and Gaia (though she is sometimes regarded as the wife or, as she is later described by the Chorus, daughter of Zeus). She came to be seen as an abstract divinity closely associated with law and justice (the Greek word *themis* usually means simply 'lawful'). She was also connected with oaths and unwritten law, which explains her significance here.

Artemis was the daughter of Zeus and Leto, and sister of Apollo. Her significance here is harder to discern. She is not directly concerned with oaths or marriage, but had a close connection with women.

183 *those in there*: i.e., the children.

188 *bull . . . cubs*: Medea's eyes were earlier likened to those of a bull (92). The simile involving the lioness guarding her cubs involves dramatic irony, as Medea's relations to her children will prove far more ambivalent than the simile suggests.

200 *If music could cure*: The idea that music is a cure for distress also appears in the Watchman's opening speech in *Agamemnon* (see p. 11).

223 *even citizens*: In fifth-century Athens foreigners could not become Athenian citizens.

232 *bought a husband*: Brides in ancient Greece were required to pay a dowry to the husband's family.

246 *A cure for boredom*: The main form of entertainment for Greek men of high social standing was the symposium, which involved a banquet followed by entertainment from girls (not free women but trained slaves) who sang, danced, engaged in conversation and provided sexual services. Free women were not permitted to attend symposia.

256 *I was taken as booty*: This is not strictly true; Medea came of her own accord (although Jason later suggests, rather conceitedly, that Medea's coming was Aphrodite's doing inasmuch as she was stricken with love for him).

258 *no mother, brother*: She omits to mention here that she, in fact, horribly murdered her brother (though she does draw attention to this detail of her chequered past earlier; line 167).

335 *Here, men*: This suggests that Creon is accompanied by guards.

340 *this one day*: The action of tragedy generally takes place over a single day (this is more strictly observed in Sophocles and Euripides than Aeschylus; see p. 28).

375 *my husband*: The mention of Jason among those Medea will seek to kill is not a mistake but a reflection of the fact that she is not

entirely clear in her mind about what action she will take (see below).

394 *kill them both*: Medea must mean Creon's daughter and Jason here rather than Creon and his daughter; it is, after all, unlikely that Creon shares a bedroom with his married daughter. The inconsistency between Medea's earlier declared intent to kill Creon, his daughter and Jason (see the previous note), what she says here, and her eventual murder of Creon's daughter and her own children (strictly speaking, the death of Creon is not planned) may be seen as part of Medea's uncertain state of mind at this point, and her unpredictability more generally.

395 *Hecate*: Hecate was originally a fertility goddess but came to be associated with, amongst other things, the underworld and sorcery.

405 *the Sun-God*: Medea's father Aeëtes was the son of Helios, and the brother of the divine witch Circe (see genealogical table, p. 305).

407 *tribe / Of Sisyphus*: Sisyphus was a Corinthian hero associated with trickery and known for his famous punishment in Hades (endlessly pushing a boulder up a hill, from which it always rolled back down). Here he is seen by Medea as the founder of the royal house of Corinth and ancestor of Creon.

424 *lyric inspiration*: Not all lyric poetry was composed by men; Sappho was a female lyric poet.

000 ENTER JASON: He arrives not from his house but from the palace, where he has taken up residence with his new bride.

476 *fire-breathing bulls*: Medea's father, king Aeëtes, was reluctant to part with the golden fleece and so set Jason a number of dangerous tasks in the hope of putting him off his quest (see Preface to the play, p. 132).

522 *clever speaker*: The speech that follows, like Jason's first speech, is strongly oratorical in feel. The tendency of Euripidean characters to speak in a strongly oratorical fashion is something at which comic writers such as Aristophanes often poked fun (see Aeschylus' remarks in *Frogs*, pp. 215–16).

544 *voice sweeter than Orpheus*: Orpheus, the child of one of the Muses, was a celebrated musician and singer, with a voice sweet enough to charm wild beasts and trees, and halt rivers.

550 *No, keep quiet*: Medea, at this point, presumably threatens to interrupt.

574 *Without the female sex*: A similar misogynistic wish that procreation were possible without women is expressed by Hippolytus in Euripides' play of that name.

636 *dread Cyprian*: Aphrodite was also known as the Cyprian (she was born on, or just off, Cyprus).

666 *Aegeus, son of Pandion*: Aegeus was king of Athens. His father Pandion was the son of Cecrops, one of the legendary early kings of Athens.

668 *The centre of the earth*: i.e., Delphi. It was called the *omphalos gês* (literally 'the navel of the Earth').

674 *Phoebus*: Phoebus was an alternative name of Apollo, though the two are often found in conjunction (Phoebus Apollo).

683 *king of Troezen*: Troezen is in the Argolid at the eastern edge of the Peloponnese, slightly inland from the Saronic Gulf. Pittheus, the founder of Troezen, was the son of Pelops (and the brother of Atreus and Thyestes).

688 *I hope you will get*: In fact, when Aegeus went to see Pittheus, though the latter understood the oracle (as meaning that Aegeus should not drink until reaching Athens because he would conceive next time he was drunk), he pretended not to. His intention was to get Aegeus drunk and have him sleep with his daughter Aethra. Aegeus did both of these things, and the child born of this union was Theseus, the greatest of Athenian heroes.

709 *bear it bravely*: There seems to be more than a pinch of sarcasm in this remark.

791 *kill my sons*: This is the first explicit mention of infanticide. Significantly, Medea's plan to kill her children is only formed after she has secured a place of refuge with Aegeus in Athens. Her initial declared intentions were to kill Jason and his bride, and possibly Creon (see notes to lines 375 and 394).

809 *dangerous . . . and loyal*: This view of justice is very similar to the popular definition of it, namely helping one's friends and harming one's enemies, contested by Socrates in book 1 of Plato's *Republic*.

824 *sons of Erechtheus*: Erechtheus, a son of Gaia (Earth), was the legendary founder of Athens. A substantial part of a temple dedicated to him (the Erechtheon), including the well-known caryatid porch, remains on the Acropolis.

833 *Muses of Pieria*: The Muses were thought, according to one tradition, to live in the area of Pieria, near Olympus (according to another they lived on Mount Helicon in Boeotia). Harmony here seems to be an abstract idea and not the figure of myth who married Cadmus.

837 *Cephisus*: Cephisus is a river that flows close to Athens, a little way to the north and west of the Acropolis.

842 *sends the Loves*: The Loves are presented as abstract forces somehow connected with Aphrodite. This image suggests that human virtue and excellence require more than knowledge or wisdom alone; they also require 'the Loves', an abstract representation of desire as a prerequisite of virtue and excellence.

910 *a second wife*: It was not customary for ancient Greek men to engage in bigamy. It should, however, be borne in mind that the status of the marriage between Jason and Medea is uncertain.

1021 *a city and a home*: The 'city and home' Medea has in mind for the children is the underworld realm of Hades.

1034 *people would envy me*: For the ancient Greeks being buried by one's own children was one of the marks of a happy life.

1060 *I will not leave sons of mine*: Though Medea briefly entertains the happy scenario of taking her sons with her to live in Athens, she quickly realizes that this is wishful thinking now that the boys have been allowed to stay in Corinth with Jason. It seems to her that killing the children is the only viable alternative to leaving them with their father. She reassures herself of this with what she says in the lines that immediately follow.

1078 *I know the full / Horror*: It is essential to the tragic quality of the play that Medea does what she does knowingly and wilfully in spite of her understanding the horror of it.

1134 *tell me how they died*: Usually characters who hear such messenger speeches relating offstage violence or death are horrified by the news, since the victims tend to be persons to whom they are attached. The present situation is both unusual and macabre; not only does Medea delight in the appalling account, but the events described are the fruits of her own grim handiwork.

1171 *the anger of Pan*: Pan was seen as one of the possible sources of sudden possession or seizure.

1256 *for mortals . . . veins of gods*: The Chorus's point here is that, while it is always wrong to kill members of one's own family, the crime is even worse if the family in question has divine ancestry, as is the case with Medea and her children, who are descended from the Sun-God.

1263 *blue Symplegades*: See note on line 2.

0000 SCREAM IS HEARD: Violence in Greek tragedy was not, as a rule, shown onstage (the only exception, in an extant play, is Ajax's suicide in Sophocles' *Ajax*). Often, however, suspense and excitement were created by having voices heard offstage (compare the murder of Agamemnon in Aeschylus' *Agamemnon*, p. 56).

1276 *We must attempt*: The Chorus, as a rule, do not intervene physically in the action of the play, though in scenes of drastic action or extreme emotion, as here, they sometimes seem on the point of doing so (compare the Chorus in the *Agamemnon* during Agamemnon's murder, p. 57, and in the final scene with Aegisthus, p. 66).

1284 *Ino*: Ino was the daughter of Cadmus and Harmonia. She nursed the infant Dionysus, son of her sister Semele, but fell victim to Hera's rage. Hera was envious of Dionysus because he was living evidence of another of Zeus' infidelities. Hera drove Ino mad, with the result that she, like Medea, killed her two children. Ino subsequently took her own life.

oooo ABOVE THE ROOF: Evidence from several vase-paintings of this scene suggest that in the ancient theatre Medea would have appeared in a chariot drawn by winged serpents on the roof of the stage-building, an area usually reserved for the appearance of the gods. Besides her appearance in a supernatural vehicle, there is much about Medea in this final scene that makes her resemble a god, particularly the fact that she is beyond the reach of other characters, and that she proceeds to reveal the future with complete authority in a way that is usually the role of a god. There are strong reasons to suppose that originally Medea would have made her appearance and exit in this scene via the *mêchanê* (see the Introduction, pp. xxviii–ix, for details about the staging of tragedies); this reinforces the sense that she has a quasi-divine status by the end of the play.

1328 *May the gods strike you down*: This is wishful thinking in view of the fact that, as Media has just said, it is her ancestor, the Sun-God Helios, who has given her the flying chariot in which she and the children appear.

1338 *mere sexual jealousy*: This emphasis on sexual jealousy makes Medea seem more like an avenging deity, not less; goddesses such as Hera and Aphrodite often meted out harsh punishment as a result of sexual jealousy.

1343 *Tuscan Scylla*: Scylla was a sea monster that lived on one side of the straits of Messina, the other being the home of Charybdis, a giant whirlpool. Scylla used to devour sailors as they passed through if they strayed towards her in attempting to avoid Charybdis, and wore the heads of her victims on a necklace. Clytemnestra in Aeschylus' *Agamemnon* is also compared to Scylla (see p. 52).

1377 *temple / Of Hera Acraea*: The temple of Hera Acraea was on a large promontory in Perachora (modern-day Peiraeum) at the east end of the Corinthian Gulf, north of the Isthmus and opposite ancient Corinth. Hera was closely associated with marriage and childbirth.

1381 *an annual feast*: Euripides often links his version of mythological events to local cults or festivals. Here the origin of a Corinthian festival in which the deaths of Medea's children were expiated annually is explained within the play.

1387 *a falling relic*: After returning from his quest for the golden fleece, Jason had dedicated a piece of the Argo as a thank-offering in the temple of Hera. Later, after the events of this play, during a visit to the temple the relic fell on him and killed him.

1389 *The curse* . . .: The section from this line to the end of the play is not in the usual metre of dialogue but a lyric metre (anapaests). In this translation this is indicated by shorter lines (generally iambic tetrameters but with the occasional trimeter and one pentameter).

1419 *the conclusion of this story*: Endings almost identical to the Chorus's final lines are used by Euripides in four other extant plays (*Alcestis*, *Andromache*, *Helen* and the *Bacchae*).

FROGS

53 *Andromeda*: Andromeda is a lost play of Euripides. It involves the hero Perseus's rescue of Andromeda, who was chained to a rock as a victim for a sea monster (punishment for her mother Cassiope's claim that her daughter was more beautiful than the divine sea nymphs, the Nereids). The play is extensively parodied by Aristophanes in his *Thesmophoriazusae*, in which Euripides and his kinsman act out the parts of Perseus and Andromeda respectively, in an attempt to escape from their captors (the women at the festival of the Thesmophoria, after whom the play is named).

55 *Molon's size*: Molon was a well-known actor and, according to scholiasts, a very large man.

59 *little bro*: Heracles refers to Dionysus as his brother because they are both sons of Zeus, the former by Alcmene and the latter by Semele.

73 *Iophon*: Iophon was the son of Sophocles. Very little is known of his work. The tragedian's art was often passed from generation to generation. Aeschylus and Euripides also had family members who wrote tragedies.

79   *on his own*: The implication is either that Sophocles had helped
     his son while he was alive or that he would do so if brought back
     to life.

82   *Lived life contented*: Sophocles was known for his extremely
     affable nature. Euripides' supposed shiftiness seems to be a comic
     inference from the wiliness of many of the characters in his
     plays.

83   *Agathon*: Agathon was a successful tragedian from the generation
     after Sophocles and Euripides. He appears as a character in
     Aristophanes' *Thesmophoriazusae*, where he is portrayed as
     excessively effeminate and avant-garde.

85   *The banquets of the Blest*: Agathon left Athens for the royal court
     of king Archelaus of Macedon, where Euripides also spent the
     final years of his life. Dionysus' remark may imply that he stayed
     there in luxury.

92   '*Choirs of swallows*': A quotation from a lost play of Euripides
     (*Alcmene* fr. 88).

100 '*Ether, boudoir of Zeus*': These are all quotations (or misquo-
     tations) of Euripides. 'Ether, boudoir of Zeus' is from *Melanippe
     the Wise* fr. 487 (originally 'abode' not 'boudoir'); 'the tread of
     time' is from *Bacchae* 889; the clumsily paraphrased quotation
     involving the 'heart averse . . .' and 'tongue . . . but not the mind'
     is from *Hippolytus* 612 (quoted again, and more accurately, at
     Frogs 1471).

105 '*Seek not . . .*': A quotation; possibly from Euripides' *Andromeda*
     (fr. 114).

108 *Never a word*: One of several complaints by Dionysus' slave
     Xanthias in the opening scene about the heavy luggage he has to
     carry.

763 *dining rights*: This granting of dining rights in Hades reflects the
     practice in the 'upper world' of Athens, where victors at the
     Dionysia would be dined at the State's expense.

764 *Pluto himself*: Pluto was the sovereign god of the underworld.

791 *Cleidemides*: Nothing certain is known of Cleidemides; he may
     have been a friend of Sophocles.

811 *his familiarity*: While Dionysus is portrayed largely as a buffoon
     (as is typical in Old Comedy) he is, nevertheless, the patron god
     of the theatre.

840 *allotment queen*: Aeschylus insults Euripides on account of his
     mother, Cleito, being a seller of groceries. The origin of this joke,
     which appears frequently in Aristophanes, is obscure; there is no
     evidence for Euripides' mother having had any connection with

the grocery business and it is in fact likely that she was of high birth. The line used by Aeschylus is probably an adapted quotation of a line from an unknown play of Euripides (fr. 885), addressed originally to Achilles. The unaltered line is 'Is that so, you child of the sea-goddess' (Achilles' mother Thetis was a goddess of the sea).

842 *rag-stitcher*: Euripides was regularly mocked by Aristophanes for presenting characters who were disguised as beggars, or who appeared in rags on account of their unfortunate circumstances. In many cases the appearance of the heroes is determined by the myths themselves, but Euripides seems to have had a fondness for treating such material, and for accentuating the wretched appearance of the characters involved.

844 *'Warm not . . .'*: Probably a parody of a line of Aeschylus.

845 *cripple-maker*: Euripides was also seen as fond of presenting characters who were lame or had suffered injuries. A number of such heroes, all from lost plays, are mentioned by Euripides himself during his brief appearance in Aristophanes' *Acharnians*: Phoenix, who was blind; Philoctetes, who had a festering foot; Bellerophon, who was lamed after a fall (from Pegasus); and Telephus, who had a septic war wound.

847 *black lamb . . . hurricane*: Black lambs were sacrificed to placate storm-gods. The god in this instance is Typhos, whose name is translated here as 'hurricane'.

849 *Cretan arias . . . perverted unions*: Euripides was fond of composing monodies or solo arias. It is not clear why these should be seen as Cretan. There may be a general association of Crete with sexual excess; both Phaedra and Pasiphae (another Euripidean character who indulged in shocking sexual behaviour – she mated with a bull – in the lost *Cretans*) are heroines of Cretan origin.

   The mention of 'perverted unions' probably refers to Euripides' lost play *Aeolus*, in which Aeolus' daughter Canace has sexual relations with her half-brother Macareus, though it may also refer to Pasiphae and the bull in *Cretans*. Aeschylus, Sophocles and Euripides all dealt with myths involving unnatural acts. The Oedipus myth, for example, involves a union that is hardly less unnatural than that of Canace and Macareus, and all three tragedians treated this part of the Oedipus story (though only Sophocles' play survives). But Aeschylus' claim seems to be that Euripides deliberately focused on, or sensationalized, mythological characters who wilfully engaged in shocking behaviour.

855 *Telephus*: On *Telephus* see the note below.

863 *Peleus . . . Telephus*: The plays that Euripides mentions are all
     lost, but they were probably not only well-known but also
     regarded as controversial (hence his defiant mention of them
     here). *Telephus* was a play that fascinated Aristophanes. It con-
     cerns the attempts by the Mysian king Telephus (a son of Her-
     acles) to infiltrate a meeting of the Greek leaders at Argos (in
     disguise) to argue against the launching of another Greek attack
     against the Mysians and, possibly, to seek a cure for his war
     wound. It is the play that Aristophanes parodies most regularly
     and extensively throughout his works.

868 *my poetry hasn't died*: Aeschylus' point is that while Euripides'
     plays are with him down in the underworld, his own plays are
     not because they are still being re-performed at the festival of the
     Dionysia. Aeschylus is the only tragedian who is known to have
     been given this privilege posthumously. Aristophanes refers to
     such a posthumous production of a play by Aeschylus in the
     opening scene of his *Acharnians* (*Ach*. 10).

886 *Demeter . . . Mysteries*: Aeschylus was from Eleusis, the town
     close to Athens where the temple of Mysteries was situated. The
     two goddesses associated with the Mysteries were Demeter and
     her daughter Persephone. It is therefore fitting that Demeter
     should be of special significance to Aeschylus. His prayer to
     Demeter is also fitting both in the presence of Dionysus, who
     under the name Iacchus was the third significant divinity in the
     cult of the Mysteries, and before the Chorus, who are initiates of
     the Mysteries. (*Frogs* has two choruses and takes its name from
     the first Chorus of frogs that sing as Dionysus crosses the river
     Styx to reach Hades.)

890 *gods . . . of your own*: Avant-garde intellectuals such as Euripides
     and Socrates are often presented by Aristophanes as worshipping
     new gods. Socrates, in the *Clouds*, rejects Zeus in favour of the
     Clouds and Vortex. While Socrates' gods are linked to meteoro-
     logical phenomena, here Euripides' gods are mostly connected
     with the senses.

906 *As for myself*: Euripides' style, like that of his characters, is
     strongly oratorical (compare Jason's first speech in Medea,
     p. 150). In Aristophanes' *Peace*, Hermes refers to Euripides dis-
     paragingly as 'the poet of the law courts'. Aristotle, when dis-
     cussing argumentation in *Poetics*, distinguishes between this
     oratorical style and a more statesmanlike style (see *Poetics* 4.4).

909 *Phrynichus*: Phrynichus was a former tragedian who pre-dated,

but overlapped with, Aeschylus. In Aristophanes, Phrynichus and Aeschylus are often seen as representatives of 'the good old days'.

911 *Achilles or Niobe*: The references are to two lost plays, *Myrmidons* and *Niobe*. The former, part of a trilogy, dealt with selected events of the *Iliad* – the death of Patroclus, the re-arming of Achilles and the death of Hector. The latter, also part of a trilogy, dealt with the story of Niobe. She boasted that she was luckier than Leto (the mother of Apollo and Artemis) because she had more children than her (either twelve or fourteen). Artemis and Apollo then killed them all, and Niobe, maddened with grief, killed herself. Both plays seem to have involved the main characters sitting on stage in prolonged silence.

914 *four rounds / Of lyrics*: For a long string of choral odes see the Chorus's entry-song in *Agamemnon* (pp. 12–20), where Clytemnestra is a silent presence on stage for some time before she eventually speaks.

923 *a dozen bulldozing words*: The general impression Euripides seeks to give is that Aeschylus' style is old-fashioned and that his plays have an outmoded heroic or martial tenor.

932 *tawny Hippocock*: A hippocock is presumably some kind of hybrid beast – part horse, part bird. In his lost play *Myrmidons*, Aeschylus mentions how the emblem of a hippocock, painted on a Greek ship, drips into the sea when struck by fire (during Achilles' abstention from the fighting, Hector set fire to many of the Greek ships; see *Iliad* 12).

941 *a course / Of wordlets*: The image is a medical one. When Euripides takes tragedy over from Aeschylus – Sophocles is conveniently overlooked here – it is in a state of being swollen or obese. His remedy, possibly a parody of prescribed treatment for a disease such as dropsy, involves stringent dieting followed by careful re-feeding.

944 *Cephisophon*: Cephisophon was a friend of Euripides who assisted him in his writing and may, to some extent, have collaborated with him.

946 *better than your own*: In questioning Euripides' background Aeschylus is again hinting at the jibe about Euripides' mother being a seller of groceries.

947 *no character idle*: A noticeable feature of Euripidean tragedy is that minor characters – nurses, servants, tutors and so on – seem to have a greater or more prominent role than they do in plays by Aeschylus and Sophocles. In *Medea*, for example, during the whole of the opening scene (prologue), the only two characters

that are on stage with speaking parts – Medea makes an offstage exclamation and the children are present but silent – are the Nurse, who delivers the opening speech, and the Tutor, who discusses Medea's problems with the Nurse.

952 *democracy*: The view of democracy implied by Euripides, in which women and slaves participate on equal terms, is far from conventional; to partake of Athenian democracy one had to be male, free and Athenian.

954 *not best qualified*: Euripides spent the last few years of his life (during the final decade of the fifth century) at the court of king Archelaus of Macedon (as did the tragedian Agathon; see note to line 83). Such a departure to a foreign monarchy, when democratic Athens was in severe danger in its long war with Sparta, may have been seen as cowardly or treacherous.

991 '*You witness . . .*': A quote from Aeschylus' lost play *Myrmidons*. The context is probably an appeal to Achilles by the chorus of Myrmidon soldiers, in the face of the Greek army's suffering at the hands of Hector, to rejoin (and let them rejoin) the fighting.

1012 *Death*: The joke, of course, is that Euripides is already dead; death here means staying in the underworld rather than being sent down to it.

1017 *sevenfold ox-hide*: According to Homer, Ajax's shield was made of seven layers of ox-hide. Ajax was synonymous with unstinting courage.

1022 *Seven Against Thebes*: This play deals with the attempt by one son of Oedipus, Polyneices, to capture Thebes by siege from the other, Eteocles. The two brothers had agreed to rule in yearly turns, but after the first year Eteocles was reluctant to relinquish his rule. The play reaches its climax with the two killing each other in a duel, in accordance with a prophetic curse laid by Oedipus. The same story is treated by Euripides in his *Phoenissae*, and the subsequent attempt by Polyneices' sister Antigone to provide him with proper burial, against the wishes of her newly crowned uncle Creon, forms the subject of Sophocles' *Antigone*.

1039 *Patroclus . . . Teucer*: Patroclus appears in the lost *Myrmidons*; Teucer, the half-brother of Ajax, appears in one or more of Aeschylus' lost plays about Ajax.

1041 *whores / Like Phaedra*: Phaedra appears in both versions of Euripides' *Hippolytus* (we possess only the second), and Stheneboea appears in the lost plays *Stheneboea* and *Bellerophon*. The story of Stheneboea was not unlike that of Phaedra: though married, she fell hopelessly in love with a younger man,

Bellerophon, only to be rejected and then wrongly accuse him of assault.

The reason why these heroines are seen as whores is that they openly express, and try to act upon, sexual feelings; to the conventional Athenian male mentality this was unacceptable (in freeborn women, at any rate). But Phaedra's initial reaction to her plight – Stheneboea's is harder to discern, as both of the plays in question are lost – is presented as laudable, though her subsequent actions are shown in a more ambivalent light.

1045 *sit heavily on you / And yours*: Cephisophon was rumoured to have had sexual relations with Euripides' wife.

1051 *exist already*: This suggests that Stheneboea's suicide by taking poison was a Euripidean invention, while Phaedra's suicide was already an established part of her story in myth.

1052 *the duty of the poet . . . good*: The view of poetry as having a primary moral function is pervasive in Greek attitudes to art. It is evident in Plato's wary attitude to poetry in the *Republic*, and may be reflected in the use of the term *didaskalos* (literally 'teacher') for a dramatist (though this usage may originally have had more to do with the task of instructing actors and others involved in the production of a play than with the idea of instructing the public). Moral or political advice is also a key part of the contest between Aeschylus and Euripides towards the end of the play (see lines 1420–65).

1057 *Lycabettus . . . Parnassus*: Lycabettus is a prominent hill in Athens, north-east of the Acropolis; Parnassus is a large massif in Phocis with Delphi standing on its southern face (see map, p. 306).

1060 *demigods*: A large number of tragic heroes or heroines were demigods or of divine lineage (e.g., Medea; see genealogical table, p. 305).

1063 *royal birth wear rags*: Telephus, for example, appeared before the Greek army disguised in rags.

1065 *rich men . . . warships*: Wealthy Athenians were expected to pay for a warship as a form of compulsory public service. Exemption could be sought on the grounds of diminished wealth if the person in question could suggest someone richer; if that second person wished to contest the claim, a court case would follow. Aeschylus is suggesting that in such cases men of high birth try to outdo each other in evoking the jury's pity by wearing tattered clothes to court.

1079 *Didn't he show . . .*: There are a number of allusions here. The most likely candidates are as follows: Phaedra's nurse in

Hippolytus acts as a bawd by trying to persuade Hippolytus to sleep with her mistress; in Euripides' lost play *Auge*, the eponymous heroine gives birth to Telephus (her son by Heracles) in the temple of Athena, whose priestess she was; Aeolus' daughter Canace has sexual relations with her half-brother Macareus in Euripides' *Aeolus*; in Euripides' lost play *Polyidus*, a mother (possibly Pasiphae) wonders whether life is death and existence in the underworld is in fact life (fr. 638).

1088 *run the torch*: Torch races were a feature of a number of Athenian festivals, including the Panathenaic festival.

1126 *'Netherworld Hermes ...'*: The first three lines of Aeschylus' *Libation Bearers*, the play that follows *Agamemnon* in the *Oresteia* trilogy.

1144 *Hermes Eriounios*: One of Hermes' functions was to escort the dead to the underworld. The epithet *Eriounios* appears a number of times in Homer. In the last book of the *Odyssey*, Hermes is seen leading the souls of the dead suitors to Hades, where they encounter the recently murdered Agamemnon.

1149 *grave robber*: Dionysus interrupts with a joke. Hermes was known as the divine thief. If he holds the underworld as a paternal inheritance then he is an underworld thief, which Dionysus interprets as tantamount to being a grave robber or tomb-raider.

1151 *'Be my ally now. . .'*: *Libation Bearers* 4–5.

1167 *Orestes didn't return*: It may not be a coincidence that this is more or less what Orestes does in Euripides' own *Electra*, which deals with the same part of the myth of Agamemnon's family as Aeschylus' *Libation Bearers*.

1172 *'And by this burial mound. . .'*: *Libation Bearers* 6–7.

1179 *extrinsic to the plot*: Euripides' emphasis on the primacy of 'plot' here is interesting in view of Aristotle's later view of 'plot' as 'the soul of tragedy' (see p. 246).

1182 *'Oedipus was a fortunate man ...'*: The opening line of Euripides' lost *Antigone*. The second line is given shortly below at 1187.

1202 *the way you write*: The point Aeschylus is making is that, in metrical terms, Euripides tends to have a predictable word-break at a particular point in the line. Iambic trimeters involve three feet, or units, consisting of four metrical quantities arranged in iambic sequence (this is a simplification of the iambic trimeter – there are a number of variations and rules – but it gives sufficient indication of what Aeschylus is about to do here). The predictable word-break comes after the first quantity of the second foot or unit (i.e., the fifth quantity out of the twelve that make up the line). In this translation, during the scene with the 'oil-flask' the Euripidean word-break always comes at the fifth syllable of an English iambic hexameter (which is quantitatively equivalent to a Greek iambic trimeter because the Greek unit is four quantities instead of two).

1206 *'Aegyptus, as the story . . .'*: The source is uncertain; it may be from one of two Euripidean plays by the name of *Archelaus*.

1211 *'Dionysus, bedecked . . .'*: The opening of Euripides' lost play *Hypsipyle* (fr. 752). The play is about the fifty daughters of Danaus, who all vowed to murder their husbands (the fifty sons of Aegyptus) because they had been forced to marry. Hypsipyle, however, was in love with her husband and spared him.

1216 *'There lives no man . . .'*: The opening of Euripides' *Stheneboea*.

1225 *'Long ago Cadmus . . .'*: The opening of Euripides' second play by the name of *Phrixus*.

1232 *'Pelops, the son of Tantalus . . .'*: The opening of Euripides' *Iphigenia in Tauris*. The play deals with the visit by Orestes and Pylades (exiled after the murder of Clytemnestra and Aegisthus) to the land of the Taurians. Upon arrival they are seized and are about to be sacrificed until they are recognized and saved by Iphigenia, Orestes' sister. She – it turns out – was saved from being sacrificed by Agamemnon at Aulis by Artemis, and was transported by the goddess to the land of the Taurians, where she became a priestess of the goddess.

1237 *'On his lands Oeneus . . .'*: These lines are from Euripides' *Meleager*. Oddly, they do not seem to be the opening lines, which are known from alternative sources, but are probably from the prologue. They are presumably used here because of their comic suitability; both lines have word breaks at the required point, allowing Aeschylus to interrupt twice.

1251 *Chorus*: For the brief choral section that follows there are two possible texts that differ considerably. The version used here is the revised script (used for the restaging of the *Frogs* the winter after the original performance). *Frogs* was the only play from Old Comedy known to have received a second performance.

1258 *More – and better – lyrics*: Aeschylus was generally considered a particularly fine, and prolific, composer of choral lyrics in his tragedies. Here Euripides claims that they are full of obscurity, repetition and archaisms.

1264 *'Phthian Achilles . . . to the rescue'*: The lines are a patchwork. The first is from *Myrmidons* (fr. 132), the second from the *Ghost*

Raisers (a play dealing with Odysseus' visit to the underworld during his travels; fr. 273). Euripides strings together lines that are monotonous – they are all dactylic in rhythm – and seem nonsensical because they are followed by the same line (in 1265, 1267, 1271, 1275 and 1277), namely the second line of *Myrmidons*, fr. 132. According to a scholiast, the line repeated by Aristophanes is spoken in the original by envoys who plead vainly with an unmovable Achilles.

1270 '*Noblest of the Achaeans . . .*': The first line is of uncertain origin (fr. 238), but is an address to Agamemnon from a lost play of Aeschylus.

1273 '*Keep Silence! . . .*': Lines 1273–4 are from Aeschylus' *Priestesses* (fr. 87). The priestesses, who form the play's chorus, are priestesses of Artemis. Artemis was associated with bees (among other things); her priestesses at Ephesus were called Bee-priestesses (*melissonomoi*).

1285 '*How the twin-throned . . . to Ajax*': This section (1285–95) is a patchwork of parodic quotations based primarily on a choral passage from *Agamemnon*, with three lines inserted from other plays. Lines 1285 and 1289 are from *Agamemnon* 108–11; 1287 is probably from Aeschylus' lost satyr-play the *Sphinx*; 1291–2 is from an unknown play (fr. 282), though it resembles the *Agamemnon* passage; 1294 is possibly from Aeschylus' lost *Thracian Women* (fr. 84), which deals with the death of Ajax. *Phlattothratt* is a humorous imitation, or misrepresentation, of stringed accompaniment used in Aeschylean choral lyrics.

1297 *rope-winders' songs*: The reference is unclear; it may be to songs sung while hauling up pails of water from wells. Marathon is probably mentioned because Aeschylus fought at the battle of Marathon (490 BC).

1300 *the same / 'Sacred mead*: Phrynichus was mentioned earlier by Euripides as someone from whom Aeschylus inherited the art of tragedy (see 908–10). Here Aeschylus seems to be wary of the charge that he followed too closely in Phrynichus' footsteps.

1302 *Meletus . . . from Caria*: Meletus was a composer of erotic verse (possibly sixth century). Caria, in south-west Asia Minor, was associated with emotive pipe music suited to symposia (and used in funeral music).

1308 *the Lesbian way*: This remark about Euripides' muse (probably a ridiculously dressed, and possibly ugly, woman) potentially carries two connotations: 1) that her music is not in the dignified style of the high lyric poets of Lesbos, such as Terpander, or 2) that she does not – or, if she is very unattractive, that she has never been asked to – perform fellatio (a sexual act sometimes associated with Lesbos).

1309 '*You halcyons . . . child*': Lines 1309–22 are a parody of Euripidean choral lyric. The basic metre is Aeolic. While it is metrically coherent, its sense is ridiculous and it is full of stylistic excesses, some musical and therefore difficult to discern with any certainty. There may be some linguistic parody of Euripides' *Hypsipyle*. It seems likely that the song is meant to be accompanied by the banging together of pot shards by the muse of Euripides as Aeschylus sings. There is probably also meant to be a parody of the style of singing, as suggested by the absurd lengthening of 'spi-i-i-i-i-i-n'.

1330 *monodies*: Lines 1331–63 are a full-blown parody of Euripidean monodies. We see a number of Euripidean traits both in stylistic terms and in terms of content. The basic idea is to take everyday matters and subject them to a range of exaggerated Euripidean stylistic habits.

1331 *gloom of night . . . extended talons*: In this section we find a preoccupation with night and dreams; the presence of bizarre and extreme emotions; paradox/oxymoron (e.g., 'lifeless life'), and melodramatic repetition.

1345 *Nymphs of the mountains*: Here the mention of 'attendants' and 'nymphs of the mountains' may be suitable for a tragic heroine, but seems wholly out of place for this humble housewife who calls on her 'housemates' and her one slave, Mania. The crisis – the theft of a cockerel – is also comically mundane.

1357 *Take up your bows*: A parodic appropriation from Euripides' *Cretans* (fr. 471).

1382 '*Would that the Argo . . .*': The opening line of *Medea*.

1383 '*River Spercheius . . .*': This line is from Aeschylus' *Philoctetes* and was probably spoken by Philoctetes himself. As with the story of Oedipus' terrible discovery of his crimes against his parents, the fetching of Philoctetes from Lemnos by the Greek army was something treated in a tragedy by Aeschylus, Sophocles and Euripides where only the Sophoclean version survives.

1386 *pre-soaking his wool*: As wool is generally sold by weight, if it is pre-soaked then it is possible to gain more money for the same quantity of wool.

1391 '*Persuasion . . .*': This is from Euripides' *Antigone* (fr. 170).

1392 '*For Death alone . . .*': This is from Aeschylus' *Niobe* (fr. 161.1).

1400 '*Achilles threw*': The line is of uncertain origin. The second part looks like a comic invention – stylistically it cannot belong to tragedy or satyr-play – but the first part, 'Achilles threw . . .' could easily be from Euripidean tragedy, as one would expect in the context. The 'two singles and a four' refer to dice scores. Achilles and Ajax playing dice is a common scene on painted vases, making a comic adaptation of something from tragedy or satyr-play a possibility.

1403 *'He took up . . .'*: This is from Euripides' *Meleager* (fr. 531).

1404 *'For chariot on chariot . . .'*: This is from Aeschylus' *Glaucus in Potniae* (fr. 38).

1406 *Egyptians*: Egyptians were often associated by the Greeks with hard labour, such as the carrying of bricks or other burdensome objects.

1413 *The one I regard*: This remark has provoked a great deal of speculation (as has the similarly cryptic remark at 1434). There is disagreement over which remark refers to which tragedian. In general, there seems a plausible case for suggesting that Aeschylus is the 'master' and Euripides the poet Dionysus simply enjoys. But it is possible to contend the opposite. Dionysus has expressed a simple enjoyment of some things Aeschylean (e.g., the silences, 915) and Euripides is seen as masterful ('I simply have to listen to / The lexical precision of your openings', 1180–1). Euripides has also generally spoken first of the two, whether questioning Aeschylus or reciting lines into the pans, suggesting that he is 'the one' (i.e., 'the master') and Aeschylus 'the other' (i.e., the poet whom Dionysus enjoys). It is, of course, possible that Aristophanes intends the remark to be mischievously ambivalent.

1423 *About Alcibiades*: Alcibiades was the most flamboyant, controversial and unpredictable of Athenian leaders during the latter half of the Peloponnesian War. In 415 BC he was arrested on the charge of profaning the Mysteries. He escaped and went over to the Spartans. His advice may have proved telling in the subsequent gaining of the upper hand by Sparta. But he soon fell out with the Spartans, possibly because of an affair with the wife of one of the Spartan kings. In 412–11 he had dealings with the new oligarchs who had taken power in Athens (he also had dealings with the Persians). The following year, he joined the Athenian fleet and, as general, defeated the oligarchs. He continued the war at sea with some success, and was reinstated in Athens in 407. But Alcibiades still had enemies in Athens, and was soon stripped of his rank, after which he withdrew to a fortress on the Hellespont. At the time of *Frogs*, there was still uncertainty as to what should be done about him; he was still seen by some as the best (or only) hope of a revival of fortunes in the war, but by others as a dangerous, volatile character.

1434 *One spoke with insight*: As with 1413, it is difficult to tell which remark applies to which poet. Generally, Euripides is prone to paradox and overly clever thinking; Dionysus even tells him to speak less cleverly and more intelligibly a little later at 1445. But equally, Aeschylus is seen as obscure and difficult to understand during the early part of the contest between the two tragedians (see esp. 923–32). Looking at the advice on Alcibiades in particular, it may be suggested that Euripides' remark seems more obvious and straightforward, and so 'intelligible', than Aeschylus' offering, which involves a paradox.

1440 *I've got an idea*: There is considerable textual uncertainty about the entire passage 1437–66. The translated selections of this section of text are based on what is supposed here to comprise the revised script. For detailed discussions of the passage see K. J. Dover's commentary on the relevant lines in *Frogs* (Oxford: Oxford University Press, 1993) and A. H. Sommerstein's argument in *Tragedy, Comedy and the Polis*, eds. Sommerstein et al. (Bari: Levante Editori, 1993), pp. 469–75.

1458 *woollen cloak*: The woollen cloak was winter wear for smart townsfolk; the goatskin mantle was also a warm garment for winter but tended to be used more by country folk. Aeschylus' point is that a man who refuses to wear either of these will be left feeling cold.

1465 *The fleet as their wealth*: Aeschylus' advice seems to be to put all resources into shipbuilding and naval warfare.

1468 *'I'll choose. . .'*: This looks very much as if it is a tragic quotation, and as such one would expect it to be Euripidean (in keeping with the subsequent parodic quotations of Euripides in 1471, 1475 and 1477–8).

1471 *'It was my tongue . . .'*: The first half is a well-known line from *Hippolytus* (*Hipp.* 612) inaccurately quoted by Dionysus at the beginning of the play (101–2). Here Dionysus hints at the situation in Euripides' play. In the original, when the nurse accuses Hippolytus of going back on his promise not to say anything to Theseus about Phaedra's uncontrollable desire for him, the self-righteous Hippolytus declares that it was his tongue that swore but not his mind (or conscience). Here, Euripides asks Dionysus to remember his promise (which does not appear in the text), but Dionysus adds insult to injury by replying that even though he did promise he is simply going to break his promise because he feels like it.

1475 '*What is low* ...': Again Dionysus uses a misquotation of Euripides as a humorous riposte. The line comes from *Aeolus*, where Macareus, after committing incest with his half-sister, asks, 'What is low, if it seems not so to the participants?'

1476 *watch me die*: The joke here, of course, is that Euripides is already dead, and so will simply remain dead.

1477 '*Who knows if living* ...': The first line is from Euripides' *Polyidus* (fr. 638), where a mother (possibly Pasiphae) wonders whether life is death and existence in the underworld is life (the line is alluded to in 1082; see earlier note). The line is, in fact, comically appropriate here, as the action in the underworld seems every bit as lively as the world above. Dionysus continues with a line of complete nonsense.

1491 *sit / Next to Socrates*: Euripides and Socrates are both portrayed as leading lights of the intellectual avant-garde, a group that comes in for heavy ridicule at the hands of writers of Old Comedy.

1499 *a mindless man*: The play continues for another thirty or so lines, in which Pluto wishes Aeschylus well as he departs with Dionysus, and the Chorus, singing the closing lines, hope that Aeschylus will benefit the city.

POETICS

1   *field of enquiry*: Aristotle says that he will focus on the criticism of existing works ('The effect which each species of poetry has') and the composition of works as yet unwritten ('the correct way to construct plots . . .').

2   *imitations*: On imitation (*mimêsis*) see Preface to *Poetics* §1.

3   *a different manner*: The three respects in which Aristotle sees *mimêsis* as differing, literally translated, are by imitating 'in different forms'(media), by imitating 'different things'(objects), and by imitating 'in a different way'(mode); see Preface to *Poetics* §1.

4   *of the voice*: The art form in question is probably mimicry of sounds, such as animal noises.

5   *present day*: The nearest contemporary terms for artistic language in prose or verse are 'literature' and 'fiction'.

6   *Socratic dialogues*: Sophron was a writer of the late fifth century working in Syracuse. His sketches of everyday life and the

dialogues of Plato are cited by Aristotle as examples of mimetic (i.e., imitative or representational) prose writing.

7   *than a poet*: Empedocles, like most other early Greek philosophers, wrote in the same dactylic hexameter verse that Homer used for the *Iliad* and *Odyssey* (the first major philosopher to use prose was Heraclitus, although his dense, figurative, aphoristic style is arguably more 'poetic' than the verse philosophy of his contemporaries). Aristotle seems to have admired Empedocles. It therefore seems likely that here he is not expressing an aesthetic preference for Homer over Empedocles – he may or may not have felt one – but simply distinguishing between the poet and natural scientist as different kinds of exponent of the same verse form.

8   *nomic poetry*: Dithyrambic and nomic poetry are both types of choral lyric.

9   *same sort*: These categories suggest a somewhat rigid view of character, but Aristotle does say later that tragic figures may comprise a combination of faults and positive qualities (see 53b–54a).

10   *worse people)*: Hegemon and Nicochares were both contemporaries of Aristophanes, though Nicochares was younger than the other two. Aristotle describes Hegemon as the inventor of parodies (works in hexameter verse involving mock-imitation of the language and style of Homeric epic). Given that the form can be traced back to Hipponax, who was writing during the sixth century, Aristotle probably means that Hegemon was instrumental in the establishment of public competitions for parodies. The title of Nicochares' *Deiliad*, which means 'The Tale of the Coward' (*deilos* = 'coward'), is a pun on the *Iliad* ('The Tale of Ilium'; Ilium = Troy). Hegemon and Nicochares both wrote comedies as well as parodies.

11   *in activity*: The three modes to which Aristotle seems to be referring are narrative, lyric and dramatic respectively. Aristotle considers the dramatic mode as preferable to the narrative mode. Elsewhere he praises Homer for using narration as sparingly as the form of epic allows (60a; not included here). This is effectively the reverse of Plato's view in the *Republic*, where the dramatic is seen as inferior to narrative because a character's words are at a remove from the author's own words (i.e., the narrative), which are themselves at a significant remove from the truth (on Plato see Preface to *Poetics*, p. 228). Aristotle explains his preference of the dramatic over the narrative in a brief comparison of epic

and tragedy towards the end of *Poetics* (61b–62b; not included here).

12   *doing things*: Aristotle's point is that Sophocles and Aristophanes, while the former shows people as better and the latter worse, nonetheless have in common the fact that they both write dramatic rather than narrative poetry. The Greek word 'drama' (literally: 'action' or 'thing done') is etymologically linked to the verb *drân* ('to do').

13   *of them natural*: The two causes are a natural desire to imitate and an instinctive sense of melody/rhythm.

14   *capacity for it*: Aristotle sees philosophers as superior to all other kinds of people.

15   *other reason*: While emphasizing, as Plato does in the *Republic*, the importance of knowledge in the full appreciation of art – we enjoy recognizing things for what they are – Aristotle also places considerable importance on purely artistic criteria.

16   *rhythm*: Rhythm may, in principle, be extended ad infinitum. A verse is therefore a rhythmic unit or segment.

17   *and encomia*: Aristotle's position is a highly inflexible, strongly intentionalist one, in which the characteristics of a work are directly correlated with the character or disposition of the author. In *Frogs* Aristophanes makes comic use of such an idea by characterizing Aeschylus and Euripides in accordance with the characteristics of their respective works.

18   *dramatic*: By 'dramatic' Aristotle means that though Homer wrote narrative fiction, he tended to use dialogue as often as possible (also see n.11).

19   *do to tragedy*: The *Margites* is a humorous poem written partly in iambics (the metre of invective and the spoken sections of tragedy and comedy) and partly in hexameters (the metre of epic and parodies of epic). The poem's authorship is disputed. It is unlikely to have been written by Homer (as was widely supposed in antiquity); other possible candidates include Archilochus and a shadowy figure called Pigres. Its date is probably seventh or sixth century, depending on authorship. Little is known about the poem except that it concerns a ridiculous hero, Margites, and his far-from-heroic adventures (Don Quixote is perhaps a suitable modern comparison). Only a few scraps survive, one of which describes the drunken Margites wetting himself, while another suggests that he is (perhaps temporarily) impotent. Uncertainties notwithstanding, the poem may, as Aristotle suggests, be considered a forerunner of comedy.

20   *than the others*: Aristotle sees comedy as the evolved, or perfected, form of lampoons and other less clearly defined forms of humorous writing (including *Margites*; see n.19), and tragedy as the evolved, or perfected, form of epic.

21   *many cities*: Dithyramb is entirely choral. There is an example of a phallic song in Aristophanes' earliest surviving play *Acharnians*, performed by the hero Dicaeopolis and his family.

22   *leading role*: Although Aeschylus is credited with reducing the choral part and expanding the role of the actors, the role of the chorus in Aeschylean tragedy remains far greater than it is in Sophoclean and Euripidean tragedy.

23   *by Sophocles*: Sophocles and Euripides both make considerable use of the third actor in their extant plays. There is also evidence for the use of stage machinery in performance. Euripides seems to have made regular use of a stage crane (the *mêchanê*), a device for lowering characters (usually gods) from the stage roof to the stage itself, or for showing characters as moving aerially: there are elaborate visual and textual parodies of Euripidean scenes involving the use of the stage crane in two plays of Aristophanes (*Peace* and *Thesmophoriazusae*). It is also widely supposed that a wheeled platform (the *ekkuklêma*), which could be brought out through the main stage doors, was used to show interior scenes on stage, but its precise workings and function remain unclear. There is no sure evidence of the use of the *ekkuklêma* by Aeschylus or Sophocles, but Aristophanes twice presents tragedians who pointedly mention that they are wheeled on and off stage by means of this device: Euripides in *Acharnians*; and Agathon, a younger contemporary of Euripides, in *Thesmophoriazusae* (on Agathon see n.52).

24   *trochaic tetrameter*: Satyr-plays were short mythological burlesques involving a chorus of satyrs – drunken, playful followers of Dionysus with a mixture of human and animal features and characteristics – who generally rescue the hero (often their leader, e.g., Dionysus, Silenus) from an oppressor. Satyr-plays were written by tragedians as part of the tragic competition (each tragedian entered three tragedies and a satyr-play). By the time Sophocles and Euripides were well-established as tragedians, the comic and satyric elements that Aristotle mention were no longer present in tragedy.

25   *involve pain*: The standard comic masks were grotesque but nonetheless comic. This may be contrasted with certain tragic masks, such as that of the disfigured Oedipus (after his self-

blinding), which would have been genuinely shocking and therefore inappropriate for a character in a comedy.

26 *stories and plots*: By universalized Aristotle means fictional or hypothetical but in accordance with causal laws and realist principles (see 51a–b and n.37). Crates belonged to the generation of comic playwrights before Aristophanes.

27 *in this respect*: Later European critics falsely ascribe to Aristotle strict unities of time and place based on this remark. Aristotle's observation, however, that tragedies tend to take place over a single day, but that earlier tragedy did not necessarily do so, is not necessarily meant in a doctrinal or prescriptive way.

28 *of such emotions*: On problems concerning the interpretation of this passage see Preface to *Poetics* §3.

29 *thing of all*: Aristotle's stressing of the primacy of plot, and the secondary importance of character, differs from the more marked emphasis on character in so much of modern drama (from Shakespeare to Chekov to Pinter) and, to some extent, in our own interpretation of Greek tragedy.

30 *speak rhetorically*: This view, that the poets of the past used more elevated language than more rhetorical-sounding contemporary poets, may be compared to the view expressed in the *Frogs* that Aeschylus wrote in a more dignified style than Euripides, who is accused (by Aeschylus, at any rate) of debasing tragedy stylistically as well as in other ways.

31 *that of the poets*: Aristotle strongly privileges the action of the written play above the particulars of the presentation of that action in any given performance.

32 *the stated forms*: The suggestion that complete plots require a beginning, a middle and an end may sound somewhat obvious, but this is largely because it is something that has become deeply ingrained both in how audiences or readers approach plays and in how playwrights compose them (the same may be said of film audiences and screenwriters). In suggesting that middle follows necessarily from the beginning, and likewise the end from the middle, Aristotle is laying the ground for his view of the unity of plot and determinate structure (see 51a).

33 *held in memory*: Aristotle's remarks about the magnitude of tragedy are a pragmatic observation rather than a dogmatic prescription: since a tragedy is performed in its entirety it makes sense for the plot to be limited, in terms of its complexity, to that which can readily be held in memory. The same rule is not

applicable to epic, since poems such as the *Iliad* and *Odyssey* were performed in manageable sections.

34   *art or instinct*: Aristotle is ambivalent about what makes a good poet; he suggests that it may be technical expertise or natural ability (or a combination of both).

35   *true of the* Iliad: The single action of the *Odyssey* is the successful return of Odysseus to his homeland. This includes resuming his position both as head of his own household and as ruler of Ithaca. The action of the *Iliad* is based around a single event: the anger of Achilles. This begins with his quarrel with Agamemnon, continues for most of the poem, and is brought to an end by a sequence of events starting with the death of Patroclus and ending with Patroclus' funeral and the return of the body of Hector (killed by Achilles) to Priam for burial.

36   *a part of the whole*: Aristotle's point is that everything which makes up the action of a play (or poem) must be causally related, or consequential.

37   *probability or necessity*: Aristotle defends poetry's fictional status (which Plato condemns on both moral and metaphysical grounds in books 3 and 10 of the *Republic*; see Preface to *Poetics*, p. 231) by arguing that what is fictional is hypothetical and, therefore, universal; what is factual, by contrast, remains particular.

38   *as the lampoonists do*: In referring to comedy here Aristotle means, above all, New Comedy, which conforms closely to the principles he applies to tragedy (determinate structure, accordance with necessity and probability, unity of action and so on).

39   *the opposite result*: The man in question is the Messenger, the Corinthian shepherd who received the infant Oedipus from the Theban shepherd whom Laius had charged with ensuring the child's death. This Messenger hoped to rid Oedipus of the fear of sleeping with his mother by revealing that queen Merope of Corinth was not his real mother. This announcement starts off a series of questions and answers that lead inexorably to Oedipus' discovery of the terrible truth that he had already been sleeping with his mother for several years and had had children by her.

40   *like the one in* Oedipus: The recognition by Oedipus that Jocasta is his mother is, at the same time, a reversal of fortune. Recognition may, however, involve a change from bad to good fortune, such as Electra's recognition of Orestes in Aeschylus' *Libation Bearers*, Sophocles' *Electra* and Euripides' *Electra*.

41 *error of some kind*: Aristotle's notion of error (*hamartia*), which was questionably reinterpreted in later European criticism as the 'tragic flaw', has been much debated; see Preface to *Poetics* §4.

42 *plot will be simple*: This sense of simple is not to be confused with the earlier use of the term (in 52a) in the context of overall action, where it is contrasted with a complex plot rather than a double one.

43 *better and worse people*: In the *Odyssey*, the noble Odysseus triumphs and the morally reprehensible suitors perish.

44 *the plot of* Oedipus: Aristotle again strongly privileges text over performance.

45 *Creon in the* Antigone: In Sophocles' *Antigone* Creon's son Haemon is distraught at his father's actions, which have played a major part in the suicide of Antigone; after trying to kill his father, he turns his sword upon himself. This is perhaps the only criticism of Sophocles in the whole of *Poetics*, and it is interesting to note Aristotle's slight diffidence in making it.

46 *the last case is best*: By the last case Aristotle means being on the verge of acting but not doing so because of a recognition of someone or something (e.g., the mutual recognition between Orestes and Iphigenia in *Iphigenia in Tauris*).

47 *generally speaking inferior*: Aristotle's views about what makes men, women and slaves good or bad, while involving questionable evaluative judgements, are based largely on notions of relativity and appropriateness.

48 *already been stated*: This remark is somewhat unclear. By likeness Aristotle probably means verisimilitude or plausibility.

49 *consistently inconsistent*: A possible example of consistent inconsistency is Euripides' Medea. There are glaring inconsistencies between what she says in her two encounters with Jason, and she is inconsistent in what she says during her exchange with Creon; nonetheless, such inconsistencies form part of a consistent motive of revenge.

50 *in the* Medea: By theatrical device Aristotle is referring to the presentation of Medea on the stage roof in a flying chariot at the end of the play; this may have involved the use of the stage crane (*mêchanê*).

51 *to be overlooked*: Aristotle places importance on the author's ability to imagine the action of the play and to perceive situations from the perspective of his characters. In suggesting that the poet may be naturally gifted or mad, Aristotle acknowledges that poetry is, to a significant extent, instinctive, although this does

not undermine the additional importance or value of technical expertise.

52   *things to happen*: Sisyphus was a figure of myth known for trickery and deceit. Agathon was a tragedian who wrote during the last two decades of the fifth century and into the early fourth century. He appears as a character in Aristophanes' *Thesmophoriazusae* (411 BC), where he is presented as effeminate and as an innovator. He also appears, along with Aristophanes, in Plato's *Symposium*, where he is described as having just won the tragic competition.

53   *but as in Sophocles*: As a rule, the Chorus in tragedy does not participate physically in the action, but Aristotle's point is that in Sophoclean tragedy the Chorus tends to be more involved in the verbal action of the play than in Euripidean tragedy, in which the Chorus generally remains more detached.

Genealogical Tables

THE HOUSE OF PELOPS (AND ATREUS)

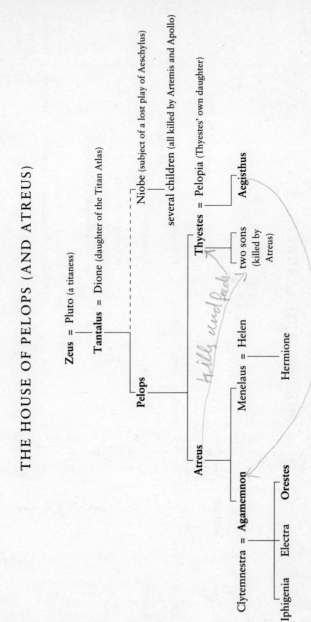

Zeus = Pluto (a titaness)

Tantalus = Dione (daughter of the Titan Atlas)

Pelops

Niobe (subject of a lost play of Aeschylus)

several children (all killed by Artemis and Apollo)

Thyestes = Pelopia (Thyestes' own daughter)

Aegisthus

two sons (killed by Atreus)

Atreus

Menelaus = Helen

Hermione

Clytemnestra = Agamemnon

Iphigenia   Electra   Orestes

kills and feeds

THE HOUSE OF LABDACUS

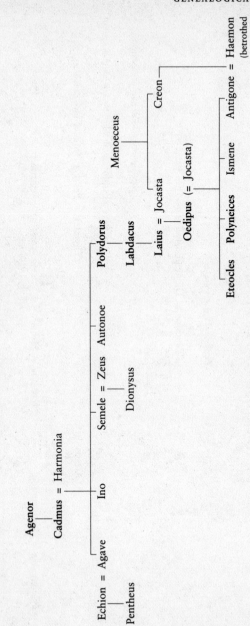

GENEALOGIES OF MEDEA AND JASON

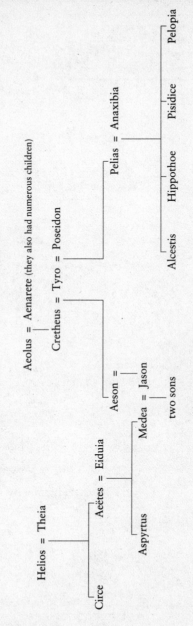

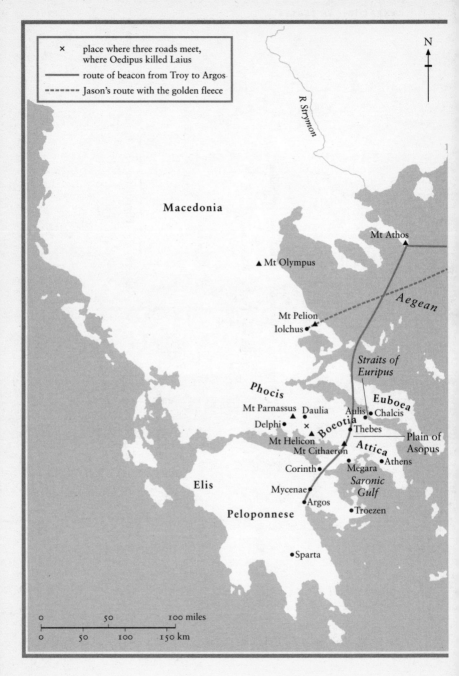

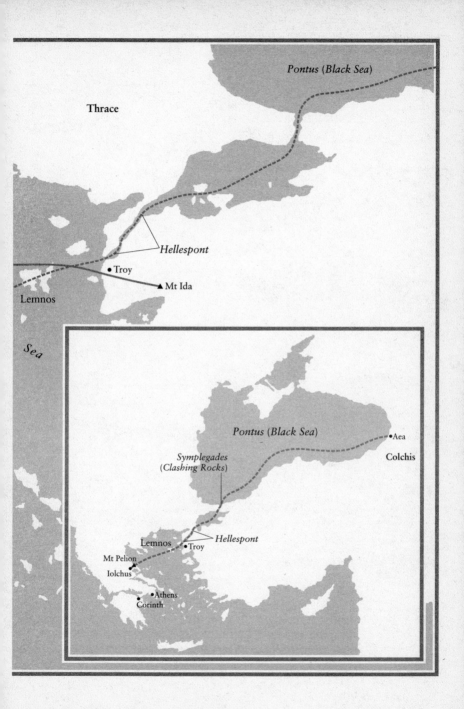